Kristie Thomas

Assessing Intellectual Property Compliance in Contemporary China

The World Trade Organisation TRIPS Agreement

Kristie Thomas
Aston University
Birmingham, UK

Palgrave Series in Asia and Pacific Studies
ISBN 978-981-10-3071-0   ISBN 978-981-10-3072-7   (eBook)
DOI 10.1007/978-981-10-3072-7

Library of Congress Control Number: 2016958728

Cover image © Pinar Gözen Ercan
Cover design by Oscar Spigolon

Printed on acid-free paper

This Palgrave Macmillan imprint is published by Springer Nature
The registered company is Springer Nature Singapore Pte Ltd.
The registered company address is: 152 Beach Road, #22-06/08 Gateway East, Singapore 189721, Singapore

Palgrave Series in Asia and Pacific Studies

Series Editors

May Tan-Mullins
The University of Nottingham Ningbo Chin
Ningbo, China

Adam Knee
The University of Nottingham Ningbo Chin
Ningbo, China

Aims of the Series

The Asia and Pacific regions, with a population of nearly three billion people, are of critical importance to global observers, academics, and citizenry due to their rising influence in the global political economy as well as traditional and nontraditional security issues. Any changes to the domestic and regional political, social, economic, and environmental systems will inevitably have great impacts on global security and governance structures. At the same time, Asia and the Pacific have also emerged as a globally influential, trend-setting force in a range of cultural arenas. The remit of this book series is broadly defined, in terms of topics and academic disciplines. We invite research monographs on a wide range of topics focused on Asia and the Pacific. In addition, the series is also interested in manuscripts pertaining to pedagogies and research methods, for both undergraduate and postgraduate levels. Published by Palgrave Macmillan, in collaboration with the Institute of Asia and Pacific Studies, UNNC

More information about this series at
http://www.springer.com/mycopy/series/14665

PREFACE

When I commenced my doctoral research in 2004, the topic of China's potential compliance with its World Trade Organization (WTO) commitments was of great scholarly interest and also fitted well with my own academic background in both law and Chinese Studies. With China's accession to the WTO on 11 December 2001, China formally committed to comply fully with the WTO Agreement on Trade-Related Aspects of Intellectual Property Rights (TRIPS) immediately and without any transition period. This commitment to comply with the stringent TRIPS standards was a major undertaking for a country in which modern intellectual property (IP) laws had only begun to be drafted in the 1980s, and thus China's subsequent compliance with the TRIPS Agreement was of significant interest to various groups of stakeholders—the WTO itself, trading partners and rights-holders. Although I was not an expert on IP law, I also found China's IP system and attempts to comply with the TRIPS Agreement to be a fascinating area for research.

It quickly became clear that China swiftly amended its legislation to transplant TRIPS-compliant rules into the domestic IP system. However, a gap was soon perceived between the substantive legislation and enforcement practices experienced by rights-holders on the ground. I explored this "enforcement gap" in my first phase of fieldwork in 2005–6 through the use of a survey as well as a series of follow-up interviews with a wide variety of business and legal professionals working on the ground in China. IP remained a key area of interest in the intervening decade, and then I returned to China for a second phase of fieldwork in early 2015 in order to see how the post-TRIPS IP system was being adapted to local conditions in the longer term. With WTO accession already 15 years in the past, this book can now provide a powerful and unique perspective both of the short-term transplant of TRIPS standards into the formal substantive law and of the longer-term adaptation of these standards into local enforcement practices through the voices of those actually working within the system.

This study would not have been possible without generous financial support from Nottingham University Business School to whom I am very grateful. Not only did I receive funding for my doctoral study, but I was also the recipient of significant internal research funding to support my 2015 fieldwork in China, as well as a semester of study leave which enabled me to write up my findings. I am also grateful to the University of Nottingham's Institute of Asia and Pacific Studies which also offered a small grant to support my 2015 fieldwork. I would also like to express my thanks to Christy Liu and Jingyi (Jane) Yuan who offered invaluable practical guidance and research assistance in both phases of the research study. I am also hugely indebted to the scores of individuals in China and beyond who generously gave their time to participate in this study and to share their experiences so candidly. This study would not have been possible without them, although they must remain anonymous. Finally, thanks to my family, in particular my husband, Gordon, not only for supporting my fieldwork but also for putting up with my grumpiness throughout the writing process.

Aston University   Kristie Thomas
Birmingham, UK

CONTENTS

LIST OF FIGURES

LIST OF TABLES

CHAPTER 1

Introduction

1.1 THE SIGNIFICANCE OF INTELLECTUAL PROPERTY IN CONTEMPORARY CHINA

With its accession to the World Trade Organisation (WTO) on 11 December 2001, China formally committed to comply fully with the WTO Agreement on Trade-Related Aspects of Intellectual Property Rights (TRIPS) immediately and without any transition period. This commitment to comply with the stringent TRIPS standards was a major undertaking for a country in which modern intellectual property (IP) laws had only begun to be drafted in the 1980s, and thus China's subsequent compliance with the TRIPS Agreement is of significant interest to various groups of stakeholders: the WTO itself, trading partners and rights-holders. With WTO accession now already 15 years in the past, surveying the evolution of China's intellectual property system from this point can provide a powerful and unique perspective of both the short-term transplant of TRIPS standards into the formal substantive law and the longer-term adaptation of these standards into local enforcement practices. It is clear that China swiftly amended its legislation to transplant TRIPS-compliant rules into the domestic IP system; however, a gap was soon perceived between the substantive legislation and enforcement practices experienced by rights-holders on the ground. Furthermore, many of China's key trading partners such as the United States (US) and the European Union (EU) still express disquiet about the effectiveness of IP enforcement on the ground, with China continuing to be the source of 80% of counterfeit goods detected at the EU's borders (European Commission 2015).

Nevertheless, it is undeniable that significant changes have been made to the IP system in China since accession to WTO, and further improvements to the IP system are now seen as a key government priority, as encouraging entrepreneurship and innovation is seen as key to rebalancing the Chinese economy which has previously relied on manufacturing low-cost exports as a key source of growth.

© The Author(s) 2017
K. Thomas, *Assessing Intellectual Property Compliance in Contemporary China*, Palgrave Series in Asia and Pacific Studies, DOI 10.1007/978-981-10-3072-7_1

As costs such as labour increase, low-end manufacturing has been losing its competitiveness, and thus China needs to look elsewhere for alternative sources of economic development to sustain the remarkable rates of growth that have continued throughout the 'reform and opening-up' era since 1978. The People's Republic of China's (PRC's) central government clearly sees investing in start-ups, high-tech companies and the service sector as the nation's economic future, with Premier Li Keqiang claiming at the National People's Congress (NPC) in March 2016 that 12,000 companies were founded every day in 2015. Many of these newly formed companies also benefit from substantial state benefits and handouts with the aim of inculcating a culture of 'mass entrepreneurship' to support future economic growth (Schuman 2016). Indeed, according to the Global Innovation Index 2016, China became a 'top 25' innovative economy for the first time, also becoming the first middle-income country to do so (WIPO 2016a, p. xviii). Nevertheless, despite impressive expansion in innovative activity in China, it is evident that an effective functioning IP system is a key foundational prerequisite upon which such an innovative knowledge-based economy can be constructed. Thus, intellectual property is of great significance in contemporary China and this study seeks to assess the evolving state of IP in China primarily through the experiences of respondents based on the ground in China to measure how China's compliance with the TRIPS Agreement has changed since WTO accession in 2001.

This chapter will next consider the significance of international intellectual property by laying out the development of IP, from the national level in the early years of IP, to the international with the signing of the Paris and Berne Conventions in the late nineteenth century, to the global with the inclusion of international IP standards in the WTO system. Then the significance of WTO accession for China will be outlined as well as giving an overview of the key agencies involved in the IP system as well as considering the implications for the current IP system of the instrumentalist nature of the post-WTO legal system in China. The fourth section will describe the development of intellectual property in China prior to WTO accession, which occurred in four phases: during imperial China; introduction of IP laws in the early twentieth century by the Nationalist Guomindang government; the changes made after the Chinese Communist Party founded the PRC in 1949; and finally the modern IP laws passed since the 'reform and opening-up' period began under Deng Xiaoping in 1978. The final section will provide an outline of the research project, detailing the key research questions as well as offering an overview of the structure of the book and the content of the subsequent chapters.

1.2   The Significance of International Intellectual Property

1.2.1   Definitions and Context

According to the World Intellectual Property Organisation (WIPO), intellectual property "refers to creations of the mind: inventions, literary and artistic works, and symbols, names, images, and designs used in commerce" (WIPO 2005).

This is similar to the definition used by the WTO, which states that "Intellectual property rights are the rights given to persons over the creations of their minds. They usually give the creator an exclusive right over the use of his/her creation for a certain period of time" (World Trade Organisation 2005a). These definitions emphasise the origins of intellectual property in the mind of the creator or inventor. It is clear that intellectual property can include various categories of rights, apart from the traditional protection for copyright, trademark and patent. Indeed the TRIPS Agreement is exhaustive in its approach to the IP rights covered by the Agreement. TRIPS Article 1(2) provides that "for the purposes of this Agreement, the term 'intellectual property' refers to all categories of intellectual property that are the subject of Sections 1 through 7 of Part II" (World Trade Organisation 1994). Therefore, the TRIPS Agreement covers a total of seven areas of intellectual property:

- Copyright and related rights (Part II(1));
- Trademarks (Part II(2));
- Geographical indications (Part II(3));
- Industrial designs (Part II(4));
- Patents (Part II(5));
- Layout designs (Topographies) of integrated circuits (Part II(6));
- Protection of undisclosed information (Part II(7)).

Consequently, for the sake of brevity, intellectual property or IP shall be referred to throughout this book, but it should be borne in mind that the definition of intellectual property that is used is the broad definition above, as used in the TRIPS Agreement.

In order to appreciate the significance of the TRIPS Agreement in terms of international intellectual property protection, it is necessary to first understand the origins of intellectual property rights. Intellectual property protection began around the time of widespread industrialisation across Europe, although the recognition of marks of ownership clearly existed long before this period. Indeed, one of the first known references to intellectual property protection dates from 500 BC when chefs were granted year-long monopolies for creating culinary delights in the Greek colony of Sybaris (Moore 2001, p. 9). However, a recognised system of intellectual property protection was not formally introduced until much later. Patents came into existence in Venice around 1500 and had spread to most of the main European powers by 1550 (Ostergard 2003, p. 12). The first formal patent system in Venice was highly significant as "for the first time a legal and institutional form of intellectual property rights established the ownership of knowledge and was explicitly utilized to promote innovation" (May and Sell 2006, p. 58). The origins of copyright, on the other hand, trace to the establishment of printing; copyright emerged from a concern to control this new technology. This concern led to the world's first copyright act, the Statute of Anne in 1710, entitled "An Act for the Encouragement of Learning, by vesting the Copies of Printed Books in the Authors or Purchasers of such Copies, during the Times therein mentioned" (Goldstein 2001, p. 5). Furthermore, early legislative developments in Britain in the seventeenth and eighteenth centuries covering intellectual property are frequently seen as the dawn of modern intellectual property law (May and Sell 2006, p. 73).

Various countries enacted intellectual property laws over the next century, but it was not until the late nineteenth century that international intellectual property protection was considered necessary. This need "became evident when foreign exhibitors refused to attend the International Exhibition of Inventions in Vienna in 1873 because they were afraid their ideas would be stolen and exploited commercially in other countries" (WIPO 2006). This led to the Paris Convention for the Protection of Industrial Property in 1883, which was the first international agreement to deal with IP rights (WIPO 2016b). This was followed by the Berne Convention for the Protection of Literary and Artistic Works of 1886, which dealt specifically with creative works such as books, plays and music (WIPO 2016c).[1] These two international conventions originally had few signatories, but included a secretariat from the outset. The Paris Convention had 14 initial member countries when it came into force in 1884 (WIPO 2004, p. 241) and the Berne Convention had eight original members in 1887. The respective secretariats merged in 1893 and eventually became the World Intellectual Property Organisation (WIPO) in 1967, which then became part of the United Nations (UN) system of specialised agencies in 1974 (WIPO 2004, p. 5).

Hence, intellectual property has a long history of protection at an international level, but the WIPO-administered system was widely criticised as insufficient as IP began to grow in importance in the 1970s and 1980s. Thus, it was proposed that intellectual property protection be incorporated into the existing multilateral trading system under the General Agreement on Tariffs and Trade (GATT) 1947. Therefore, the development of intellectual property protection could be said to have three distinct phases: *national*, from the fifteenth to the late nineteenth century; *international*, from the passing of the Paris and Berne Conventions in the 1880s until the final decades of the twentieth century; and *global*, from the inclusion of IP in the multilateral trading system with the establishment of the TRIPS framework in 1994. As a result, the TRIPS Agreement can be seen as highly significant from the perspective of the historical evolution of IP protection as it began a new phase of development—that of global protection.

Although the Paris and Berne Conventions were significant at the time they were agreed for embodying the principles of non-discrimination and national treatment, they "neither created new substantive law nor imposed new laws on member states; rather, they reflected a consensus among member states that was legitimated by domestic laws already in place" (Sell 2003, pp. 10–1). Accordingly, the Conventions allowed wide variation in IP protection offered by the signatories and recognised that different countries may require different levels of IP protection according to their different levels of economic development. As the TRIPS Agreement downplays this inherent flexibility in favour of the promotion of universality, it is indeed a significant step in the progression of IP protection, and its inclusion in the GATT/WTO system will now be examined in more detail.

1.2.2 The Development of Intellectual Property in the International Trading System

Although the GATT, the forerunner to the WTO, was not established until 1948, consideration of the benefits of multilateral trade agreements had begun as early as the 1930s. Due to the Great Depression, import tariffs and other discriminatory barriers were raised. However, as:

> many large economies became protectionist simultaneously or in retaliation, so more rather than less suffering resulted from these policies...Hence the belief that there must be gains from getting together to sign a multilateral trade agreement to prevent such destructive trade policy lapses in the future. (Anderson 1996)

After the Second World War, the desire to establish an international trade organisation grew stronger. Although the primary aim of such an agreement was economic, there was also the issue of political stability to consider. Therefore, initially countries wanted to establish a trading organisation for reasons of political stability as well as economic gains.[2] Subsequently, the GATT came into being in January 1948, with 23 initial contracting parties, which included China.

In terms of intellectual property, the provisions of GATT were very limited with scant mention of IP protection, as the primary focus of GATT, at least initially, was tariff reduction. However, GATT Article XX(d) did allow contracting parties a general exception to the rules on trade barriers to allow signatories to adopt or enforce measures "necessary to secure compliance with laws or regulations which are not inconsistent with the provisions of this Agreement, including... the protection of patents, trade marks and copyrights, and the prevention of deceptive practices."[3] This Article was invoked in two disputes under the GATT dispute settlement process. In the first from 1983, the panel held that patent protection was an area in which a contracting party could take action which did not otherwise conform to their GATT obligations. In the second case from 1989, the panel held that although domestic patent law could not be challenged, the contracting parties had an obligation to try to enforce their intellectual property legislation in accordance with their GATT commitments (Gervais 2003, p. 7).

Therefore, although GATT 1947 did mention intellectual property protection in brief, it was not a major concern of the multilateral trading system until the 1970s. The complex drafting history of the TRIPS Agreement and negotiations that took place during the Uruguay Round from 1986 to 1994 will be further detailed in Chap. 3, as the characteristics of the TRIPS Agreement are discussed in the context of their possible impact upon subsequent compliance by WTO members. It is important to note that IP protection is now one of the major issues in the international trading system, particularly in the past few decades as the emphasis has shifted from tariff barriers to trade to non-tariff barriers, such as inappropriate IP protection. As a result, compliance with the TRIPS Agreement is a matter of great concern for many WTO members.

On the other hand, it could be argued that evaluating compliance with the TRIPS Agreement is futile and ineffective as we move into a "post-TRIPS" era. Since the TRIPS Agreement was signed more than 20 years ago, many countries (particularly developed countries) around the world have continued to negotiate and pressure trading partners to assent to a wide array of free trade agreements (FTAs). Such bilateral and regional agreements have frequently included IP standards in their discussions and the resulting mess of criss-crossing free trade agreements has even been described as a "spaghetti bowl" (Antons and Hilty 2015). In addition, it was not only the developed industrialised nations which sought to negotiate differing IP standards from those contained within the TRIPS Agreement. Developing countries were also subsequently dissatisfied with the contents of the TRIPS Agreement and in particular, those focused on the provisions affecting public health, human rights, biodiversity and plant genetic resources (Helfer 2004, p. 4), which led to the Doha Declaration in November 2001. Looking back to when the TRIPS Agreement was accepted in 1994, "it soon became clear that TRIPS only represented the starting point for more substantial demands" (Kur 2016, p. 136) and for many members, TRIPS was never enough (Sell 2011).

The reality today is that the post-TRIPS system of unilateral, bilateral and regional standards of IP rules undeniably goes beyond the multilateral norms found in TRIPS and creates an increasingly fragmented system of 'TRIPS-plus' protection and enforcement around the globe (Ruse-Khan 2016, p. 163). In other words, it could be argued that compliance with the TRIPS Agreement is of little or no significance in the so-called post-TRIPS era in which many countries have entered into subsequent unilateral, bilateral or regional agreements involving intellectual property standards which frequently go beyond the minimum standards defined in the TRIPS Agreement which was concluded more than two decades ago in 1994.

However, I would argue that China's compliance with the TRIPS Agreement is of considerable interest for many reasons. Firstly, China's compliance or otherwise with the obligations imposed upon it by the TRIPS Agreement can act as an indicator of likely compliance with other trade-related agreements to which China may accede in the future. Furthermore, the TRIPS Agreement remains the key global agreement containing the international intellectual property standards. Compared to the subsequent trade agreements incorporating IP standards such as the Anti-Counterfeiting Trade Agreement (ACTA) and Trans-Pacific Partnership (TPP), the TRIPS Agreement is seen as "in many respects still the better Agreement" as it is more balanced, fairer and more flexible (Jaeger 2016, p. 641). Furthermore, it is also undeniable that TRIPS is still the key Agreement laying down the international intellectual property standards because although subsequent agreements have expanded the levels of protection, such agreements have largely either failed to be ratified and implemented, are still under negotiation, or are only bilateral Free Trade Agreements (FTAs) affecting those trading partners only.

In addition, ACTA, TPP and the Transatlantic Trade and Investment Partnership (TTIP) have all been negotiated in complete secrecy which not only prevents public comments on the negotiation process but also leads to considerable suspicion about the provisions contained within the final agreements and thus to consequent reluctance to ratify and implement the agreed provisions. ACTA was "different from other multilateral IP agreements to the extent that it was conceived as an agreement between like-minded nations" (Drexl 2016, p. 67). In other words, the arena of international intellectual property rule-making shifted from an inclusive approach seeking to establish minimum standards to which all trading partners can commit, to a "country club" approach in which like-minded nations break away to form their own agreement and instead seek to set a "gold standard" in IP rights, particularly in enforcement. Compared to TRIPS, ACTA was widely felt to embed tougher standards entirely for the benefit of rights-holders (Jaeger 2016, pp. 625–6). Consequently, the TRIPS Agreement is still recognised as offering an acceptable balance between rights-holders and users, whereas subsequent agreements are generally regarded as tipping the balance further towards rights-holders.

Furthermore, the narrative of China's shifting compliance with the TRIPS Agreement over the past 15 years since formal WTO accession can offer valuable lessons to other countries, particularly developing countries acceding to trade agreements. For example, Russia joined the WTO in December 2011, a decade after China, and experienced similar issues in implementing WTO commitments due to ingrained "institutional challenges" (Lane 2013). Finally, China's compliance with the TRIPS Agreement, as a recognised and respected set of international intellectual property rules, is of continued interest to rights-holders in China—both foreign and domestic. Having considered why China's compliance with the TRIPS Agreement remains of interest, I will now consider the specifics of China's accession to the WTO.

1.3   The Significance of WTO Accession for China

The PRC, formed in 1949 following the victory of the Communist Party in China's civil war, has a long and uneven history of interaction with the international trading system of GATT/WTO. Nationalist "China" became an original contracting party to GATT on 30 October 1947, as the Republic of China (ROC). However, China's initial membership in GATT came to an end in 1950, when in March 1950, "the Taiwan authority informed the UN Secretary-General of its intention to withdraw from GATT" (Li 1998). From 1950 until the early 1970s, Taiwan participated in GATT proceedings as an observer. However, following a thaw in relations between China and the US, the UN shifted diplomatic allegiance from the ROC (Taiwan) to the PRC based on the mainland and governed by the Chinese Communist Party. In 1971, the UN General Assembly passed resolution 2758 (XXVI) that recognised the PRC government as the sole representative of

China and expelled Taiwan. Subsequently, GATT followed suit and nullified Taiwan's observer status.

As China commenced the process of opening up to trade with the outside world from 1978 onwards, greater interest began to be shown in the benefits and membership of various international financial organisations. In 1980, China became a member of the World Bank and International Monetary Fund (IMF) and started to show an interest in GATT. However, China did not immediately apply to resume its membership of GATT, although it began to participate in GATT as an observer from 1982 (Pearson 1999, p. 169). It was not until July 1986 that this application to resume full membership was made (GATT 1986). Subsequently, GATT acted swiftly to consider China's application with a working party established to negotiate for China's full membership in June 1987 (GATT 1987).

Initially, the GATT working party made steady progress in the admission process. However, the events in Tiananmen Square in June 1989 halted further negotiations; "although the working party continued to meet periodically, its members developed a more hardened attitude, despite their declaration of support for China's accession in principle" (Pearson 1999, p. 169). China's application to GATT was further complicated by Taiwan's application to join GATT as a separate customs territory in January 1990. In effect, the accession process halted from 1989 to around 1992. Nevertheless, as China had at that time applied to resume GATT membership, "China was permitted to participate fully in the Uruguay round of multilateral trade negotiations," and as part of this participation, Chinese representatives had been included in TRIPS discussions "in 1991 and before that time" (Zheng 1997, p. 243). Therefore, China attempted to follow TRIPS provisions in subsequent amendments to its intellectual property laws, and the influence of TRIPS on the Chinese IP system should thus be considered as beginning much earlier than China's eventual formal WTO accession in December 2001.

Although China failed to join GATT in time to become a member of the newly established WTO in 1995, negotiations resumed soon after and good progress was made towards accession. Several factors did stymie this process, including the bombing of the Chinese embassy in Belgrade in May 1999 (Hamada 2004, p. 28). However, after furious negotiations, China finally entered the WTO on 11 December 2001 and from that date, had to formally comply with all the agreements that together make up the framework of the WTO. In the case of the TRIPS Agreement, China agreed to comply with its TRIPS obligations immediately upon accession, with no transition period (World Trade Organisation 2001).

The issue of intellectual property protection in China was one of the key issues in China's WTO accession negotiations. Furthermore, the importance of IP protection can be witnessed in the final Working Party Report on China's WTO accession, which devoted 55 paragraphs out of a total of 343 paragraphs to China's commitments under the TRIPS regime.[4] In addition, China's capacity to fully implement its TRIPS commitments was "one of the most frequently aired concerns" prior to entry in December 2001 (Gregory 2003, p. 321). These concerns arose from the recognition that "government commitment and a sound legal framework would not suffice to ensure enforcement, as IPRs involve millions of enterprises and hundreds of millions of individuals" (Long 2003, p. 169).

Therefore, China's compliance with the TRIPS Agreement as evidence of the maturity of its intellectual property system as a whole is an area of considerable interest for several of China's trading partners and given the level of concern regarding China's TRIPS implementation prior to accession; it is clearly an issue worthy of further study. Furthermore, as 15 years have passed since accession, now is an ideal time to research both the short-term and longer-term impact of the TRIPS Agreement on China's IP system.

1.3.1 The Nature of the Post-WTO Chinese Legal System

In order to fully comprehend the current IP system in China, it is necessary to first grasp an appreciation for the complex interplay between the state and the law in China and how this relationship has developed. Firstly, China could be said to have only benefited from an independent legal system since 1912; in Imperial China, all power was vested in the emperor and the legal codes that did exist were aimed at protecting the state's interests rather than individual rights. Moreover, many legal matters were dealt with informally by local groups without recourse to formal legal structures (Cohen 1966, p. 470).

Furthermore, since the establishment of the PRC in 1949, the formal legal framework has also periodically been sidelined in favour of extrajudicial mechanisms, particularly during the Cultural Revolution from 1966–76 (Wang 1995, p. 132). As the contemporary legal framework of courts and personnel has only been established for less than four decades, since the start of the reform period in the late 1970s, the juvenile nature of the legal system still has its legacy in the current IP system, particularly in the lack of experience of key personnel, an issue compounded by the fact that specialised IP courts were only more recently established. In addition, although the legal system has been subject to sweeping reforms in the past decades, these changes cannot be considered in isolation.

> Regardless of how much legislation is promulgated and how many judges are trained and installed in the courts, legality will not grow unless the Party-state fosters and maintains a commitment to it and alters the allocation of power between the courts and the rest of the Party-state. (Lubman 1999, p. 299)

In other words, consideration of the legal system necessarily incorporates discussion of the political system in China as well. The legal system in China is also subject to lingering suspicions that, despite committing to establishing a rule-of-law state in a constitutional amendment of 1999, it is still subject to the policy whims of the Party (Liu 1991, pp. 7–8). Indeed, China's legal system is frequently judged to be following an instrumentalist model of the law, whereby law is merely the vehicle by which policy goals are achieved, whether they be social control, class emancipation or economic development. This instrumentalist model could be seen as originating in the traditional Chinese legal system, but also as arising from adoption of a Marxist legal model (Yu 2001, p. 72).

The instrumentalist nature of the legal system in China has several implications for the current IP system. It is certainly true that legislation is often drafted to be "intentionally ambiguous" (Potter 2001, p. 11) in order to allow for shifts in policy emphasis and with detailed regulations issued later to fill the gaps. This could also be a consequence of the traditional preference in China for bureaucratic discretion over legislative certainty. In addition, there is a traditional preference in China for informal dispute resolution mechanisms, such as mediation which leads to a continued dominance of public enforcement mechanisms in the legal system generally.[5] The obvious corollary of this is a corresponding weakness in the judicial system. Although the principle of judicial independence is officially accepted, the interpretation of this principle refers to the elimination of direct interference in individual cases rather than a wider separation of powers recognised as central to judicial independence in other jurisdictions (Keith 1994, p. 18). Finally, the decentralisation that has taken place in the reform era, as China has moved away from a centrally planned command economy, has conversely led to problems in the legal system; as provinces are now more powerful, local protectionism cannot be easily confronted as local interests are deeply entrenched.

In terms of the IP system specifically, there are a number of official agencies charged with administering the current IP system in China. The State Administration for Industry and Commerce (SAIC) is responsible for trademark registration and enforcement, which is often carried out administratively through local-level AICs. The General Administration of Customs is the body responsible for enforcement of IP at the border, whilst copyright is dealt with by the National Copyright Administration (under the General Administration of Press and Publication). Finally, despite the wider-ranging name, the State Intellectual Property Office is only responsible for patent registration and enforcement and was formerly known as the Chinese Patent Office. In addition, the Supreme People's Court is the body responsible for judicial enforcement of intellectual property in China.

Apart from the Supreme People's Court, all of these organisations are directly responsible to the State Council. The Supreme People's Court is overseen by the National People's Congress (NPC) and its permanent Standing Committee. According to Article 67 of the PRC constitution,[6] it is also the role of the NPC's standing committee to oversee the work of the State Council. Thus, the main IP agencies are not subordinate to a particular ministry. However, as they are powerful bodies reporting directly to the State Council, they are highly resistant to any attempts to merge them or delegate their powers to other bodies. As a result, the IP system is often accused of lacking coordination between these multiple channels (Mertha 2005, p. 111).

Therefore, the role of the law and of the state in China and the developing relationship between the two has a variety of implications for the current system of IP protection. These consequences will be discussed further in this book as analysis of the current IP system develops. The following section will now examine the development of IP in China.

1.4   INTELLECTUAL PROPERTY IN CHINA PRIOR TO WTO ACCESSION

China's WTO entry in December 2001 and consequent obligation to comply with the TRIPS Agreement had a significant impact on the IP system in China and, to appreciate this full impact, it is necessary to first understand the development of intellectual property protection from imperial China until the reform era. The development of intellectual property protection in China can be divided into four stages: firstly, the initial steps towards IP protection taken in the final years of the Qing Dynasty under pressure from Western powers; secondly, the early IP laws enacted by the Guomindang (Nationalist party) government in the period from 1912 to the 1940s to try to modernise the law; next, the preliminary Communist reforms during the early years of the PRC; and finally, the extensive period of law reform which has taken place since the reform and opening-up period began in the late 1970s. These four stages of development will be outlined below in order to place the significance of China's accession to the TRIPS regime in context.

1.4.1   Intellectual Property in Imperial China

It is widely accepted that there was "no comprehensive, centrally promulgated, formal legal protection for either proprietary symbols or inventions" in imperial China, despite some evidence of limited protection of brand names and controls regarding publications (Alford 1996, p. 15). On the contrary, these feeble efforts made to protect intellectual property were regarded as solely aimed at maintaining the state's authority by controlling the dissemination of ideas (Yu 2002, p. 5). It is also undeniable that several commentators have been bemused by the lack of rudimentary intellectual property protection in imperial China, given China's considerable advances in science and technology.

Furthermore, despite some scanty evidence suggesting that the concept of intellectual property was ingrained in imperial society, the written legal codes did not reflect the private proprietary rights of intellectual property. In the Qing dynasty, the formal legal Code "dealt with almost all aspects of a citizen's and an official's life", but all "in penal form and China had no other (civil) code of law" (Tay 1969, p. 160). In fact, "the law was only secondarily interested in defending the rights- especially the economic rights- of one individual or group against another individual or group and not at all in defending such rights against the state" (Bodde and Morris 1967, p. 4). This concurs with the finding that the scant intellectual property protection that did exist in imperial

China was not concerned "with the rights of individuals or their claims for their own sake, but with the social order and the interests of the State" (Tay 1969, p. 161). In other words, Qing legal codes did not cover individual rights as modern conceptions of IP do.

In the late Qing dynasty, international pressure to introduce protection for intellectual property in China began to gain momentum in the late nineteenth century following the Paris Convention on Industrial Property (1883) and the Berne Convention for the Protection of Literary and Artistic Works (1886), as discussed above. Pressure on China from Western powers to improve intellectual property protection also increased at this time as many Chinese traders used foreign trademarks in order to avoid taxes to which Chinese, but not foreign, goods were subject (Feder 1996, p. 233). By the turn of the twentieth century, there were some efforts within the treaty ports to register marks belonging to foreign nationals, but without effective enforcement powers, these efforts proved worthless (Alford 1996, p. 35). Furthermore, treaties concluded with Britain, Japan and the US in the early twentieth century[7] included clauses on intellectual property, but these provisions were unclear and contradictory.

China did make some effort at this time to bring Chinese law in line with Western jurisprudence in order to escape from the extraterritorial regime, specifically by establishing a Law Codification Commission in 1904 (Lee 1969, p. 136). This process of westernisation focused on Japan as a recommended model for reform (Chen 2000, p. 22). China also attempted to introduce some basic intellectual property laws during the final years of the Qing Dynasty, such as the Law of Authorship of 1910, but the short life of this law meant that any evidence of its implementation was absent (Qu 2002, p. 22). Thus, despite this period from the late nineteenth to the early twentieth century of "unprecedented international attention to intellectual property" (Alford 1996, p. 34), no effective formal legal measures were instituted to protect intellectual property in imperial China.

1.4.2   *Reforms in Intellectual Property Under the Guomindang*

Following the fall of the Qing Dynasty in 1912, China experienced several years of political upheaval before the country was largely united under the government of the Nationalist Guomindang Party in 1927. When the Guomindang (GMD) first came to power, efforts were made to stimulate invention and creativity. The Guomindang carried out an extensive programme of legislation, first soon after the end of the Qing Dynasty and further, more extensive, reforms after 1927. For example, soon after the fall of the Qing dynasty, the Guomindang announced the Temporary Statute on Technology Reward of 1912. The Guomindang also introduced a trademark law which saw 50,000 trademark registrations by 1948, a detailed copyright law and the first patent law in Chinese history (Yang 2002, p. 6).

Additionally, the first copyright law was passed in 1928, which borrowed extensively from the German model via the Japanese version and was amended in 1944 to grant more equal treatment to both Chinese and foreign authors (Qu 2002, p. 26). A comprehensive trademark law was passed in 1931 which was still in force when the Communists came to power in 1949; according to some sources, this law was again transplanted from the Continent via Japan (Carter 1996, p. 11). The patent law drafted in 1944 formalised the system previously established by the Measures to Encourage Industrial Arts of 1932. These laws could thus be seen as the first introduction of formal IP protection to China.

Nevertheless, despite the promulgation of these landmark intellectual property laws, "these laws failed to achieve their stated objectives because they presumed a legal structure, and indeed, a legal consciousness, that did not then exist in China and, most likely, could not have flourished there at that time" (Alford 1996, p. 53). These fundamental IP laws called for administration through well-organised central agencies and modern courts, which simply were not present in China at that time. As a result, despite detailed legislation being adopted, there were very little changes in Chinese IP practice during Guomindang rule.

1.4.3 Development of Intellectual Property in the PRC

After the victory of the Chinese Communist Party and subsequent establishment of the PRC in 1949 following many years of bitter civil turmoil, all Guomindang laws and decrees were abolished, as they were seen as tools for the repression of the masses (Blaustein 1962, p. 41). Consequently, the preliminary intellectual property protection system that had been established by the Guomindang was dismantled, and the new PRC government began to consider a Communist alternative. This dismantling of the Guomindang legal system and codes for ideological reasons clearly left a legal vacuum (Chen 2000, p. 30). Therefore, the question became how could inventions and outstanding works be encouraged and rewarded in a way which was consistent with Communist ideology?

The Provisional Regulations on the Guarantee of Invention Rights and Patent Rights which were promulgated on 11 August 1950 were the first regulations passed to fill this legal vacuum. These Provisional Regulations from 1950, "closely paralleled western patent laws in granting exclusive rights of exploitation of the patented device to the patentee" (Gale 1978, p. 336). It is also significant that rights granted under these Regulations were inheritable and transferable under Article 7, as these rights reflect Western notions of personal property rights. However, the relatively liberal 1950 Provisional Regulations were soon amended by the Provisional Regulations on Awards for Inventions, Technical Improvements and Rationalization Proposals Concerning Production, approved on 6 May 1954.[8] These Regulations provided for monetary awards for improvements to any production process, calculated according to the money saved in the 12 months after the invention.

However, in these revised regulations, "patents as such were ignored" (Gale 1978, p. 337). The focus of these Regulations on monetary awards rather than the granting of property rights reinforces the notion that Communist legislation at this time was firmly aimed at promoting the state's interests and not at promoting individual proprietary rights. This supports the proposition that early intellectual property legislation was patterned on the Soviet model, with just a few modifications to allow for the gap in development between the Chinese and Soviet economies. The abandonment of personal property rights in the limited rewards offered to inventors also reflects classic Marxist thought (Marx 1963, p. 157). Thus, under Communist ideology, the notion of privately owned property rights effectively became meaningless (Hsia and Haun 1973, p. 280).

The patent system was further amended by the 1963 Regulations on Awards for Inventions and the separately published Regulations on Awards for Technical Improvements, which permanently eliminated the certificate of ownership in favour of a lump sum payment system. As a result, the 1963 Regulations were even more radical than the previous system in operation, with much fewer rewards and legal rights for inventors. This more radical approach is also reflected in a *People's Daily* editorial from 1963 which emphasised the position of inventions as collective property and added:

> This is totally different from the old society... it is not necessary for us to regard the inventions and technical improvements of a certain individual or a certain unit as personal property which deserves 'protection'. This is different in nature from the so-called 'patent rights' under the capitalistic system.[9]

The trademark system could also be considered to be fairly radical compared to that established in the Soviet Union. Trademarks were not retained in order to assist businesses, but rather to assist the consumer, individual or collective, to identify the quality of a product. Thus, they were predominantly used on products made for export (Hsia and Haun 1973, pp. 285–6) as individual consumers did not play a role in a centrally planned economy.

In contrast to the Regulations passed to govern patents and trademarks, the PRC did not enact any statute on copyright following the abolition of the Guomindang Copyright Law from 1928, amended in 1944; indeed the only protection available to Chinese authors was in the form of model contracts from 1957 (Hsia and Haun 1973, p. 289). This lack of copyright protection exemplifies attitudes to intellectual property in the early years of the PRC. Patent law was codified in order to encourage industrial innovation, much needed to stimulate economic growth; trademark law was tolerated in order to promote consumer interests and potential exports; but copyright law did not promote any public interest and thus was simply at odds with Communist ideology.

Overall, the provisional IP regulations and reward systems put in place from 1949 to the 1970s did not succeed in promoting innovation and steadily moved away from the initial position of recognising an individual's IP rights to a more radical socialist approach that viewed IP as collective property. Consequently, between 1950 and 1963 only four patent rights and five inventions were granted in China (Xue and Liang 2010). The Soviet intellectual property laws were also quite influential in the early IP regulations adopted in the 1950s, although the Soviet model was not always appropriate due to the differences in industrialisation between the Soviet Union and China. Furthermore, during the Chinese Cultural Revolution which took place from 1966 to 1976, even the system of lump sum bonuses was abolished in favour of a strict policy that all inventions and creations were national assets (Kolton 1996, p. 416). As a result, the research and development system was virtually paralysed throughout much of the pre-reform years of the PRC, with many individuals reluctant to acknowledge their role in a creation or invention, for fear of the potentially capitalist or individualistic stigma that would be attached to them. As China began to face the post-Mao era in the late 1970s, it was clear that the existing intellectual property system was inadequate to stimulate the necessary economic development and foreign investment.

1.4.4　Development of Intellectual Property in the Reform Era

As the reform era began in 1978 and China began to open up to the outside world, intellectual property protection was in a parlous state. Despite the lack of formal functioning intellectual property laws, indeed the perceived lack of the entire concept of intellectual property, protection of intellectual property was soon prioritised in China's dealings with its trade partners. For instance, the China–US Agreement on Trade Relations of 7 July 1979 committed China to implementing formal rules for intellectual property protection. In effect, this committed China to introducing laws and regulations that offered the same high level of protection as the equivalent laws in the US.

Although intellectual property laws took several years to be drafted and promulgated, new regulations were passed in 1978 to encourage innovation (Sit 1983, p. 497), which shows the early recognition by the central government of the importance of innovation to economic development. As a result, in the early 1980s, China did attempt to draft and adopt several intellectual property laws to replace the outdated provisional regulations passed in the 1950s. However, the introduction of such laws was no easy task, as they raised difficult ideological questions about the future of Chinese socialism. For example, advocates of a new patent law argued that reform was necessary to stimulate industrial innovation and foreign investment. Conversely, opponents of the new patent law argued that rewarding inventors was contrary to key socialist principles and that a liberal patent system "would allow foreign enterprises to control and dominate Chinese technology" (Bachner 1997, p. 449).

Consequently, the new statutes passed in the first years of the reform era reflected the Communist government's unease with the introduction of private property rights and still had socialist principles at their core (Yu 2000, p. 36). Notwithstanding these ideological difficulties, China did push ahead with intellectual property reform, joining the World Intellectual Property Organisation (WIPO) in 1980 and the Paris Convention on Industrial Property in 1984, as well as passing the PRC Trademark Law in 1982 and the aforementioned PRC Patent Law in 1984. Copyright protection lagged behind protection for patents and trademarks, perhaps because industrial property was considered to be more commercially necessary to stimulate short-term economic development. The PRC Copyright Law was finally passed in 1990, although copyright had been mentioned in the 1986 General Principles of Civil Law (Bachner 1997, p. 444).

Despite establishing a comprehensive framework of statutory protection for intellectual property rights by the 1990s, China was still subject to heavy criticism from several trading partners, especially the US. Bilateral tensions concerning IP protection escalated in the mid-1990s and sanctions were threatened on several occasions before agreements were reached. Therefore, by the turn of the twenty-first century, there was a clear need for a new approach to intellectual property both within the international trading system and in China specifically to break the cycle of unilateral pressure and growing resentment. This alternative was provided by the accession of China to the WTO and the consequent obligation to comply with the TRIPS Agreement which is the focus of this book.

1.5   Outline of the Research Project

As this chapter has explained, protection of intellectual property rights by individual nations has evolved over many centuries and has emerged as worthy of international consideration only in the past hundred years or so. Furthermore, the concept of intellectual property rights in China has also developed beyond recognition over the past hundred years and is now acknowledged to be an area of crucial importance for the modern Chinese legal system. As intellectual property became more and more significant for the international trading system in the 1980s and 1990s, the TRIPS Agreement began to emerge from the Uruguay Round of trade negotiations that led to the establishment of the WTO. The TRIPS Agreement represented an important step in the development of international IP rights as the Agreement included provisions on enforcement previously neglected by international IP Conventions. Compliance with the TRIPS Agreement by individual WTO members is thus highly significant as it affirms the legitimacy of the TRIPS Agreement and the WTO system of rules as a whole, and continues to be of interest even as we enter the post-TRIPS era of international intellectual property rule-making.

Accession to the WTO and the associated commitment to fully comply with the provisions of the TRIPS Agreement is also highly significant for China. Despite previous attempts to introduce a comprehensive system of protection for IP rights in China, the pre-WTO intellectual property system was still subject to strong criticism from key trading partners such as the US. Thus, the impact of the TRIPS Agreement was hoped to not only assist with the continuing development of the IP system, but also to alleviate IP-related tensions with trading partners, as well as to contribute towards economic development in China. As a result, it can be seen that compliance with the TRIPS Agreement would signify an important step forward for the intellectual property system in China.

As WTO entry took place in December 2001, the time is now pertinent to make a systematic attempt to evaluate the post-WTO system of intellectual property protection in China. Thus, compliance theory can be a useful tool with which to examine both the immediate short-term impact of TRIPS accession on the IP system in China and also the continuing effects on the current system. Existing theories of compliance from both international law and international relations will be discussed in more detail in Chap. 2. Previous studies of the legal system in China have largely relied on subjective judgements about the effectiveness of the system without any attempt to provide an overall model of the development of this system in response to external and internal influences, and this study aims to rectify this deficit.

The key research questions which I will be attempting to answer in this study are thus as follows: what are the characteristics of the TRIPS Agreement that may affect a member's compliance with it? What has the impact of WTO accession and related TRIPS obligations been on the IP system in China in both the short term and the longer term? How effective is the current system of IP protection in China? Is China fully complying with its obligations under the TRIPS Agreement? If there are continuing areas of non-compliance, what are they and why is China not fully complying with TRIPS? How can any outstanding areas of non-compliance with TRIPS be resolved?

In order to address these questions, the remainder of the book will be structured as follows: Part I will consider how to assess 'compliance' with the TRIPS Agreement generally by outlining the key concepts and methods. Chapter 2, the first in this section, will outline the central concept of compliance and key theories and models of compliance that have been proposed in both international law and international relations literature before identifying a comprehensive model of compliance to be applied specifically to evaluating China's TRIPS compliance. Chapter 3 will discuss the TRIPS Agreement in more detail, analysing the drafting history of the Agreement, characteristics of the Agreement that may affect compliance, as well as the international environment surrounding IP rights in order to fully describe the development of the system of global rules for intellectual property protection. Because TRIPS imposes such detailed obligations on members not only limited to legislative changes but also including enforcement, application, appeal and remedies, it is necessary to look behind and beyond the law on paper in order to gain a deeper understanding of the Chinese IP system in practice. It is also desirable to see the law as a continuum and as a process (Lam 2009, p. 148); in other words, there is a clear scale of compliance from complete TRIPS compliance to complete non-compliance which needs to be gauged. This deeper level of understanding was achieved through a combination of research methods including a questionnaire, detailed interviews and document analysis which will be outlined in Chap. 4 to offer an inclusive framework for assessing compliance with the TRIPS Agreement.

Part II of the book looks in more detail at compliance with the TRIPS Agreement in the Chinese context. Chapter 5 considers the implementation of the TRIPS Agreement in China, compliance with the TRIPS Agreement and the overall effectiveness of the Agreement in transforming the IP system in China. Chapter 6 then focuses more specifically on the short-term effects of the TRIPS Agreement on the IP system in China. This chapter is substantially built upon surveys and interviews conducted in China in 2005–6 and seeks to explore the gap which was identified as existing between the laws on paper and the enforcement witnessed on the ground. Chapter 7 then considers the post-TRIPS intellectual property system in China in the longer term with further data and interviews collected in 2015. This chapter considers how the post-TRIPS IP system has adapted to the local conditions and needs of contemporary China. Finally, in Chap. 8 the comprehensive model of compliance will be revisited and a revised model of China's compliance with the TRIPS Agreement will be proposed. The book will close with a summary and some thoughts on the implications of these findings for China, the WTO, key trading partners such as the US and for individual rights-holders.

Notes

1. Other relevant international intellectual property conventions are also available via the World Intellectual Property Organisation website at http://www.wipo.int/
2. Indeed, prevention of military conflict by channelling trade disputes into the WTO's dispute settlement process is still one of the stated aims of the WTO: World Trade Organisation (2005b).
3. For the full text of the 1947 GATT Agreement, see: World Trade Organisation (2016).
4. As noted by Long (2003, p. 165).
5. With the official standpoint that mediation should be attempted prior to litigation (Article 122 PRC Civil Procedure Law (2012)): Thomas (2016, p. 134).
6. Full text of China's Constitution available at: PRC National People's Congress (2004).
7. The texts of the Great Britain and China Treaty 1902, US–China Treaty 1903 and the Japan–China Treaty 1903 are all available in: MacMurray (1921, pp. 342–52; 411–5; 23–32).
8. Full text available from: Blaustein (1962, pp. 523–33).
9. Cited by Gale (1978, p. 341).

REFERENCES

Alford, William P. 1996. *To Steal a Book Is an Elegant Offense: Intellectual Property Law in Chinese Civilization*. Stanford: Stanford University Press.

Anderson, Kym. 1996. Why the World Needs the GATT/WTO. In *Strengthening the Global Trading System: From GATT to WTO*, ed. Kym Anderson. Adelaide: Centre for International Economic Studies, University of Adelaide.

Antons, Christoph, and Reto M. Hilty. 2015. Introduction: IP and the Asia-Pacific 'Spaghetti Bowl' of Free Trade Agreements. In *Intellectual Property and Free Trade Agreements in the Asia-Pacific Region*, ed. Christoph Antons and Reto M. Hilty, 1–23. Heidelberg: Springer.

Bachner, Bryan. 1997. Intellectual Property Law. In *Introduction to Chinese Law*, ed. Chenguang Wang and Xianchu Zhang. Hong Kong: Sweet & Maxwell.

Blaustein, Albert P., ed. 1962. *Fundamental Legal Documents of Communist China*. South Hackensack: Fred B. Rothman & Co.

Bodde, Derk, and Clarence Morris. 1967. *Law in Imperial China*. Cambridge, MA: Harvard University Press.

Carter, Connie. 1996. *Fighting Fakes in China: The Legal Protection of Trade Marks and Brands in the People's Republic of China*. London: The Intellectual Property Institute.

Chen, Jianfu. 2000. Coming Full-Circle: Law-Making in the PRC from a Historical Perspective. In *Law-Making in the People's Republic of China*, ed. Jan Michiel Otto et al. The Hague: Kluwer Law International.

Cohen, Jerome. 1966. The Criminal Process in the People's Republic of China: An Introduction. *Harvard Law Review* 79(3): 469–533.

Drexl, Josef. 2016. The Concept of Trade-Relatedness of Intellectual Property Rights in Times of Post-TRIPS Bilateralism. In *TRIPS Plus 20: From Trade Rules to Market Principles*, ed. Hanns Ullrich, Reto M. Hilty, Matthias Lamping, and Josef Drexlg. Heidelberg: Springer.

European Commission. 2015. Report on EU Customs Enforcement of Intellectual Property Rights: Results at the EU Border 2014. http://ec.europa.eu/taxation_customs/resources/documents/customs/customs_controls/counterfeit_piracy/statistics/2015_ipr_statistics.pdf. Accessed 19 Aug 2016.

Feder, Gregory S. 1996. Enforcement of Intellectual Property Rights in China: You Can Lead a Horse to Water But You Can't Make It Drink. *Virginia Journal of International Law* 37(1): 223–254.

Gale, Barden N. 1978. The Concept of Intellectual Property in the People's Republic of China: Inventors and Inventions. *The China Quarterly* 74: 355–334.

GATT. 1986. Ministerial Declaration on the Uruguay Round. http://www.wto.org/gatt_docs/English/SULPDF/91240152.pdf. Accessed 20 Oct 2015.

———. 1987. Document L/6191 Working Party on China's Status as a Contracting Party. http://gatt.stanford.edu/bin/object.pdf?91280113. Accessed 20 Apr 2005.

Gervais, Daniel. 2003. *The TRIPS Agreement: A Drafting History*. 2nd ed. London: Sweet & Maxwell.

Goldstein, Paul. 2001. *International Copyright: Principles, Law and Practice*. Oxford: Oxford University Press.

Gregory, Angela. 2003. Chinese Trademark Law and the TRIPS Agreement-Confucius Meets the WTO. In *China and the World Trading System: Entering the New Millennium*, ed. Deborah Cass. Cambridge: Cambridge University Press.

Hamada, Koichi. 2004. China's Entry into the WTO and Its Impact on the Global Economic System. In *Doha and Beyond: The Future of the Multilateral Trading System*, ed. Mike Moore. Cambridge: Cambridge University Press.

Helfer, Laurence R. 2004. Regime Shifting: The TRIPS Agreement and New Dynamics of International Intellectual Property Lawmaking. *Yale Journal of International Law* 29(1): 1–84.

Hsia, Tao-Tai, and Kathryn A. Haun. 1973. Laws of the People's Republic of China on Individual and Intellectual Property. *Law and Contemporary Problems* 38: 274–291.

Jaeger, Thomas. 2016. Merging ACTA into TRIPS: Does TRIPS-Based IP Enforcement Need Reform? In *TRIPS Plus 20: From Trade Rules to Market Principles*, ed. Hanns Ullrich, Reto M. Hilty, Matthias Lamping, and Josef Drexl. Heidelberg: Springer.

Keith, Ronald C. 1994. *China's Struggle for the Rule of Law*. London: The Macmillan Press.

Kolton, Gregory S. 1996. Copyright Law and the People's Courts in the People's Republic of China: A Review and Critique of China's Intellectual Property Courts. *University of Pennsylvania Journal of International Economic Law* 17(1): 415–460.

Kur, Annette. 2016. From Minimum Standards to Maximum Rules. In *TRIPS Plus 20: From Trade Rules to Market Principles*, ed. Hanns Ullrich, Reto M. Hilty, Matthias Lamping, and Josef Drexl. Heidelberg: Springer.

Lam, Esther. 2009. *China and the World Trade Organization: A Long March Towards the Rule of Law*. Alphen aan den Rijn: Kluwer Law International.

Lane, William P. 2013. Trapped in China's Shadow? Intellectual Property Protection in Post-WTO Accession Russia. *Boston College International and Comparative Law Review* 36(1): 183–218.

Lee, Luke T. 1969. *China and International Agreements: A Study of Compliance*. Leiden: A. W. Sijthoff.

Li, Yuwen. 1998. Fade-Away of Socialist Planned Economy: China's Participation in the WTO. In *International Economic Law with a Human Face*, ed. Friedl Weiss, Erik Denters, and Paul J. De Waart. London: Kluwer Law International.

Liu, Peixue. 1991. Tan Tan <<Yao Fazhi Bu Yao Renzhi>> De Kouhao" (Discussing the Slogan 'Rule of Law Not Rule of Man'.) *Neibu Wengao* (Internal Manuscripts), 7.

Long, Yongtu. 2003. Implications of China's Entry into the WTO in the Field of Intellectual Property Rights. In *China in the WTO: The Birth of a New Catching-Up Strategy*, ed. Carlos A. Magarinos, Yongtu Long, and Francisco Sercovich. New York: Palgrave Macmillan.

Lubman, Stanley. 1999. *Bird in a Cage: Legal Reform in China After Mao*. Stanford: Stanford University Press.

MacMurray, John V.A., ed. 1921. *Treaties and Agreements with and Concerning China 1894–1919, Vol. 1, Manchu Period (1894–1911)*. New York: Oxford University Press.

Marx, Karl. 1963. *Early Writings*. Trans. Thomas B. Bottomore. London: Watts & Co.

May, Christopher, and Susan K. Sell. 2006. *Intellectual Property Rights: A Critical History*. London: Lynne Rienner Publishers.

Mertha, Andrew. 2005. *The Politics of Piracy: Intellectual Property in Contemporary China*. Ithaca: Cornell University Press.

Moore, Adam D. 2001. *Intellectual Property and Information Control: Philosophic Foundations and Contemporary Issues*. New Brunswick: Transaction Publishers.

Ostergard, Robert L. 2003. *The Development Dilemma: The Political Economy of Intellectual Property Rights in the International System*. New York: LFB Scholarly Publishing LLC.

Pearson, Margaret M. 1999. China's Integration into the International Trade and Investment Regime. In *China Joins the World: Progress and Prospects*, ed. Elizabeth Economy and Michel Oksenberg. New York: Council on Foreign Relations.

Potter, Pitman B. 2001. *The Chinese Legal System: Globalization and Local Legal Culture*. London: Routledge.

PRC National People's Congress. 2004. Constitution of the PRC. http://www.npc. gov.cn/englishnpc/Constitution/node_2825.htm. Accessed 21 July 2016.

Qu, Sanqiang. 2002. *Copyright in China*. Beijing: Foreign Languages Press.

Ruse-Khan, Henning Grosse. 2016. IP and Trade in a Post-TRIPS Environment. In *TRIPS Plus 20: From Trade Rules to Market Principles*, ed. Hanns Ullrich, Reto M. Hilty, Matthias Lamping, and Josef Drexl. Heidelberg: Springer.

Schuman, Michael. 2016. Venture Communism: How China Is Building a Start-Up Boom. *New York Times*, 3 September.

Sell, Susan K. 2003. *Private Power, Public Law: The Globalization of Intellectual Property Rights*. Cambridge: Cambridge University Press.

———. 2011. TRIPS Was Never Enough: Vertical Forum Shifting, FTAs, ACTA, and TPP. *Journal of Intellectual Property Law* 18(2): 447–478.

Sit, Victor F.S., ed. 1983. *Commercial Laws and Business Regulations of the People's Republic of China 1949–1983*. Hong Kong: Tai Dao Publishing.

Tay, Alice Erh-Soon. 1969. Law in Communist China-Part I. *Sydney Law Review* 6(2): 153–172.

Thomas, Kristie. 2016. Dynamism in China's Civil Procedure Law: Civil Justice with Chinese Characteristics. In *The Dynamism of Civil Procedure- Global Trends and Developments*, ed. Colin B. Picker and Guy I. Seidman, 119–139. Heidelberg: Springer.

Wang, James C.F. 1995. *Contemporary Chinese Politics: An Introduction*. Englewood Cliffs: Prentice-Hall International.

WIPO. 2004. *WIPO Intellectual Property Handbook: Policy, Law and Use*. http://www. wipo.int/about-ip/en/iprm/index.htm. Accessed 14 Jan 2007.

———. 2005. What Is Intellectual Property? http://www.wipo.int/about-ip/en/. Accessed 15 May 2005.

———. 2006. WIPO Treaties- General Information. http://www.wipo.int/treaties/ en/general/. Accessed 5 Jan 2006.

———. 2016a. Global Innovation Index 2016. http://www.wipo.int/edocs/pub-docs/en/wipo_pub_gii_2016.pdf. Accessed 6 Sept 2016.

———. 2016b. Paris Convention for the Protection of Industrial Property (1883). http://www.wipo.int/treaties/en/text.jsp?file_id=288514. Accessed 25 Aug 2016.

———. 2016c. Berne Convention for the Protection of Literary and Artistic Works (1886). http://www.wipo.int/treaties/en/text.jsp?file_id=283698. Accessed 25 Aug 2016.

World Trade Organisation. 1994. Agreement on Trade-Related Aspects of Intellectual Property Rights. http://www.wto.org/english/docs_e/legal_e/27-trips.pdf. Accessed 20 Oct 2015.

———. 2001. Protocol on the Accession of the People's Republic of China. *Document WT/L/432*. https://docsonline.wto.org/dol2fe/Pages/SS/DirectDoc.aspx?filena me=t%3A%2Fwt%2Fl%2F432.doc&. Accessed 25 Aug 2016.

———. 2005a. What Are Intellectual Property Rights? http://www.wto.org/english/ tratop_e/trips_e/intell_e.htm. Accessed 13 May 2005.

———. 2005b. The WTO… in Brief. http://www.wto.org/english/thewto_e/ whatis_e/inbrief_e/inbr00_e.htm. Accessed 1 Feb 2005.

———. 2016. General Agreement on Tariffs and Trade (GATT 1947). http://www.wto.org/English/docs_e/legal_e/gatt47_01_e.htm. Accessed 25 Aug 2016.

Xue, Lan, and Liang Zheng. 2010. Relationships Between IPR and Technology Catch-Up: Some Evidence from China. In *Intellectual Property Rights, Development, and Catch-Up: An International Comparative Study*, ed. Hiroyuki Odagiri et al. Oxford: Oxford University Press.

Yang, Deli. 2002. The Development of the Intellectual Property in China. *Bradford University School of Management Working Paper* 02/24.

Yu, Peter. 2000. From Pirates to Partners: Protecting Intellectual Property in China in the Twenty-First Century. *American University Law Review* 50: 131–244.

Yu, Xingzhong. 2001. Legal Pragmatism in the People's Republic of China. In *Chinese Law and Legal Theory*, ed. Perry Keller. Aldershot: Ashgate Publishing Limited.

Yu, Peter. 2002. The Second Coming of Intellectual Property Rights in China. *Occasional Papers in Intellectual Property from Benjamin N. Cardozo School of Law, Yeshiva University* Number 11.

Zheng, Chengsi. 1997. *Intellectual Property Enforcement in China: Leading Cases and Commentary*. Hong Kong: Sweet & Maxwell Asia.

PART 1

How to Assess Compliance with the TRIPS Agreement: Concepts and Methods

CHAPTER 2

The Concept of "Compliance"

2.1   Defining the Concept of "Compliance"

A broad concept is necessary to be able to fully evaluate China's interactions with the WTO Agreement on Trade-Related Intellectual Property Rights (TRIPS). This may be provided by the concept of "compliance," which is a key term with its origins in international law (Chan 2006, p. 4). Compliance and law are "conceptually linked because law explicitly aims to produce compliance with its rules: legal rules set the standard by which compliance is gauged" (Raustiala and Slaughter 2002, p. 538). Indeed, the concept of compliance has become a "central preoccupation" in international law scholarship in recent years (Howse and Teitel 2010) and has also been increasingly used by political scientists and those in the field of international relations since the 1980s. However, despite such academic attention, there is still little consensus regarding the nature of compliance and how it can be measured. This chapter will first attempt to define the concept of compliance before reviewing and categorising some of the existing theories of compliance. The comprehensive framework of compliance which will be used in this study will then be introduced and previous studies of compliance in the Chinese context will also be outlined.

Compliance is desirable not only to tackle the problem that the rule was created for in the first place, but also "both to protect the rule and to protect the entire system of rules" (Fisher 1981, p. 21). In other words, China's compliance with the TRIPS Agreement is sought after not only to contend with the problem of intellectual property (IP) infringements, but also to protect the TRIPS Agreement itself and the entire World Trade Organisation (WTO) system. As a result, China's compliance with the TRIPS Agreement is worthy of study for various reasons, not only to analyse the development of the IP system in the People's Republic of China (PRC), but also to judge the effectiveness of imposing international IP standards through the framework of the WTO.

© The Author(s) 2017
K. Thomas, *Assessing Intellectual Property Compliance in
Contemporary China*, Palgrave Series in Asia and Pacific Studies,
DOI 10.1007/978-981-10-3072-7_2

However, operationalising compliance as a variable is problematic. It is clear that "one cannot simply read domestic legislation to determine whether countries are complying" (Jacobson and Brown Weiss 1998a, p. 2). The substantive measures that the state takes in order to make the specific international accords applicable to domestic law should rather be referred to under the concept of *implementation* or what has also been descriptively called "paper compliance" (Webster 2014). However, it is clear that *compliance* goes beyond mere implementation of international commitments into domestic law; compliance "refers to whether countries in fact adhere to the provisions of the accord and to the implementing measures that they have instituted" (Jacobson and Brown Weiss 1998a, p. 4). In other words, to what extent are the substantive laws on paper actually applied and upheld in practice? Compliance also needs to be differentiated from *effectiveness*, which is related to compliance but is not identical. Effectiveness can be seen from two perspectives: in achieving the stated objectives of the treaty and in addressing the problems that led to the treaty. Effectiveness may be achieved without compliance and equally, compliance might be fully achieved without effectiveness. Thus, "compliance" is a difficult concept both to define and to measure.

Furthermore, even with a clear definition of the concept, compliance is difficult to assess in practice. This is because it is clear that perfect compliance never occurs; "in reality, there is a level of acceptable practical compliance in the light of regime norms and procedures" (Kent 1999, p. 232). Therefore, despite an abstract concept of full and complete compliance, something less than this is usually accepted in most international accords. Even within a specific international accord, there may not be a fixed judgement of what level of compliance is acceptable. "Consequently, what is compliance to some may not be regarded as such by others. Seen in this light, the nature of compliance and the standards for measuring compliance are by and large relative rather than absolute" (Chan 2006, p. 66). These variations in the standard of acceptable compliance have implications for the study of China's compliance with its TRIPS obligations as, "in the end, assessing the extent of compliance is a matter of judgment" (Jacobson and Brown Weiss 1998a, p. 4). However, despite these difficulties in objectively analysing compliance, it is still an important aim.

2.1.1   Theories of "Compliance"

The question of compliance with international commitments has given rise to various theories of compliance in the past few decades. The main question behind these various theories, which have appeared in both international relations and international law literature in recent years, is simply: why do states comply (or not) with their international obligations? Obviously, "in general states are induced to do so because, in their overall strategic assessment, positive outcomes resulting from compliance outweigh negative ones" (Chan 2006, p. 66). However, there is no clear agreement on the exact processes that lead to compliance, or indeed that even make compliance more likely. Louis Henkin, in one of the earliest attempts to consider the issue of compliance, famously stated that it is "probably the case that *almost all nations observe almost all principles of international law and almost all of their obligations almost all of the time*" (Henkin 1979, p. 47).[1] However, he was less clear on why nations comply and offered a "remarkably rich" list of factors to explain state compliance (Raustiala and Slaughter 2002, p. 540).

Henkin's realist model of compliance revolves around a simple cost-benefit analysis, whereby violation would offer more advantage than compliance, although he did acknowledge, "that nations act on the basis of cost and advantage may seem obvious, but the notions of cost and advantage are not simple and their calculation hardly precise" (Henkin 1979, p. 50). This straight forward cost-benefit analysis approach is also taken by neorealist theorists such as Neuhold, whose analysis of state behaviour focuses on strategic incentives at both international and domestic levels. Neuhold proposed that decision-makers focus on three variables when deciding whether to comply: the magnitude and consequences of possible sanctions; the probability of the sanctions being imposed; and the likelihood of their non-compliance being detected (Neuhold 1999, p. 88). However, neorealist theories such as Neuhold's work best where nation-states remain the main players in global politics and in many areas of international law, this is no longer the case. Certainly in the case of intellectual property, companies and individual rights-holders also have a significant role to play in ensuring compliance with international commitments.

Challengers to cost-benefit-based theory have arguably proposed more precise models of a state's compliance. For example, Franck (1995) offered a detailed theory of compliance based on legitimacy and fairness, both substantive and procedural. In this theory of compliance, legitimacy is the key factor; "the legitimacy of rules exerts a 'compliance pull' on governments that explains the high observed levels of compliance of international law" (Raustiala and Slaughter, p. 541). However, although legitimacy is clearly an important factor in compliance, Franck's theory of compliance based on the legitimacy of the rules has been criticised as circular; that the rules are complied with because they are legitimate, but they derive their legitimacy from nations complying with them. Thus, although the issue of the perceived legitimacy of the rules, in this case of the TRIPS Agreement, may play a crucial role in compliance, ultimately Franck's theory does not go far enough to satisfactorily explain compliance with international law and other factors also need to be included.

In recent decades, other theorists have attempted to bridge the divide between compliance theory in international relations and in international law, a case in point being the managerial theory of compliance presented by Chayes and Chayes, which "rejected sanctions and other 'hard' forms of enforcement in favour of collective management of (non)-performance." Chayes and Chayes (1995) sought to offer an alternative to "enforcement" models of compliance based on the possibility of sanctions. They contend that the reasons states do not fully comply are either ambiguity in the treaty language; limitations in capacity to carry out their undertakings; or the magnitude of the social, economic and political changes required to comply. Therefore, "if we are correct that the principal source of non-compliance is not wilful disobedience but the lack of capability or clarity or priority, then coercive enforcement is as misguided as it is costly" (Chayes and Chayes 1995, p. 22). Chayes and Chayes thus provide a powerful challenge to enforcement models of compliance based on realist theory that states make an active choice to comply or not based on an assessment of the associated costs and benefits, by shifting the emphasis of compliance to a state's capacity to comply. However, the Chayes and Chayes approach has also been criticised as being incomplete: "As long as one is only interested in coordination games, it provides a good guide to compliance and national behaviour" (Guzman 2002, pp. 1832–3). Furthermore, Chayes and Chayes give the impression that there is a stark choice between the enforcement model and their own managerial model, whereas in fact, they may complement each other (Burgstaller 2005, p. 145).

In the 1990s, dissatisfaction with existing theories and the rise of constructivist theory led to a more normative approach to compliance theory, an example of which is Koh's theory of "obedience" with international law. Koh (1996) claimed that "obedience is compliance motivated not by anticipation of enforcement but via the incorporation of rules and norms into domestic legal systems." This obedience theory has three sequential components, interaction, interpretation and internalisation. According to this model, public and private actors first interact in a variety of fora to create the legal rule; these actors then interpret the rule and finally, through interaction, internalise the rule; "it is through this repeated process of interaction and internalisation that international law acquires its 'stickiness'" (Koh 1996, p. 204). However, Koh provides no explanation of how these legal norms are eventually internalised and "without an understanding of why domestic actors internalise norms of compliance in the international arena, and a theory of why this internalisation tends towards compliance, the theory lacks force" (Guzman 2002, p. 1836). It may be true that international legal norms need to be internalised as a precondition for full compliance, but Koh does not offer a clear explanation of this process of internalisation.

Another competing theory of compliance which emerged in the late 1990s was proposed by Andrew Guzman, whose theory of compliance relies on reputational factors to explain a state's compliance and instances of violation. In his model, when a state considers whether or not to comply with an international obligation, the possible sanctions it would face are paramount. These sanctions "include all costs associated with such a failure, including punishment or retaliation by other states, and reputational costs that affect a state's ability to make commitments in the future" (Guzman 2002, p. 1845). Guzman cites several factors which affect the reputational impact of a violation, which include the severity of the violation, the reasons for the violation, the extent to which other states know of the violation, and the clarity of the commitment and the violation. This reputational theory is similar to the Chayes' managerial approach in that it places reputational concerns at the centre of a state's compliance.

However, Guzman himself recognises the limitations of his reputational theory in its applicability to areas where the stakes are high.

In the past few years, the scope of theories of compliance has moved beyond the traditional question of why states comply with international agreements. For example, recent theories of compliance have sought to diminish the distinction between "hard" law, such as formal treaties, and "soft" law, such as bilateral Memoranda of Understanding (Guzman 2002, p. 1828). There is also a growing recognition in international relations theory that states are not the only relevant actors in international relations. Liberal theories of compliance such as those proposed by Slaughter and Moravcsik rest on a "bottom-up" view of politics, in which the demands of domestic interest groups are crucial (Burgstaller 2005, p. 166). Although it is undeniably important to acknowledge the role of individual actors in the international arena, focusing on these diverse and multifarious interest groups can also lead to overly complex theories of compliance.

Therefore, over the past few decades, there have been various theories advanced to explain a state's compliance or otherwise with its international obligations, but no single theory has yet achieved recognition as complete. There are still clear gaps in the theories, with some theories suiting some legal obligations better than others. It is important to recognise that although compliance is a significant area of study in contemporary international relations and legal study as outlined in discussion of the key theories above, "compliance remains a relatively young field. Many core concepts are debated and empirical testing of compliance theories is limited" (Raustiala and Slaughter 2002, p. 548). Furthermore, using compliance theory as a source of solutions to non-compliance and as a tool to evaluate strategies to reduce non-compliance have been identified as key priorities for policy researchers to pursue (Downs and Trento 2004, p. 19). Consequently, this study of China's compliance with international IP standards as embedded in the TRIPS Agreement can contribute to this ongoing development of compliance theory. Furthermore, as there is not yet any agreement over a model of compliance for individual states with international obligations, it is difficult to decide exactly which model of compliance should be applied in this study.

It is clear that although the study and theory of compliance in both international law and international relations literature has been underway for several decades, there is no clear agreement on why a state complies with or reneges on its obligations. There are also clear differences between these theories based on the approach they have taken to compliance. Compliance theories have been clustered into six broad conceptual categories and it is useful to explore these categories in the context of China's compliance with international IP standards.[2] The first category of compliance theories considers the *problem structure*. In the case of IP, it is both a large problem and pervasive in all developing countries at a similar stage of economic development. The problem is further complicated because infringing behaviour is often hidden. The second category of compliance theory is that of *solution structure*, which focuses on the specific institutional design or framework of the agreement. In the case of the TRIPS Agreement, it is consequently important to consider whether the framework of the institutional structure of the TRIPS Agreement itself raises or lowers the cost of compliance.

The third category of compliance theory is that of *solution process*, which includes the methods and processes by which the institution operates. In other words, the rules themselves must be seen as inclusive, fair and legitimate to encourage compliance; the TRIPS Agreement must be seen as fair by China and other members for full compliance to follow. This echoes the approach taken by Franck, focusing on the legitimacy of the rules themselves. The fourth category of compliance theory is *norms*. Through a process of socialization, new norms may be adopted by the country leading to changes in behaviour. Thus, it is important to not only consider the pre-existing legal and cultural norms in China, but also the norms associated with the TRIPS Agreement and the congruence between them. The fifth category is that of *domestic linkages* or "structural links between international institutions and domestic actors" (Raustiala and Slaughter 2002, p. 546).

Some theories have taken this category a stage further by proposing a general relationship between the type of domestic regime and its inclination to comply with international commitments. Under this general relationship, "liberal" states are more likely to comply and under the definition often used, China is not a liberal state. Thus, this type of compliance theory would hold that China is automatically less likely to comply given the nature of the Chinese state as non-liberal. The final group of compliance theory is based on *international structure*. This considers the institutionalisation of the international system and suggests that "highly institutionalised systems may create positive spirals of compliance by embedding states in regularized processes of cooperation that are mutually reinforcing" (Raustiala and Slaughter 2002, p. 548). This kind of compliance theory would focus on the WTO as an international trading system and ask how the WTO institutions such as the Council for TRIPS and the dispute resolution body encourage compliance.

The significance of these disparate categories is that ideally all of these categories need to be included in order to broaden existing discussions of compliance in the Chinese context. It has been stated that ideally scholars concerned with China's rule conformity should aspire towards an overarching framework encompassing a host of domestic and external factors to explain compliance (Mushkat 2011, p. 68). Moreover, as an emerging field, it is also crucial not to discount any important influences on China's TRIPS compliance. Therefore, this study will seek to incorporate elements of all these different categories of compliance theory in a comprehensive model of compliance as outlined in the following section.

2.1.2   *Towards a Comprehensive Model of Compliance*

The theories of compliance related above attempt to explain a country's compliance with international accords in general terms. It is clear from these various theories that many factors may affect a country's compliance with international rules, including the characteristics of the activity involved, the characteristics of the accord to be complied with, the international environment (i.e. are other countries complying?) and factors involving the country itself (Jacobson and Brown Weiss 1998a, pp. 6–7). It is crucial to combine these rather abstract theories of compliance gathered above into a more detailed model of specific factors which affect compliance.

These factors can be combined into a comprehensive model of factors which affect implementation, compliance and effectiveness of international accords (as shown in Fig. 2.1 [adopted from Jacobson and Brown Weiss 1998b, p. 535]). This model of specific factors initially developed to explain a state's (non-)compliance with environmental accords will be applied to the context of international IP protection under the TRIPS Agreement in this study. The factors affecting compliance can thus be divided into country-specific and non-country-specific factors. The latter type of factors relate to the specific activity involved, namely IP infringements; the characteristics of the TRIPS Agreement, including the substantive and procedural provisions; and the international environment, including the number of countries already in compliance with TRIPS, international NGOs concerned with IP protection and coverage of IP issues in the media. In terms of the characteristics of the activity involved, it is believed that the smaller number of actors involved in the activity, then the easier it is to regulate it. Furthermore, economic incentives may act towards compliance and the presence of multinational corporations (MNCs) may contribute towards compliance as they are easier to influence than smaller less-visible firms. Finally, the activity is more likely to be easily regulated if it is concentrated in a few major countries (Jacobson and Brown Weiss 1998b, p. 522). The specific activity involved in the TRIPS Agreement is IP infringements and this activity may well be particularly problematic in ensuring compliance, as discussed in Chap. 3.

Turning to the characteristics of the accord, the eight characteristics identified as possibly affecting implementation of that accord can be divided into substantive provisions and procedural provisions of the accord (Jacobson and Brown Weiss 1998b, p. 528). The accord under consideration in the international IP arena is the TRIPS Agreement and thus, the substantive provisions to consider include the perceived equity of the obligations and the precision of the obligations. The procedural provisions of the TRIPS Agreement include the role of the secretariat (specifically the Council for TRIPS) and those related to monitoring. The TRIPS Agreement does contain several relevant substantive and procedural provisions that may affect WTO members' compliance and these will also be considered in more detail in Chap. 3. The final aspect of non-country-specific factors to consider is the international environment which can also play a role in strengthening compliance with an international agreement. Consequently, it is also important to consider the presence of international NGOs concerned with IP and media pressure in this field, as well as the number of WTO members already complying with TRIPS obligations, which will all be considered in Chap. 3.

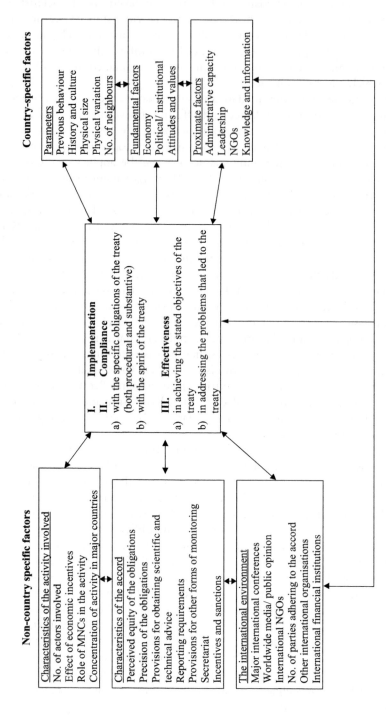

Fig. 2.1 Jacobson and Brown Weiss' comprehensive model of factors that affect implementation, compliance and effectiveness

Turning to the specific context of compliance in China, specific factors involving the country are some of the most important ones determining a country's compliance with its international obligations. Indeed, the consideration of domestic factors is often the most glaring gap in explorations of compliance with international rules by China (Mushkat 2011, p. 64). These factors may be divided into parameters, fundamental factors and proximate factors. Parameters comprise essential characteristics of the country which may affect its tendency to comply. The relevance of the history and culture of a country cannot be denied. Other parameters to consider include the physical size and variation of the country, the number of neighbours and the country's previous behaviour in this field which are all considered in Chaps. 6 and 7. The second category of China-specific influences to consider is fundamental factors. In general, fundamental factors affecting a country's compliance include political and institutional factors, as well as economic considerations. Economic factors seem to be indirectly relevant and the level of government ownership of production seems to be particularly important as, "governments seem to be better at regulating the activities of nongovernmental entities than they are at regulating activities under their own control" (Jacobson and Brown Weiss 1998b, p. 532). Thus, economic factors may affect compliance more in countries where the government and government ownership play a more important role in the economy such as China. Both economic and political fundamental factors will also be considered in Chaps. 6 and 7. The final category of country-specific factors which may influence China's TRIPS compliance are proximate factors. These may include administrative capacity, the attitude of the leadership and the influence of NGOs. It is undeniable that, "a crucial factor contributing to the variance among the performance of countries is administrative capacity," which includes funding for administrative agencies, powers assigned to these agencies and having sufficient numbers of trained personnel (Jacobson and Brown Weiss 1998b, p. 530). Proximate factors such as administrative capacity will also be discussed in Chaps. 6 and 7.

In addition to consideration of both non-country-specific and country-specific factors, the comprehensive model of compliance represented in Fig. 2.1 also distinguishes between implementation of the specific obligations, compliance—both substantive and procedural—and effectiveness of the resultant system. This distinction may be particularly pertinent to China's TRIPS compliance as China's implementation of TRIPS obligations into its substantive black letter law (as described in Chap. 5) is widely praised, yet compliance is sometimes doubted and the effectiveness of the current IP system is certainly criticised on a frequent basis. Overall, the model above suggests which factors may be important in affecting a country's compliance with international agreements, but does not describe how the dynamic process of change in a country's compliance may occur.

Changes within countries can be explained in two dimensions: the intention to comply and capacity to comply. Factors endogenous to the country concerned are important, such as changes in the government or major changes in the domestic economy. Exogenous factors such as financial and technical assistance can also play a role. However, intention to comply is meaningless without the capacity to comply. Therefore, "external pressure may contribute to a country's resolve to comply, but its role is limited" (Jacobson and Brown Weiss 1998b, p. 540). In the end, "the level of a country's compliance... depends crucially on the leaders and citizens of the country understanding that it is in their self-interest to comply, and then acting on this belief" (Jacobson and Brown Weiss 1998b, p. 541). It is also important to recognise that even if less than full compliance is confirmed, there is no straightforward explanation for this lack of compliance. "A lack of reach of the law could be a sign of government impotence, a reservation of government discretion, or a way for the government to conserve its resources, or any or all of these" (Lee 1997, p. xiv). Therefore, the dynamic processes of change will be considered in Chap. 7 when China's longer-term TRIPS compliance is considered in detail, and in the Chap. 8 which draws together the observations from both China's short-term and longer term attempts to comply with the TRIPS Agreement.

2.2   PREVIOUS STUDIES OF COMPLIANCE IN THE CHINESE CONTEXT

Detailed studies into China's compliance with international commitments are limited, but are beginning to emerge in various areas of international law. In the context of international economic law specifically, China has been highlighted as an interesting test case of the effectiveness of international multilateralism as it can act as a "least-likely" case to comply with (neo-) liberal institutions such as the WTO (Kent 2007, p. 2). Additionally, China's pattern of compliance is also of interest, because it exhibits such extreme differential levels of compliance, depending on the international regime in question (Webster 2014, p. 4). Existing studies of China's compliance have focused mainly on the areas of arms control, trade, environmental protection and human rights, as well as some broad-brush multidisciplinary analyses of China's compliance with its international obligations more generally.

One of the earliest studies of compliance in China was an early study of China's compliance with international treaty agreements from the 1960s which found that overall, "with respect to trade agreements, except for difficulties in connection with the Great Leap Forward and the Cultural Revolution, the PRC has enjoyed an excellent reputation for meeting its obligations" (Lee 1969, p. 119). Due to China's lack of diplomatic recognition at this time, trade agreements were concluded at the Associational level, for example, between the Canadian Wheat Board and the China Resources Corporation regarding grain imports and exports. Lee (1969, p. 119) concluded that "the consensus appears to be that, while negotiation with Peking is not always an easy matter, once an unambiguous agreement is reached, compliance likely will follow." Applying this finding to China's compliance with WTO obligations, it must not be forgotten that China actively negotiated the trade agreements of the

1960s and furthermore, these agreements were bilateral. Conversely, China's commitment to the WTO, specifically in the field of IP protection was based on a multilateral agreement (the TRIPS Agreement), the terms of which had already been fully negotiated prior to China's entry. It is therefore conceivable that any problems that China experiences in fully complying with the TRIPS Agreement may be created by the nature of accession to the WTO on "take it or leave it" basis.

In terms of more recent multidisciplinary studies of China's engagement with international legal regimes in the reform era, Feinerman (1995) was unable to find a unifying pattern of compliance spanning the disciplines. Just over a decade later, Potter (2007) used the concept of "selective adaptation" to explain China's compliance (or otherwise) with a variety of international legal regimes. By suggesting that China was acting in pursuit of its own national interest through actively selecting which norms to comply with, this analysis adhered to a realist approach. A more explicitly realist approach was also taken by Kim (1994, p. 419) who described China's engagement with the international legal order as following a "maxi/mini principle." In other words, China was said to be seeking the maximum benefits in terms of technical assistance and trade benefits and linkages but making minimal concessions in terms of reforming domestic laws and institutions.

In another multidisciplinary study of China's interactions with global legal institutions, Kent (2007, pp. 26–7) proposed five levels of international and domestic compliance, which could also be applied to China's compliance with its IP commitments: first, accession to treaties or agreements; second, procedural compliance with reporting and other requirements; third, substantive compliance; fourth, *de jure* compliance—the implementation of international norms in domestic legislative provisions; and finally, *de facto* compliance or compliance at the level of domestic practice, which can also be further divided into political and social implementation. The first three levels represent international compliance and could also be considered as "superficial" compliance as the norms embodied in the international accord are not necessarily accepted and absorbed. The final two levels of compliance in this model represent domestic compliance and could also be considered as "deep" compliance, as the norms are thus internalised into domestic practice. Thus, this model or "spectrum" of compliance is useful for further considering compliance which falls short of full compliance; problems with compliance can be identified at a specific level of acceptance. This model also reflects the distinction in compliance theory between implementation, compliance and effectiveness. Kent (2007, p. 3) also distinguishes between compliance and *cooperation* as a more comprehensive test of the internalisation of international norms, further underlining the need to look beyond the formal legal rules to obtain a fuller, richer picture of compliance.

China's pattern of entry into and implementation of international accords has also been studied in the context of single disciplines such as compliance with international environmental agreements. Oksenberg and Economy

(1998, p. 356) found that China acceded to international accords only after careful consideration of the costs, benefits and responsibilities involved. This corresponds with the impression given from the historical research on China's compliance with international agreements discussed above: that China takes a long time to commit to an international accord, but once it has committed, then compliance should follow as China has already weighed up the costs and benefits of the agreement. This study of China's implementation of and compliance with environmental accords also found several factors which determine the success of implementation. These ranged from the status of the implementing agency and the level of support from high-level political leaders, to the visible nature of the agreement and whether the requirements "are congruent and converge with the path China was pursuing prior to signing the agreement" (Oksenberg and Economy 1998, p. 358). However, in terms of codification of these environmental agreements, Oksenberg and Economy (1998, p. 392) also found that China was often ahead of the necessary timescale for commitments and the real problem lay in the enforcement of these domestic laws and regulations.

China's arms control compliance has also been analysed. Frieman's study of China's compliance with international arms control agreements set up a framework of costs and benefits to understand how China responds to different arms control regimes (Frieman 2004, p. 149). The potential costs Frieman identified include: provision of data, prevention and limitation of exports, refraining from testing or use, making legal commitments, making verifiable commitments, submitting to inspection or other international verification and setting up monitoring stations. The potential benefits include enhanced security, economic or financial gain, avoidance of censure, access to new technology or new information and the ability to shape the international regime and gain prestige (Frieman 2004, p. 149). Many of these costs and benefits such as the desire to access the latest technology also apply to compliance with international IP commitments. However, Frieman's main conclusion was that "despite the absence of compelling tangible benefits, China has been willing to bear substantial costs" (Frieman 2004, p. 171). China has been willing to pay substantial costs for only marginal benefits because the international arms control regime is seen as inevitable and thus, China would rather play a role in shaping the future regime from the inside. This desire to be able to influence the system could also apply to China's implementation of the obligations associated with the TRIPS Agreement. Johnston (1996) also considered China's compliance in the context of arms control regimes and concluded that there was a clear distinction between learning and adaptation, with the former a result of constructivist interactions with the regime in question and the latter a realist position that true adaptation only takes place once it is matches China's national interest. On the other hand, Angelova (1999, p. 449) cautions against the application of the managerial theory of compliance to China's interactions with the missile technology control regime as she argues that Chinese compliance was ultimately only forthcoming through the use of coercive sanctions.

Compliance theory has also been directly applied to the protection of IP in China. One study which focuses more specifically on China's compliance with international IP norms is Carter's study of trademark enforcement in China in the 1990s. Carter's model of trademark enforcement is based on "four factors, inherent in the Chinese brand of Socialist legality, [that] could prevent the Western-style trademark law from gaining the acceptance of people in the PRC" (Carter 1996, pp. 41–2) and five factors inherent in Chinese culture which operate against the acceptance of trademark law. The four factors inherent to the Chinese legal system are: firstly, "as a rule, PRC laws and regulations are enacted to achieve specific, immediate policy objectives", but these objectives may be the appeasement of international pressure, rather than the effective protection of IP; secondly, "some PRC laws remain secret" and this lack of transparency does not allow for widespread public familiarity with the law which would be the first step to acceptance of the law as legitimate; thirdly, "many PRC laws are intentionally vague in order that policy-makers and implementing officers may have flexibility in interpretation." This vagueness can also operate against the acceptance of the law as legitimate. The fourth and final characteristic of the Chinese legal system that Carter (1996) identifies is that "many PRC laws are programmatic, that is, they present ideals or goals rather than implementation details." In other words, the lack of transparency and precision in the substantive law prevent effective trademark enforcement in China. It may be interesting to see whether this is equally applicable to other areas of the IP system.

The five cultural factors which Carter (1996) identified as operating against the acceptance of IP law are as follows: firstly, "traders might think that 'copying' is not wrong because emulation was seen as an exercise in deference and socialisation in Chinese society"; secondly, there is no tradition of individual property ownership; thirdly, under Marxist thought, IP is seen "as products of the society from which they emerge"; next, Chinese consumers are used to relying on brands to guide their choices; and finally, *guanxi* (relationships) and networks "override formal law-based obligations." Carter places equal emphasis on both cultural factors and systemic factors in the legal system as responsible for the current condition of the trademark system in China. According to Carter, these nine legal and cultural factors operate together to prevent the successful legal transplant of international standards of trademark law by inhibiting the legitimation of trademark protection in Chinese society. Carter's emphasis on factors based on China's legal system and cultural traditions appears to highlight the importance of factors specific to China under the Jacobson and Brown Weiss comprehensive model of compliance outlined above.

It is indeed necessary to acknowledge the role of cultural values in any legal system. "The nature and role of law are delineated in any society within its particular cultural and institutional matrix" (Haley 1991, p. 4). Thus, cultural factors are indeed significant in analysing compliance with international legal norms. Furthermore, recent analyses of IP and its role in international relations have also focused on moving beyond a formalist concept of international law to a more normative approach. This is in line with the Rawlsian approach which "maintains that international relations are not solely about states, but are also about people and peoples."[3] This corresponds with Ryan's study of the politics of international IP described as "knowledge diplomacy," which agrees that "state power offers only a superficial explanation of the multilateral diplomacy concerning intellectual property rights that has been conducted in the 1980s and 1990s" (Ryan 1998, p. 3). For example, "US patent and copyright business interest groups drove trade-related IP policy in the 1980s and 1990s, although the diplomacy was conducted on their behalf by the US executive branch" (Ryan 1998, p. 8). Accordingly, it is no longer sufficient to solely examine the law and government policy in order to analyse IP law; it is crucial to also examine the many interest groups also involved in IP law-making and enforcement. This shift of emphasis from the state as the sole actor in IP to other groups and individuals reflects the emergence of liberal theory in international relations literature which also focuses on the role of the individual. Thus, previous studies of China's compliance may be outdated if they ignore the role of actors below the level of the state.

Finally, a recent study of China's compliance in global affairs by Chan (2006) considered China's compliance with international trade agreements such as those mentioned above, as well as the previously discussed areas of arms control, environmental protection and human rights. His overall conclusion is that "it can be concluded that China's overall compliance record in global affairs is satisfactory to good, given the difficulties that it faces in its economic, social and political transitions, and given the fact that compliance measurement is difficult to make" (Chan 2006, p. 204). Chan further concluded that China's compliance with its global trade commitments is judged as "satisfactory" overall, but highlighted IP as an area in which China has had problems fully meeting its international obligations. Chan also considered the impact of different theories in China's interactions in global trade, including neorealism, liberal institutionalism and social constructivism, but overall takes a fairly neorealist approach to compliance, for example stating that "nation-states are still the main actors in international affairs" (Chan 2006, p. 210). Considering this tension between commentators who hold that, at least in China's case, the state is the most important player, and those commentators who insist that the role of other interest groups is also significant, it may be interesting to consider who exactly are the main actors in China's developing IP system.

In terms of research into China's IP system specifically, there is a persistent idea that IP "has always evolved in response to economic and political necessity" (Endeshaw 1996, p. 79). Some observers have used this idea as a basis for explaining why China lacks effective IP protection. The dominant theory draws on the experience of Taiwan and Korea to argue that a combination of *external* and *internal* pressure is truly necessary to bring about genuine change in IP protection (Maruyama 1999, p. 167). Based on the development of IP protection elsewhere in Asia (such as Korea, Japan and Taiwan), a three-phase model has therefore been proposed for the development of an effective IP regime. These three stages are as follows: first, external trade pressure leads to legal formalities such as adequate laws and regulations; then, a stop-gap form of enforcement by government edict emerges following US pressure; finally, IP agreements become self-sustaining and a genuine rule of law begins to emerge due to the development of indigenous technologies (Maruyama 1999, p. 207).

In China, the first two stages can clearly be witnessed in the US-Sino Agreements of the 1990s, which first emphasised the substantive legislation on IP and then focused on the enforcement of IP. Therefore, if this model also applies to China, in the final stage of the model, IP needs to be developed by Chinese rights-holders in order to become self-sustaining. This theory is supported by many observers who believe that if Chinese private companies possessed more IP, protection would be sought and obtained for these rights (Endeshaw 1996, p. 79).

This three-stage theory of China's development of IP protection and moves towards global IP norms also reflects some aspects of the compliance theories outlined above. It is clear that codifying international obligations into domestic legislation is insufficient for full compliance. Furthermore, this model seems to reflect Koh's theory of transnational legal process in that only when the imported norms have been internalised can full compliance be observed. Finally, this model is similar to the five stages of compliance identified by Kent, in that procedural compliance is distinguished from *de jure* and *de facto* compliance. *De jure* compliance could be seen as equating to implementation under the Jacobson and Brown Weiss model of compliance and *de facto* compliance means enforcement of these laws in practice. However, this theory of IP development has been criticised as a form of "historical determinism" that "developing countries mount a deterministic development ladder, from light assembly to heavy manufacturing and on to high-tech products, and, having achieved this degree of industrialization, they begin to create, and protect IP" (Stevenson-Yang and DeWoskin 2005, p. 10). This reflects the criticism levelled at many compliance theories that they do not adequately explain the *process* of change, which will be the focus of Chap. 7 in this book.

Furthermore, China often does not follow conventional models of development. For example, strong rule of law and clear protection for personal property rights are usually thought to be required as a prerequisite for economic development, but China appears to have experienced significant growth without either, presenting a puzzle for economists, political scientists and legal scholars alike (Peerenboom 2002, p. 19). Consequently, although strong IP may have necessarily developed elsewhere in Asia in order to maintain economic growth, "an examination of the present situation in China indicates that this historical lesson may be inapplicable to China, at least for the present" (Chow 2000). Additionally, there may be key differences between China and other Asian countries which mean that the path of IP development is different. Overall, these previous studies of IP in China are simplistic and rely on emphasising one factor such as economic development or the role of individual rights holders to the exclusion of all others. Clearly, the issue of trying to rationalise non-enforcement of IP needs further analysis before a conclusive model can be agreed upon and this "enforcement gap" will be the focus of Chap. 6.

Finally, in terms of China's compliance with its WTO obligations, there is now an emerging body of work in this area. Existing compliance theory would predict relatively higher levels of compliance with international trade rules as trade is seen as more closely aligning with national interest (Downs and Trento 2004). Kent, in her 2007 mini case study of China's WTO participation, anticipated high levels of compliance with WTO obligations not only because accession offered clear material advantages to China, but also because it was so hard won (Kent 2007, p. 234). Webster's study of China's compliance with the rulings of the WTO Dispute Settlement Body (DSB) found that "to the extent China complies, it is largely discursive rather than digestive, focusing on words... rather than deeds" (Webster 2014, p. 23). This chimes with Kent's overall judgement of China's WTO compliance, that "China is, on the whole, compliant but not wholly cooperative" (Kent 2007, p. 238). Consequently, the existing literature would suggest that China's formal laws and regulations appear to substantially comply with its WTO obligations, but actual practice may present a more mixed picture. Thus, this study will probe this purported gap between rules and practice in more depth to obtain a more complete picture of TRIPS compliance, as well as including a uniquely long-term analysis of China's changing compliance with its TRIPS obligations since WTO accession in 2001.

2.3   SUMMARY AND CONCLUSION

This chapter first outlined the key concept of "compliance" which will be used in this study to analyse China's interactions with the TRIPS Agreement. Then the main theories of compliance which have emerged from international law and international relations literature in recent decades were discussed. Previous studies of compliance in China, particularly in relation to IP commitments, were also considered. Overall, previous studies into China's compliance with international commitments, including research focusing on IP protection, have tended to mostly focus on factors specific to China without fully considering the nature of the obligations involved. Equally, existing theories of compliance often focus on characteristics of the specific agreement without allowance for the individual country.

Therefore, this study will apply a comprehensive model of compliance to China's IP protection under the TRIPS Agreement. This model will allow for consideration of factors both specific to China, as well as considering the nature of the TRIPS Agreement itself and the nature of the IP protection problem. Then, this comprehensive model of compliance will be applied to China's compliance with the TRIPS Agreement in stages: firstly in Chap. 3, the background context of the TRIPS Agreement itself will be examined, to evaluate if there are factors which are not specific to China which generally affect compliance with its provisions. Then, the methodology used in this study will be fully explained and justified in Chap. 4. Part II will then focus on applying this model to the specific context of China's TRIPS compliance by not only examining the short-term changes made at the time of accession in 2001, but also the longer term changes up to 15 years later.

NOTES

1. Emphasis in original.
2. Categorisation taken from Raustiala and Slaughter (2002, pp. 545–8).
3. Discussion of Rawls, *The Law of Peoples*, 1999 in: Mayeda (2005, p. 86).

REFERENCES

Angelova, Anastasia A. 1999. Compelling Compliance with International Regimes: China and the Missile Technology Control Regime. *Columbia Journal of Transnational Law* 38(2): 419–449.

Burgstaller, Marcus. 2005. *Theories of Compliance with International Law*. Leiden: Martinus Nijhoff Publishers.

Carter, Connie. 1996. *Fighting Fakes in China: The Legal Protection of Trade Marks and Brands in the People's Republic of China*. London: The Intellectual Property Institute.

Chan, Gerald. 2006. *China's Compliance in Global Affairs: Trade, Arms Control, Environmental Protection, Human Rights*. Singapore: World Scientific Publishing.

Chayes, Abram, and Antonia Handler Chayes. 1995. *The New Sovereignty: Compliance with International Regulatory Agreements*. Cambridge, MA: Harvard University Press.

Chow, Daniel. 2000. Counterfeiting in the People's Republic of China. *Washington University Law Quarterly* 78(1): 1–57.

Downs, George W., and Andrea W. Trento. 2004. Conceptual Issues Surrounding the Compliance Gap. In *International Law and Organization: Closing the Compliance Gap*, ed. Edward C. Luck and Michael W. Doyle. Lanham: Rowman & Littlefield.

Endeshaw, Assafa. 1996. *Intellectual Property in China: The Roots of the Problem of Enforcement*. Singapore: Acumen Publishing.

Feinerman, James V. 1995. Chinese Participation in the International Legal Order: Rogue Elephant or Team Player? *The China Quarterly* 141: 186–210.

Fisher, Roger. 1981. *Improving Compliance with International Law*. Charlottesville: University Press of Virginia.

Franck, Thomas. 1995. *Fairness in International Law and Institutions*. Oxford: Oxford University Press.

Frieman, Wendy. 2004. *China, Arms Control and Nonproliferation*. London: RoutledgeCurzon.

Guzman, Andrew T. 2002. A Compliance-Based Theory of International Law. *California Law Review* 90(6): 1823–1887.

Haley, John Owen. 1991. *Authority Without Power: Law and the Japanese Paradox*. Oxford: Oxford University Press.

Henkin, Louis. 1979. *How Nations Behave: Law and Foreign Policy*. 2nd ed. New York: Council on Foreign Relations.

Howse, Robert, and Ruti Teitel. 2010. Beyond Compliance: Rethinking Why International Law Really Matters. *Global Policy* 1(2): 127–136.

Jacobson, Harold K., and Edith Brown Weiss. 1998a. A Framework for Analysis. In *Engaging Countries: Strengthening Compliance with International Environmental Accords*, ed. Edith Brown Weiss and Harold K. Jacobson. Cambridge, MA: The MIT Press.

———. 1998b. Assessing the Record and Designing Strategies to Engage Countries. In *Engaging Countries: Strengthening Compliance with International Environmental Accords*, ed. Edith Brown Weiss and Harold K. Jacobson. Cambridge, MA: The MIT Press.

Johnston, Alastair Iain. 1996. Learning Versus Adaptation: Explaining Change in Chinese Arms Control Policy in the 1980s and 1990s. *The China Journal* 35: 27–61.

Kent, Ann. 1999. *China, the United Nations and Human Rights: The Limits of Compliance*. Philadelphia: University of Pennsylvania.

———. 2007. *Beyond Compliance: China, International Organizations, and Global Security, Studies in Asian Security*. Stanford: Stanford University Press.

Kim, Samuel S. 1994. China's International Organizational Behavior. In *Chinese Foreign Policy: Theory and Practice*, ed. Thomas W. Robinson and David Shambaugh. Oxford: Clarendon Press.

Koh, Harold Hongju. 1996. Transnational Legal Process (The 1994 Roscoe Pound Lecture). *Nebraska Law Review* 75: 181–207.

Lee, Luke T. 1969. *China and International Agreements: A Study of Compliance*. Leiden: A. W. Sijthoff.

Lee, Tahirah V. ed. 1997. *Law, the State, and Society in China*. New York: Garland Publishing Inc.

Maruyama, Warren H. 1999. U.S.-China IPR Negotiations: Trade, Intellectual Property and the Rule of Law in a Global Economy. In *Chinese Intellectual Property Law and Practice*, ed. Mark A. Cohen, A. Elizabeth Bang, and Stephanie J. Mitchell. London: Kluwer Law International.

Mayeda, Graham. 2005. A Normative Perspective on Legal Harmonization: China's Accession to the WTO. *U.B.C. Law Review* 38(1): 39–122.

Mushkat, Roda. 2011. China's Compliance with International Law: What Has Been Learned and the Gaps Remaining. *Pacific Rim Law & Policy Journal* 20(1): 41–70.

Neuhold, Hanspeter. 1999. The Foreign Policy 'Cost-Benefit Analysis' Revisited. *German Yearbook of International Law* 42: 84–124.

Oksenberg, Michel, and Elizabeth Economy. 1998. China: Implementation Under Economic Growth and Market Reform. In *Engaging Countries: Strengthening Compliance with International Environmental Accords*, ed. Edith Brown Weiss and Harold K. Jacobson. Cambridge, MA: The MIT Press.

Peerenboom, Randall. 2002. *China's Long March Toward Rule of Law*. Cambridge: Cambridge University Press.

Potter, Pitman B. 2007. China and the International Legal System: Challenges of Participation. *The China Quarterly* 191: 699–715.

Raustiala, Kal, and Anne-Marie Slaughter. 2002. International Law, International Relations and Compliance. In *Handbook of International Relations*, ed. W. Carlnaes, T. Risse, and B.A. Simmons. London: SAGE.

Ryan, Michael P. 1998. *Knowledge Diplomacy: Global Competition and the Politics of Intellectual Property*. Washington, DC: Brookings Institution Press.

Stevenson-Yang, Anne, and Ken DeWoskin. 2005. China Destroys the IP Paradigm. *Far Eastern Economic Review* 168(3): 9–18.

Webster, Timothy. 2014. Paper Compliance: How China Implements WTO Decisions. *Michigan Journal of International Law* 35(3): 525–578.

CHAPTER 3

The TRIPS Agreement: Developing Global Rules for Intellectual Property Protection

According to the comprehensive model of compliance outlined in Chap. 2, there are various categories of factors which may influence the likelihood or otherwise of compliance with a specific international accord. These categories include both country-specific factors such as the history, size and culture of the country as well as non-country-specific factors relating to the agreement and the activity concerned. In this chapter, these factors external to the Chinese context influencing compliance with the World Trade Organisation (WTO) Agreement on Trade-Related Intellectual Property Rights (TRIPS) will be considered. First, the background to the TRIPS Agreement will be outlined, in order to detail the drafting history and consequent context of compliance with this specific accord. Then, the specific characteristics of the TRIPS Agreement will be examined, to analyse their possible effect on compliance. This chapter will also include discussion of the characteristics of the activity which the TRIPS Agreement was designed to solve: intellectual property infringements. Finally, the international environment surrounding the protection of intellectual property rights will be explored.

3.1 The Drafting of the TRIPS Agreement

As detailed in Chap. 1, the pre-WTO international trading system did not offer a detailed and universal framework for the protection of intellectual property. Under the General Agreement on Tariffs and Trade 1947 (GATT), provisions relating to intellectual property had been limited and effectively no substantive terms applied (Hoekman and Kostecki 2001, p. 282). However, protection of intellectual property became prioritised by developed countries during the 1980s and 1990s due to their growing reliance on technology. It was consequently an important issue during the Uruguay Round of trade negotiations (1986–94), where it proved to be a divisive issue. Following this key round

© The Author(s) 2017
K. Thomas, *Assessing Intellectual Property Compliance in Contemporary China*, Palgrave Series in Asia and Pacific Studies,
DOI 10.1007/978-981-10-3072-7_3

of negotiations, the WTO emerged as the successor to GATT in 1995,[1] with the TRIPS Agreement at the heart of the new international organisation. The issue of intellectual property protection was first raised in the context of the GATT system at the close of the Tokyo negotiation round in 1979, where the European Community and the United States (US) unsuccessfully tried to obtain an "Agreement on Measures to Discourage the Importation of Counterfeit Goods" (Goldstein 2001, p. 53). Although the Tokyo Round had attempted to move beyond reducing tariffs as barriers to trade to consideration of non-tariff barriers, this shift in focus was taken to new levels in the years following the conclusion of the Tokyo Round.

This new emphasis on intellectual property protection arose as technology started to become more of an important factor in global competition (Correa 2000, p. 3). Developed industrialised countries were becoming conscious of the pressure that newly industrialising nations especially in Asia were beginning to place on their own economic growth. However, initial proposals regarding the inclusion of intellectual property (IP) in GATT negotiations were modest. In the early 1980s, proposals for consideration of intellectual property rights in the multilateral trading system focused almost exclusively on trade in counterfeit goods "because commercial counterfeiting had become such a serious problem for trademark owners in a number of countries" (Bradley 1987, p. 65). Thus, initial consideration of the inclusion of IP protection in the GATT/WTO system was much narrower than the broad scope of the final TRIPS Agreement.

Furthermore, the very inclusion of intellectual property in the scope of multilateral trade negotiations was strongly resisted by some of the larger developing countries such as Brazil and India, who argued that the World Intellectual Property Organisation (WIPO) was the proper forum within which to negotiate this issue (Bradley 1987). However, WIPO was widely regarded as ineffective at enforcing the various treaties it was responsible for, such as the Paris and Berne Conventions, whereas the GATT dispute settlement mechanism was admired as a potentially more efficient tool in enforcing international IP obligations (Jackson 1997, p. 311). These Conventions were also criticised for relying on the principles of non-discrimination and national treatment, rather than providing uniform minimum standards of protection. This meant that if a country did not offer any IP protection to its own nationals, then it was not obliged to offer higher protection to foreign nationals. This lack of pressure on developing countries to introduce effective protection for IP was clearly unsatisfactory to the richer industrialised nations.

In other words, the reasons why the developed countries wished to include intellectual property protection in the GATT system were twofold: first, to subject intellectual property disputes to the multilateral dispute settlement body, and second, to provide uniform standards of protection which all signatories would have to provide. The lack of enforcement provisions in the existing conventions was also seen as a weakness of the international intellectual property system then in force. The Uruguay Round of negotiations, launched in Punta del Este on 20 September 1986, included the issue of intellectual property for negotiation as follows:

> In order to reduce the distortions and impediments to international trade, and taking into account the need to promote effective and adequate protection of intellectual property rights, and to ensure that measures and procedures to enforce intellectual property rights do not themselves become barriers to legitimate trade, the negotiations shall aim to clarify GATT provisions and elaborate as appropriate new rules and disciplines. (GATT 1986, p. 7)

Therefore, the scope of intellectual property protection to be negotiated during the Uruguay Round already appeared to be broader than the narrow scope of counterfeit goods originally tabled in the Tokyo Round. From the very outset of the Uruguay Round, there were severe disagreements between developed and developing countries over the direction of the intellectual property negotiations. Australia proposed that the Berne, Paris, Rome and Geneva Conventions be incorporated into the multilateral system—a proposal with which most economically developed countries agreed. On the other hand, India proposed that negotiations be limited to practices that distort international trade—a proposal with which many developing countries concurred (Stewart 1993, p. 2270).

Resistance to the broader scope of TRIPS was not based on resistance to the idea of combating counterfeiting *per se*, rather it arose from the perception that the proposed TRIPS Agreement would embody "a policy of 'technological protectionism' aimed at consolidating an international division of labour" (Correa 2000, p. 5). This "technological protectionism" was perceived as protecting the interests of industrialised countries at the expense of the developing economies and was thus strongly resisted by many of the negotiating powers. Developing countries were concerned that greater IP protection would strengthen the monopoly power of multinational corporations (MNCs), and detrimentally affect the poor by increasing the prices of key medicines and foods (Hoekman and Kostecki 2001, p. 283). It has also been claimed that developing countries never really had a significant part to play in the TRIPS negotiations. According to one commentator, "the negotiations on TRIPS are often said to have begun properly in the second half of 1989, when a number of countries made proposals, or the first part of 1990, when five draft texts of an agreement were submitted to the negotiating group. A more sceptical view is that the negotiations were by then largely over. An even more sceptical view is to say that no real negotiations ever took place. Developing countries had simply run out of alternatives and options" (Drahos 1996, p. 171).

It is certainly undeniable that private actors had a significant role to play in the drafting of the TRIPS Agreement, a public law instrument. For example, the Intellectual Property Committee (IPC) was seen as crucial in the TRIPS negotiations (Sell 2003). The IPC was made up of representatives from major US MNCs and presented a draft text which the negotiators then fine-tuned. Thus, it could be said that the negotiators did not actually draft the full text of the final

Agreement, but rather were heavily influenced by powerful private participants in the shape of the IPC and other lobby groups. Developing countries were concerned that intellectual property protection was only being considered in the context of its commercial effects, rather than for its use in the context of national development (May and Sell 2006, p. 157). Nevertheless, these concerns were sidelined by the developed countries which dominated the TRIPS negotiations.

Indeed, as the Uruguay Round of negotiations progressed, the tensions between developing and developed countries appeared to diminish, whereas tensions grew between industrialised nations, such as the US and the European Community. This was a result of the negotiations moving towards detailed substantive provisions which were not always in congruence with the existing domestic systems of protection (Jackson 1997, p. 312). Whatever the truth about the tensions or otherwise between the countries negotiating the TRIPS Agreement, by a midterm review carried out in 1989, most countries, both developed and developing, agreed that substantive intellectual property protection was desirable and a framework for the TRIPS Agreement be put in place (Goldstein 2001, p. 55).

Furthermore, "by the time of the Dunkel text in December 1991, there seemed to be an enormous change in attitudes, including attitudes of developing countries, which led many such countries to be willing ultimately to accept the IP Agreement as part of the very broad package of the Uruguay Round" (Jackson 1997, p. 311). However, agreement between developing and developed countries, who had initially appeared diametrically opposed, was not reached based solely on the text of the proposed TRIPS Agreement alone. Instead, consensus was achieved through the common negotiating strategy of "linkage-bargaining." This "occurs when a negotiator offers something of value to a counterpart as a means of convincing the counterpart to offer concessions on matters considered valuable to the negotiator" (Richards 2004, p. 123). In other words, developed countries gained the agreement of developing countries on intellectual property issues by threatening to withdraw concessions agreed in other trade areas of concern to developing nations, such as agriculture. Put simply, the developing countries were subject to pronounced coercion on the basis of expanded market access in return for their acquiescence during the TRIPS negotiations (Sell 2003, p. 9).

This high-stakes negotiating strategy has been heavily criticised, but did lead to agreement overall, which ultimately would not have been possible in single-issue negotiations involving international standards for intellectual property protection. The final text of the Agreement on Trade-Related Aspects of Intellectual Property Rights was signed at Marrakesh, Morocco on April 15 1994 and can consequently be seen as a compromise on the part of the developing countries, in order to receive benefits from other areas of the WTO Agreements. Although the TRIPS Agreement can be seen as a highly significant step in the expansion of IP protection in the global system and is notable on many levels, TRIPS has also been the subject of various criticisms. In contrast to the existing international intellectual property Conventions, the

TRIPS Agreement removes the national autonomy which was used to decide the appropriate level of protection at a domestic level. The TRIPS Agreement instead advances a "one size fits all" approach which "defies both economic analysis and historical experience" (Sell 2003, p. 13).

Furthermore, the stated justification for the TRIPS Agreement has come under fire; the explicit aim of promoting economic development through stronger IP protection is disputed by several studies and the delicate balance between rights-holders and the public interest is tipped firmly in favour of protection. Finally, the TRIPS obligations represent a stark departure from the existing GATT system. Not only was GATT previously focused on trade in goods, but the TRIPS Agreement also contrasts with the Uruguay Round's aims of deregulation and trade liberalisation by striving for "internationally driven re-regulation" (Sell 2003, p. 15). Moreover, it could be claimed that the controversy surrounding the inclusion of intellectual property protection in the Uruguay round of GATT negotiations has its legacy in the full title of the resulting agreement, "Agreement on Trade-Related Aspects of Intellectual Property Rights," known as TRIPS. Initial negotiations had limited intellectual property protection to that relating to trade, but the final agreement is so far-reaching that "trade-related" is said to be a misleading title (Das 1999, p. 355). It has even been claimed that "the term TRIPS was invented to make the issue look GATT-relevant, but many economists think it is meaningless because intellectual property cannot be trade-specific" (Dunkley 2000, p. 187). However, as both developed and developing countries conceded that a system of IP protection was a necessary inclusion in the international trading system, this seems an overly critical stance.

The TRIPS Agreement, which resulted from these negotiations, has also been criticised as beneficial only to industrialised nations, whilst detrimentally affecting developing countries. This criticism is based on the notion that the standards of intellectual property protection it expounds are solely suitable for industrialised nations (Correa 2000, p. 5). By protecting technology already established in developed countries and restricting the development of technology in poorer countries, it has been argued that developed countries could increase exports and stifle competition. The TRIPS Agreement has also been criticised for attempting to remove intellectual property protection from the realm of global politics by ignoring the developmental implications for developing nations and redefining it solely as a legal issue (May and Sell 2006, p. 162). Therefore, the TRIPS Agreement clearly had a controversial drafting history and has also been strongly criticised as favouring developed countries over developing countries. The specific provisions of the TRIPS Agreement which resulted from this complex negotiating process will now be considered.

3.1.1 The Provisions of the TRIPS Agreement

The TRIPS Agreement is one of the three so-called pillar agreements that together make up the commitments of the WTO.[2] While the drafting of the TRIPS agreement clearly caused controversy, what provisions does the final text of the Agreement actually contain? In sharp contrast to most "negative" obligations imposed by the WTO agreements (e.g. not to use certain policies such as export subsidies or quotas), TRIPS invokes a "positive" obligation to adopt a set of substantive rules (Hoekman and Kostecki 2001, p. 274). This set of substantive rules is contained within seven major parts and 73 articles of TRIPS. The seven areas covered are: copyright, trademarks, geographical indication, industrial design, patents, layout design of integrated circuits, and undisclosed information (Das 1998, p. 115).

Among other provisions, the TRIPS Agreement:

- sets minimum standards of protection for these seven areas;
- sets minimum standards for the enforcement of intellectual property rights in administrative and civil actions;
- sets minimum standards, with regard to copyright piracy and trademark counterfeiting, for the enforcement of intellectual property rights in criminal actions and actions at the border;
- requires that, subject to limited exceptions, WTO members provide national and Most Favoured Nation (MFN) treatment to the nationals of other WTO members with regard to protection and enforcement of intellectual property rights.[3]

The extensive provisions of the TRIPS Agreement did not emerge solely from the Uruguay Round of negotiations; rather it pulls together and supplements previous intellectual property conventions (Richards 2004, p. 4). In fact, the substantive provisions on minimum levels of protection essentially incorporate existing IP conventions into the TRIPS Agreement. Part III of the TRIPS Agreement deals specifically with minimum standards for the enforcement of intellectual property rights.

The TRIPS Agreement was a result of compromise between the negotiating positions of the developed and developing countries respectively, and the provisions on enforcement demonstrate this compromise (Goldstein 2001, p. 59). In general, developed countries argued for stringently applied remedies, whereas developing countries were more concerned about maintaining their judicial discretion. Thus, members are required to give the appropriate judicial authorities the power to grant certain remedies but without further specifying the substantive form that the remedy should take. This preserves the concept of judicial autonomy, seen as crucial by some members. The enforcement provisions of the TRIPS Agreement were also seen as crucial because the lack of enforcement provisions in the existing conventions was one of the main stimuli to the negotiation of the TRIPS Agreement (May and Sell 2006, p. 173). Consequently, the TRIPS provisions on enforcement will be outlined below.

3.1.2   The TRIPS Provisions on Enforcement

Part III of the TRIPS Agreement is concerned with the *enforcement* of intellectual property rights and this Part is divided into 21 articles and five sections:

- General Obligations (Article 41)
- Civil and Administrative Procedures and Remedies (Articles 42–49)
- Provisional Measures (Article 50)
- Special Requirements Related to Border Measures (Articles 51–60)
- Criminal Procedures (Article 61)

All of these provisions on enforcement can be said to have two basic objectives: "One is to ensure that effective means of enforcement are available to rights holders; the second is to ensure that enforcement procedures are applied in such a manner as to avoid the creation of barriers to legitimate trade and to provide for safeguards against their abuse" (World Trade Organisation 2015b). Part III as a whole also complements the substantive minimum standards of TRIPS as "from a rights holder's perspective, substantive minimum rights are of little value if there are no effective procedures for the enforcement of such rights" (UNCTAD-ICTSD 2004, p. 575).

Section 1 of Part III outlines the general obligations relating to enforcement. The first paragraph of Article 41 outlines the main principles of enforcement, that enforcement procedures shall "permit effective action against any act of infringement of intellectual property rights covered by this Agreement, including expeditious remedies to prevent infringements and remedies which constitute a deterrent to further infringements." Sections 2 and 3 (dealing with civil and administrative procedures and remedies and provisional measures) are applicable to all intellectual property rights infringements, whereas Sects. 4 and 5 (special requirements related to border measures and criminal procedures) apply only to trademark counterfeiting and copyright piracy.

It is significant that, in sharp contrast to the substantive provisions, the TRIPS provisions on enforcement in Part III mark a significant departure from previous intellectual property protection offered by international agreements such as the Paris and Berne Conventions by adding teeth to the substantive provisions. Under these Conventions, adoption into domestic law was seen as sufficient to discharge a state's obligation to comply, even if the domestic law was subsequently unenforced (Reichman 1996, p. 338), whereas under TRIPS, the prescribed minimum standards of protection have to actually be implemented. Another important consideration to take into account is that Part III of TRIPS does not attempt to harmonise national enforcement procedures, but rather aims to establish general minimum standards, which can then be implemented by each member as they see fit. This approach is also laid out in the Preamble to TRIPS which states that the negotiating parties saw "the need for new rules and disciplines concerning... c) the provision of effective and appropriate means for the enforcement of trade-related intellectual property rights, *taking into account differences in national legal systems*" (emphasis added). This is important to remember when assessing China's compliance; even if China's IP system is considerably different from that of its trading partners, China could still be in compliance with TRIPS due to this inbuilt flexibility in the TRIPS Agreement.

Overall, the drafting of the TRIPS Agreement provoked controversy between the developed and developing WTO members and as a result, the final text of the Agreement reflects the compromises made in the negotiating process. This compromise is reflected most prominently in enforcement provisions in Part III. As the controversy surrounding the establishment of the TRIPS regime has now been outlined, the TRIPS Agreement will now be analysed in the context of compliance.

3.2   Analysing the TRIPS Agreement in the Context of Compliance Theory

3.2.1   The Characteristics of the Accord

According to the model of compliance presented in Chap. 2, the characteristics of the specific accord may affect the prospects of compliance with it. Thus, it is crucial to consider the TRIPS Agreement itself before judging China's compliance with its intellectual property obligations under this accord. The non-country-specific factors which may influence compliance with the TRIPS Agreement should be considered under various categories: the perceived equity of the obligations, the precision of the obligations, provisions for obtaining scientific and technical advice, reporting requirements, provisions for other forms of monitoring, the secretariat, and other incentives and sanctions.

The perceived equity of the TRIPS Agreement is in some doubt. As discussed above, negotiations over intellectual property rights within the GATT system were protracted and involved serious compromises on the part of the developing countries in return for concessions in other areas of trade negotiations. During the TRIPS negotiations, China participated as an observer and joined with the bloc of developing countries in the TRIPS negotiations. Fourteen of these developing countries, including China, submitted a draft text concerning intellectual property in May 1990 (Negotiating Group on Trade-Related Aspects of Intellectual Property Rights 1990). Unlike the three rival drafts submitted by the US, Japan and Switzerland respectively, the developing countries' draft emphasised the "need to take into consideration the public policy objectives underlying national systems for the protection of intellectual property, including developmental and technological objectives" (Negotiating Group on Trade-Related Aspects of Intellectual Property Rights 1990). This draft also emphasised that signatories should not have recourse to unilateral measures in the event of any dispute. However, the draft was heavily criticised for providing "a wide degree of latitude" to governments with respect to legislating on standards and for providing levels of protection seen as insufficient by the developed countries (Negotiating Group on Trade-Related Aspects of Intellectual Property Rights 1990b).

It was clear after the rival drafts had been submitted that tensions still existed between the objectives of the developed countries and those of the developing countries within the TRIPS negotiations. In 1991, one developing country commented that they "continued to believe that the situation of the negotiations fell far short of addressing the special needs and problems of developing countries" (Negotiating Group on Trade-Related Aspects of Intellectual Property Rights including Trade in Counterfeit Goods 1991). Therefore, it is clear that throughout the negotiating and drafting process, there were concerns amongst the developing countries that their interests and concerns were being overlooked. As a result, there may still be a lingering perception that the final Agreement is not fair as it favours the interests of industrialised nations over poorer members. If some members do hold this perception, this may decrease the likelihood of their full compliance with their TRIPS obligations.

The precision of the TRIPS Agreement is almost certainly an area of some doubt. This is not helped by the nature of the TRIPS Agreement itself, which is a minimum standards agreement. This means that each member must provide protection of at least the standard provided for in the agreement, but is free to decide exactly how to implement the specific provisions. In this minimum standards nature, it is similar to a European Union directive. The minimum standards nature of the TRIPS Agreement is provided by Article 1, which states:

> Members shall give effect to the provisions of this Agreement. Members may, but shall not be obliged to, implement in their law more extensive protection than is required by this Agreement, provided that such protection does not contravene the provisions of this Agreement. Members shall be free to determine the appropriate method of implementing the provisions of this Agreement within their own legal system and practice. (World Trade Organisation 1994b)

The precision of the obligations contained within the TRIPS Agreement is also subject to the balance between substantive precision and judicial autonomy which is a result of the hard-fought negotiations during the drafting of the Agreement. For example, many of the Articles relating to enforcement provisions are couched in language which states that the judicial authorities should have the authority to grant a particular remedy but without further guidance on how this should be implemented. An example of this is Article 44, which provides that "the judicial authorities shall have the authority to order a party to desist from an infringement." However, the exact process of granting an injunction, the evidence which must be presented in order for an injunction to be granted, or any remedies for breach of an injunction are not further specified. This vagueness of language may lead to disputes.

In general, the wording of the TRIPS Agreement has been condemned as "result-oriented" and vague. Many of the provisions require members to give judicial or other authorities the authority to do something, but these authorities are not then obliged to exercise this power (UNCTAD-ICTSD 2004, p. 576). This flexibility within the obligations, particularly contained in Part III of TRIPS, means that assessing a member's compliance can be problematic.

For example, as stated above, Article 41 outlines the general obligations regarding enforcement procedures. Article 41(1) commits members to ensuring the availability of the specified enforcement procedures "so as to permit effective action against any act of infringement". "Effective action" is not defined here and thus, there is considerable room for interpretation. It has even been stated that "any judgment about compliance should be objectively based on whether Members have made or not the required procedures available" (UNCTAD-ICTSD 2004). This test seems to be permissive; mere existence of the procedures seems to satisfy this obligation, regardless of how, or indeed if, the procedures are actually utilised.

The analytical index of the WTO offers interpretation and application for any provisions that have been interpreted in cases brought before the WTO (World Trade Organisation 2012). The formal interpretation available concerning the TRIPS provisions on enforcement includes, for example, guidance on the scope of "unwarranted delays" in Article 41(2) and the words "shall have the authority" in Article 42. As many subsequent Articles also use the wording "shall have the authority," this interpretation is signalled to be of broader application than just to Article 42. In *India-Patents (EC)*, India tried to claim that a generally available system was not required by the wording "shall have the authority" in Articles 42–8 (World Trade Organisation 1998). However, this argument was rejected by the panel who affirmed that "the function of the words 'shall have the authority' is to address the issue of judicial discretion, not that of general availability." Therefore, although it has been argued that the mere provision of these procedures is sufficient, the outcome in this case would appear to suggest that compliance requires more; the procedures actually have to be available. To date there have been 34 disputes involving provisions of the TRIPS Agreement.[4] Several of these disputes have involved legal arguments about the precise nature of the obligations and arise from the imprecise nature of these obligations. Therefore, the precision of the obligations in the TRIPS Agreement is in doubt, and this lack of precision may be a factor affecting compliance with the Agreement overall.

Turning to provisions for obtaining scientific or technical advice to assist in compliance, there are several provisions within the TRIPS Agreement which provide for technical assistance and cooperation to assist members to comply with their obligations. The main provision is contained within Article 67. Under Article 67, developed countries shall provide technical and financial cooperation in favour of developing and least-developed countries (LDCs):

> Such cooperation shall include assistance in the preparation of laws and regulations on the protection and enforcement of intellectual property rights as well as on the prevention of their abuse, and shall include support regarding the establishment or reinforcement of domestic offices and agencies relevant to these matters, including the training of personnel.

This issue of technical assistance has been central to the agenda of the Council of TRIPS and has resulted in numerous initiatives, such as conferences and training seminars. It has also led to several joint initiatives between WIPO and the WTO; specifically, "in 1998, the joint initiative on technical cooperation to assist developing countries in meeting the deadline for implementation of the TRIPS Agreement and, in 2001, the same initiative targeted the least-developed country Members" (Gervais 2003, p. 354). Following the 2005 decision to extend the TRIPS transition period for least-developed countries until 1 July 2013, the two organisations also agreed to intensify their cooperation to facilitate TRIPS compliance from these members.[5]

In addition to the WIPO-run Cooperation for Development Program, the European Patent Office offers various programmes, the World Bank includes IP in their legal training programme and the WTO, UNCTAD and NGOs all offer support. In terms of bilateral support, the US Agency for International Development (USAID) "spends around a quarter of its annual budget on legal and regulatory training" (May and Sell 2006, p. 177). Therefore, it is clear that a variety of training programmes exist under the auspices of Article 67 in order to assist developing countries to comply with the TRIPS Agreement. Furthermore, as the changes necessary to comply with TRIPS require considerable resources, many developing countries rely on this assistance (May and Sell 2006).

However, it is clear from the wording of this provision that any such cooperation must be at the request of the developing country member and cannot be imposed by the developed country partner without mutually agreed terms and conditions. Therefore, this provision may not always allow for the necessary cooperation where it is perceived by the developing country member that the assistance offered is interference in its domestic affairs rather than helpful support. In addition, the training programmes and assistance offered have also been criticised for encouraging countries to adopt "TRIPS-plus" legislation, regardless of whether it is in the country's best interests or not and for discouraging the use of autonomy or flexibility in the implementation permitted under TRIPS Agreement (May and Sell 2006). In other words, the assistance offered by developed countries may encourage recipients to model their IP system on the developed country which may not be a suitable model for emulation, particularly if it requires stronger protection than mandated by TRIPS. Furthermore, assistance offered may also breach the key TRIPS principle that each member is free to implement TRIPS provisions as they see fit. Thus, although assistance is available under Article 67 and many developing countries do need such assistance, this training and cooperation may not always benefit the developing country as intended. Indeed, it has also been claimed that despite the provisions for cooperation under Article 67, "in the years since the promulgation of the WTO treaty there has been little- if any- real effort by developed countries to meet the Article 67 obligation" (Lehman 2002, p. 12).

There is further provision under Article 69 for more general international cooperation. This article provides that members:

Shall establish and notify contact points in their administrations and be ready to exchange information on trade in infringing goods. They shall, in particular, promote the exchange of information and cooperation between customs authorities with regard to trade in counterfeit trademark goods and pirated copyright goods.

To comply with this provision, the WTO Secretariat established a list of contact points in the administration of members and the World Customs Organisation has established a database to facilitate the exchange of information regarding cross-border trade in goods which infringe intellectual property rights (Gervais 2003, p. 360). Overall, there are provisions within the TRIPS Agreement itself for assistance and cooperation regarding implementation of TRIPS provisions. However, there is some dispute over the effectiveness of some of these measures and in general, there is a perception that developed countries could do more to assist developing country members.

In terms of reporting, the main requirement is created by Article 63 of the TRIPS Agreement which concerns transparency. Article 63(2) of the TRIPS Agreement provides that members shall notify relevant laws and regulations to the Council for TRIPS "in order to assist that Council in its review of the operation of this Agreement." Relevant laws and regulations can also include final judicial decisions and administrative rulings which pertain to the subject matter of the TRIPS Agreement (Article 63(1)). There are also further reporting requirements contained in TRIPS, such as the requirement to notify contact points under Article 69 or notification of certain options relating to national treatment under Article 3. The TRIPS Council may also ask for notification regarding a member's involvement in cooperation under Article 67.

It is clear that the notification requirements arising from the TRIPS Agreement are not insignificant. For example, notifications of laws and regulations under Article 63 include: the texts of all relevant laws and regulations in their original language; translations into one official WTO language; a listing of "other laws and regulations" in a specific format; as well as responses to a checklist regarding the law and practice of enforcement (World Trade Organisation 1996, p. 4). However, the Council for TRIPS also recognises that the notification requirements may constitute a considerable burden for some members; consequently, "procedures were adopted to attempt to reduce the burdens for Members in preparing them as well as for the Secretariat in processing them" (World Trade Organisation 1996).

Therefore, the reporting requirements of the TRIPS Agreement may operate against full compliance despite some allowances made by the TRIPS Council. Although it is clearly necessary for members to inform the Council for TRIPS of laws and regulations affecting IP rights, some members, especially developing country members, may struggle to fulfil their reporting obligations, especially when combined with various other reporting requirements of the WTO. It may be necessary to offer further assistance to support some members in fulfilling these reporting requirements, such as the WIPO assistance with translation of laws and regulations into a WTO language for the purposes of Article 63.2.

Additionally, there are various bodies which monitor intellectual property standards internationally. The World Intellectual Property Organisation (WIPO) is one of the main organisations in the field of international intellectual property. WIPO's strategic goals are: (1) to promote an IP culture; (2) to integrate into national development policies and programmes; (3) to develop laws and standards; (4) to deliver quality services in global IP protection systems; and (5) to increase the efficiency of WIPO's management and support processes (WIPO 2015). Consequently, although the role of WIPO is not directly related to active monitoring of individual countries' IP standards, the development of these standards indirectly incorporates a form of passive monitoring. Thus, the role of WIPO could be said to be a form of monitoring.

There are also a number of international intergovernmental organisations which are granted observer status at meetings of the TRIPS Council (World Trade Organisation 2016c). These organisations could also be informally seen as a form of monitoring of the operation of the TRIPS Agreement, although clearly their role is not to question an individual member's compliance. Some of these organisations are:

- Food and Agriculture Organisation (FAO)
- International Monetary Fund (IMF)
- International Union for the Protection of New Varieties of Plants (UPOV)
- Organisation for Economic Cooperation and Development (OECD)
- United Nations (UN)
- United Nations Conference on Trade and Development (UNCTAD)
- World Bank (WB)
- World Customs Organisation (WCO)
- World Intellectual Property Organisation (WIPO)

In addition to these organisations which hold formal observer status, the World Health Organisation (WHO), Joint United Nations Programme on HIV/AIDS (UNAIDS), the African Intellectual Property Organisation (OAPI), the African Regional Intellectual Property Organisation (ARIPO), the European Free Trade Organisation (EFTA) and the Cooperation Council for the Arab States of the Gulf (GCC) may all also observe TRIPS Council meetings either as ad hoc observers or on a meeting-by-meeting ad hoc basis (World Trade Organisation 2016c). Additionally, there are various bodies globally that may informally monitor the operation of the TRIPS Agreement through monitoring intellectual property protection and levels of counterfeiting and piracy. These bodies will be considered further under the category of the international environment below.

In terms of the relevant secretariat monitoring and enabling compliance, the Council for Trade-Related Aspects of Intellectual Property Rights (the Council for TRIPS) is formally established by the WTO Agreement. Article IV(5) establishes that the Council for TRIPS shall operate under the general guidance of the General Council, but with the power to create its own rules of procedure and subsidiary bodies as necessary (World Trade Organisation 1994, p. 11). Article 68 of the TRIPS Agreement further details the creation of the Council for TRIPS, which is responsible for monitoring the operation of the TRIPS Agreement. Article 68 states: "The Council for TRIPS shall monitor the operation of this Agreement and, in particular, Members' compliance with their obligations hereunder, and shall afford Members the opportunity of consulting on matters relating to the trade-related aspects of intellectual property rights." It is clear that monitoring members' compliance with TRIPS "is the predominant task of the Council" (UNCTAD-ICTSD 2004, p. 744). However, as the wording of Article 68 implies, monitoring by the Council does not only relate to members' compliance, but extends to the operation of the TRIPS Agreement in general.

The Council for TRIPS is also the forum where members can consult on matters relating to intellectual property. This provision that the Council shall provide members with a chance to consult over IP issues is intended to avoid the use of the formal dispute settlement process. The Council is also responsible for providing assistance in the event of any disputes and overseeing the review of legislation in member countries. One of the first tasks completed by the Council for TRIPS was the establishment of formal links with WIPO under Article 68, for ease of cooperation. The Council for TRIPS is also the body responsible for the review and amendment of the TRIPS Agreement, after the expiration of the one-year transitional period and every two years thereafter under Article 71. Thus, there are five main functions that the Council for TRIPS performs (World Trade Organisation 2016d), which could be summarised as monitoring, consultation, technical cooperation, review and negotiation on specific subjects, and the review of the TRIPS Agreement itself.

It is clear from the detailed annual reports submitted by the Council for TRIPS that the Council performs a significant number of important tasks to ensure the full implementation of the TRIPS Agreement. For example, the annual report for 2014 lists the activities carried out in three formal meetings of the Council (Council for Trade-Related Aspects of Intellectual Property Rights 2014). The Council took note of new notifications by members regarding new or amended legislation relevant to the TRIPS Agreement; continued with the process of reviewing the legislation of members, including Montenegro and Tajikistan; held briefings on the relationship between TRIPS and the Convention on Biological Diversity (CBD) and on non-violation complaints; reviewed technical cooperation efforts; and discussed intellectual property and innovation, amongst other issues. Overall, the Council for TRIPS evidently works hard to fulfil its role of monitoring both individual members' compliance and the operation of the TRIPS Agreement in general. In addition, the Council plays a useful role in mediating between members, to try to avoid the use of the formal dispute resolution mechanism. Therefore, the role of the secretariat would appear to be a factor which encourages compliance.

Turning now to other incentives and sanctions, there are certain provisions in the TRIPS Agreement relating to least-developed country members. These provisions act in addition to the general clauses relating to technical and international cooperation outlined above. For example, under Article 66, in addition to granting the least-developed countries substantial transitional periods to comply with the TRIPS Agreement, Article 66(2) also provides that:

> Developed country Members shall provide incentives to enterprises and institutions in their territories for the purpose of promoting and encouraging technology transfer to least-developed country Members in order to enable them to create a sound and viable technological base.

In theory, this provision should increase the incentives for least-developed countries to cooperate with the TRIPS regime as they will be entitled to significant assistance in terms of technology transfer from more developed members. However, in practice, transfers are not as frequent as the Article would suggest, as many members are reluctant to transfer their technology prior to the least-developed partner enacting effective intellectual property protection.

With this reluctance in mind, on 19 February 2003, the Council for TRIPS adopted a decision that developed country members should make annual reports regarding their activities under Article 66.2 (Council for Trade-Related Aspects of Intellectual Property Rights 2003). This decision was prompted by the Ministerial meeting at Doha which had directed members to put in place a mechanism for ensuring the monitoring and full implementation of the obligations in Article 66.2. These annual reports should contain an overview of the incentives regime put in place, as well as information regarding the operation of these incentives, including details of technology transferred and recipient countries.

According to the minutes of the Council for TRIPS meeting which established the annual report mechanism to monitor Article 66.2, the proposal was well received by the developing countries. For example, the representative of Bangladesh said that:

> Implementation of Article 66.2 was of prime importance to LDCs. Developing countries, and in particular LDCs, had assumed onerous responsibilities in the TRIPS Agreement. Article 66.2 was one of the few provisions in Uruguay Round agreements that provided LDCs opportunities to build up their economies, and thereby helped them to comply with TRIPS provisions. (Council for Trade-Related Aspects of Intellectual Property Rights 2003b)

It is clear from the comments of the Bangladesh representative that Article 66 is seen as highly significant for the developing countries. In fact, Article 66 is almost seen as "payback" for agreeing to some of the most burdensome obligations contained within TRIPS and could therefore be seen as one of the "carrots" offered in the negotiating process.

In contrast to these additional incentives available for complying with the TRIPS Agreement, sanctions for non-compliance are less clear. The Council for TRIPS does not have any power to impose sanctions for non-compliance; the role it plays is positive—to facilitate members' compliance rather than identify offenders. Thus, the only route available to sanction non-complying members is through the WTO dispute resolution mechanism. Overall, although further incentives do exist to increase the likelihood of compliance, particularly the potential for technology transfer under Article 66(2), there are few coercive sanctions applicable to members that do not fully comply with their TRIPS obligations.

Overall, the various characteristics of the TRIPS Agreement itself may affect whether members fully comply with their obligations or not. The most problematic areas of the TRIPS Agreement overall are the perceived equity and the precision of the obligations contained within the Agreement. There is a general perception originating in the drafting process that the standards of protection embodied in the TRIPS Agreement protect the interests of developed country members, whilst preventing the economic development of developing country members. This perceived inequality clearly operates against compliance. The precision of the obligations is also in doubt; as TRIPS obligations are imprecise, compliance with them is difficult to measure, and thus countries may not do all that they should to comply with the accord. In addition, although the Council for TRIPS plays an important role in monitoring compliance, other monitoring provisions are largely absent. Moreover, the reporting requirements may be difficult for some members to comply with and the provisions for assistance and cooperation that exist may not be used as much as they should be.

Therefore, in relation to the TRIPS Agreement, the institutional framework as represented by the Council for TRIPS is sound, but the procedural framework in terms of available incentives, sanctions and monitoring varies in terms of promoting compliance. The features that most discourage full implementation of and compliance with the TRIPS Agreement are related to how the substantive provisions are actually written, namely the perceived unfairness and imprecision of the obligations. This may be a result of the negotiating process that led to the establishment of the TRIPS Agreement and the inevitable compromises that were made between the negotiating parties. Overall, there are certain characteristics of the TRIPS Agreement itself that may not encourage full compliance, particularly the perception that the provisions benefited certain members more than others and the imprecision of some of the provisions.

3.2.2   *The Characteristics of the Activity Involved*

According to the comprehensive model of compliance, the characteristics of the activity involved may also affect whether compliance with the international accord can be achieved. There are four elements of the activity which need to be considered: the number of actors involved; the effect of economic incentives; the role of MNCs in the activity; and the concentration of the activity in major countries. These elements will now be considered for the specific activity with which the TRIPS Agreement is concerned to resolve, namely intellectual property infringements. The first element of intellectual property infringements that may be influential in ensuring compliance with the TRIPS Agreement is the number of actors involved in the activity. Clearly, in the case of piracy and counterfeiting, large numbers of actors are involved worldwide. However, it is equally clear that it is difficult to estimate clearly the number of actors involved due to the opaque nature of the activity. Furthermore, intellectual property infringements are a problem worldwide and are not just restricted to a few developing countries. Thus, the number of actors involved in the activity is large and this may act against compliance. As a large number of actors are involved in counterfeiting and piracy, dealing with this activity is clearly not straightforward as it follows the "conventional wisdom that the smaller the number of actors involved in the activity, the easier it is to regulate it" (Jacobson and Brown Weiss 1998, p. 521).

The second element of intellectual property infringements which needs to be considered is the possible effect of economic incentives. In this case, the effect of economic incentives on the levels of intellectual property infringements needs to be considered. Undoubtedly, economic incentives are highly relevant to the specific activity of IP infringements, as economic considerations are the primary factor behind a great deal of the existing global infringements. Clearly, economic incentives may play a large role in intellectual property infringements in general; for an individual company, infringing activities offer easy profits in the short term which may seem more attractive than unknown long-term benefits from complying with intellectual property accords. The economic benefits of TRIPS compliance may be easier to appreciate on a macroeconomic level, where stronger intellectual property protection may encourage greater innovation (Maskus 2002, p. 7).

The third element of intellectual property infringements that may be important to the likelihood or otherwise of compliance with the TRIPS Agreement is the role of MNCs in the activity. The companies actually committing the majority of intellectual property infringements do not tend to be MNCs, but rather smaller, less visible enterprises. In the context of intellectual property rights, MNCs do have a strong role to play, as there is a growing recognition of the value of intangible assets to a company. However, it is only in the past couple of decades that this recognition has been widespread amongst MNCs.

Therefore, the role MNCs played in intellectual property protection was limited until the 1980s. Once MNCs did begin to seek to protect their rights, they swiftly formed a powerful lobby group, in order to pressurise governments globally to seek stronger international IP standards. This is clearly evidenced in the Uruguay Round of GATT negotiations, when, for the first time, the influence of the MNCs was notable.[6] However, this pressure from the MNCs may not necessarily be seen as a positive force; on the contrary, MNCs are sometimes perceived as just seeking to protect their own interests with little or no regard to the economic development of the developing countries. Hence, the role of MNCs in the field of intellectual property is a significant driver towards stronger protection, but may not be a wholly positive factor in encouraging compliance amongst smaller developing WTO members as vocal MNCs can cause local hostility.

The final element of the specific activity that should be taken into account as an influence on potential TRIPS compliance is the concentration of the activity in major countries. This factor is important because it could affect the concentration of pressure to comply; if the activity is limited geographically, pressure to comply is less likely to be universal. In the case of intellectual property infringements, the activity is certainly not only limited to a handful of countries. On the contrary, infringements are a global phenomenon, although rates of IP infringements do vary from country to country. For example, the Global Software Piracy Study conducted annually by the Business Software Alliance shows marked variation in levels of software piracy worldwide (Business Software Alliance 2014). The highest rate of unlicensed PC software installations observed was in the Asia-Pacific region at an average of 62%, while the lowest was in North America where only 19% of software was unlicensed. China had an overall rate of 74% which whilst high, represented a modest drop of 3% from the previous survey in 2011 (Business Software Alliance 2014, p. 7). Therefore, it is obvious that even the most developed countries suffer from intellectual property infringements and this activity is not solely concentrated in a few developing countries. However, the worst rates of infringements are to be found in the developing countries, predominantly in the Asia-Pacific region.

In addition to the overall number of countries involved in infringing activities, it is also relevant to consider the extent of the activity in one country as a proportion of the total. In other words, it may be more efficient to focus on one country which is responsible for a large proportion of the overall activity rather than several smaller countries each responsible for a small proportion of the total. In fact, this may explain why China is so consistently the focus of scrutiny regarding its intellectual property protection; as China's contribution to total IP infringements is so large, if compliance in China can be achieved, this would make a significant contribution towards decreasing the total amount of infringing activity. Conversely, this constant pressure on China may contribute to China's perception of unequal treatment and actually discourage greater compliance with TRIPS obligations. Overall, the location of an infringing activity may be of relevance to compliance for two reasons. Firstly, as infringements are not limited to just a few countries, the problem is more difficult to tackle. Secondly, certain countries may be responsible for a larger proportion of the infringing activity overall and thus more attention may be devoted to those countries, although this attention may create resentment.

In general, the characteristics of the activity involved in the TRIPS Agreement, intellectual property infringements, may play a part in affecting the implementation of and compliance with the Agreement. The most significant of these is the economic incentives involved in infringing activities and the discouraging effect that they may have on compliance with TRIPS obligations by offering individuals and private companies easy profits in the short term. MNCs also play a role in lobbying for stronger intellectual property protection. Although they played a large part in the negotiations regarding the drafting of the TRIPS Agreement, their role in the IP field today is not entirely welcome. In fact, pressure from MNCs may discourage implementation of and compliance with TRIPS obligations in some developing countries. Finally, both the number of actors and the number of countries involved in intellectual property infringements may also discourage compliance with the TRIPS Agreement. As both a large number of actors and a large number of countries are involved, it may be difficult to assess compliance reliably and there may be scope for individual enterprises and countries to not do as much as they should.

3.2.3 *The International Environment*

In addition to the characteristics of the specific accord and the specific activity involved, the international environment surrounding the specific activity and accord should also be examined. According to the comprehensive model of compliance proposed in Chap. 2, there are several elements of the international environment that may influence compliance with the specific international obligations. These include: major international conferences, worldwide media and public opinion, the presence of international non-governmental organisations (NGOs), the number of parties adhering to the accord and other international organisations including international financial organisations. As the model is not restricted to intellectual property protection, some of these factors may be more relevant than others. Thus, the international environment will be considered under three main criteria: the role of international organisations, worldwide media and public opinion and the number of parties adhering to the TRIPS Agreement.

International organisations active in the intellectual property field may include both intergovernmental organisations and industry lobby groups. The role that these organisations may play mostly consists of monitoring and pressure. Apart from the WTO, WIPO is arguably the most important international organisation operating in the field of intellectual property rights and WIPO's role in working with the Council of TRIPS to improve TRIPS compliance and assist developing countries to build effective IP systems has been discussed above. Although WIPO does play an important role in supporting the TRIPS Agreement, the organisation is also criticised for lacking any effective means of enforcing IP Agreements which it is charged with administering. However, there are also a host of other international bodies which may play a part in intellectual property protection. For example, the International Intellectual Property Alliance (IIPA) is a coalition representing US copyright-based industries in a number of sectors such as software, music, film and publishing (International Intellectual Property Alliance 2015). The IIPA has a large part to play in the Annual Special 301 Report issued by the United States Trade Representative (USTR); the IIPA issues specific recommendations for each country which can form a significant part of the USTR's final report. The Intellectual Property Owners Association (IPO) is another US-based organisation lobbying for higher levels of IP protection, with membership open to

IP rights-holders predominantly in the US. There are also a number of think tanks worldwide which contribute to the IP debate, such as the IP Institute, a London-based think tank focused on research into economic aspects of intellectual property. Despite the large number of international organisations which exist within the IP arena, their role in encouraging TRIPS compliance is minor. This is due to a number of reasons; not only do these international organisations not enjoy widespread public support, but as many of them are US-based, they may face the same feelings of resentment that MNCs do when pressuring for stronger IP protection.

Similarly, the influence of global public opinion is linked to the previous discussion of the limited role of MNCs and international organisations; as there is a lack of consensus in public opinion worldwide on the issue of IP protection, strong pressure to increase IP standards is at risk of being perceived as imposed by certain self-interested actors. Indeed, the global issue of IP protection could be seen as a delicate balancing act between weak IP protection to stimulate low-level economic growth and strong IP protection to protect innovative industries. This lack of global agreement on required IP standards differs from public opinion regarding other areas of international agreements; not everyone may benefit equally from improved IP protection. Therefore, without clear consensus in worldwide opinion, there is a lack of consistent media pressure towards TRIPS compliance.

As of 29 July 2016, the WTO has 164 members (World Trade Organisation 2016e). After the establishment of the WTO in 1995, developed countries were granted a one-year transition period, meaning they had to comply with TRIPS from 1 January 1996; developing countries and most transition economies were allowed a further period of four years until 1 January 2000 to comply, other than Articles 3, 4 and 5 dealing with general principles such as non-discrimination. In addition, least-developed countries had a longer transition period of 11 years within which to bring their IP system into compliance with the TRIPS Agreement. This was due to expire on 1 January 2006, but was extended to 1 January 2016 for pharmaceutical patents (Council for Trade-Related Aspects of Intellectual Property Rights 2002). Therefore, the majority of WTO members are now subject to the provisions of the TRIPS Agreement and must adhere to their commitments. As there are now such a large number of countries within the TRIPS system, it is possible that this may drive momentum towards greater overall compliance with the Agreement.

In general, the international environment does not play a critical role in the formulation and implementation of international intellectual property protection standards. In contrast to the field of international environmental protection, where changes in the international environment are considered to be the most important factor in the trend towards improved implementation and compliance in the 1980s and 1990s, the international environment is not as significant for intellectual property protection. The sole feature of the international environment that may encourage greater compliance with the TRIPS Agreement is the number of countries that are now WTO members and thus subject to the provisions of the TRIPS Agreement. In terms of momentum, there are few countries left out of this regime and thus individual members may not want to be seen as lagging behind. This effect may accelerate once all the transition periods applicable to least-developed countries have ended and when all countries then have to fully comply with the TRIPS Agreement.

3.3   SUMMARY AND CONCLUSION

This chapter has considered various non-country-specific factors which may have an impact on compliance with the TRIPS Agreement. Of these factors, arguably the most significant are the perceived inequity and imprecision of the obligations contained within the TRIPS Agreement. These factors arose due to the drafting history of the Agreement and the nature of TRIPS as a minimum standards agreement. Other factors related to characteristics of the TRIPS Agreement specifically include the burden of notification obligations that members must fulfil and the lack of sufficient incentives in the form of technology and cooperation from developed country members. On the other hand, the TRIPS Agreement does have several features that may have a positive effect by encouraging compliance. These include the broad role of the Council for TRIPS and the role of the WTO dispute resolution body as a multilateral forum for resolving disputes and imposing sanctions.

With regards to the characteristics of the activity that the TRIPS Agreement aims to confront, namely the problem of intellectual property infringements, and the international environment surrounding the issue of IP protection, there are also several factors which may affect compliance. The most significant of these are the large number of actors and countries involved in IP infringements; piracy is a global activity, which makes it difficult to combat. In addition, many infringers are encouraged by short-term economic gains from IP infringements. Other factors which may have a smaller adverse effect on compliance include the lack of consensus in public opinion worldwide on the subject of IP protection and a certain amount of resentment towards MNCs and international IP organisations based in powerful developed countries for the pressure they impose for stronger IP protection.

However, as with the characteristics of the TRIPS Agreement, the international environment and characteristics of the activity of IP infringements may also have a positive impact on compliance. Specifically, the role of international organisations such as WIPO and the large number of countries which are now included in the WTO system may both entice countries to comply with the TRIPS Agreement. Having examined factors relating to the TRIPS Agreement in general, the next chapter (Chap. 4) will focus on outlining the research methods used to assess China's compliance with the TRIPS Agreement specifically.

NOTES

1. For further information on the history of the WTO, TRIPS agreement and GATT, see World Trade Organisation (2015).
2. The full text of the TRIPS Agreement is available at World Trade Organisation (1994b).
3. Summary of TRIPS provisions adapted from Stewart (2004).
4. As of 19 August 2016; for details of all the TRIPS-related disputes brought to the WTO dispute settlement body to date, see World Trade Organisation (2016).
5. For an overview of the cooperation efforts undertaken by the WTO and WIPO, see World Trade Organisation (2016b).
6. See discussion in Sect. 3.1 concerning the role of the Intellectual Property Committee (IPC) in the TRIPS drafting process, for example.

REFERENCES

Bradley, A. Jane. 1987. Intellectual Property Rights, Investment, and Trade in Services in the Uruguay Round: Laying the Foundations. *Stanford Journal of International Law* 23(1): 57–98.

Business Software Alliance. 2014. The Compliance Gap: BSA Global Software Survey (2014). http://globalstudy.bsa.org/2013/downloads/studies/2013GlobalSurvey_Study_en.pdf. Accessed 20 Oct 2015.

Correa, Carlos M. 2000. *Intellectual Property Rights, the WTO and Developing Countries: The TRIPS Agreement and Policy Options.* London: Zed Books Ltd.

Council for Trade-Related Aspects of Intellectual Property Rights. 2002. Extension of the Transition Period Under Article 66.1 of the TRIPS Agreement for Least-Developed Country Members for Certain Obligations with Respect to Pharmaceutical Products. https://www.wto.org/english/tratop_e/trips_e/art66_1_e.htm. Accessed 20 Oct 2015.

———. 2003a. Implementation of Article 66.2 of the TRIPS Agreement – Decision of the Council for TRIPS of 19 February 2003. https://www.wto.org/english/tratop_e/trips_e/ta_docs_e/ipc28_e.pdf. Accessed 20 Oct 2015.

———. 2003b. Minutes of Meeting- Held 18–19 February 2003. https://docsonline.wto.org/dol2fe/Pages/SS/DirectDoc.aspx?filename=t%3A%2Fip%2Fc%2Fm39.doc. Accessed 20 Oct 2015.

———. 2014. Annual Report (2014) of the Council for TRIPS. WTO Document IP/C/68.

Das, Bhagirath Lal. 1998. *An Introduction to the WTO Agreements.* London: Zed Books Ltd.

———. 1999. *The World Trade Organisation: A Guide to the Framework for International Trade.* London: Zed Books Ltd.

Drahos, Peter. 1996. *A Philosophy of Intellectual Property.* Aldershot: Dartmouth.

Dunkley, Graham. 2000. *The Free Trade Adventure: The WTO, the Uruguay Round and Globalism- A Critique.* London: Zed Books Ltd.

GATT. 1986. Ministerial Declaration on the Uruguay Round. http://www.wto.org/gatt_docs/English/SULPDF/91240152.pdf. Accessed 20 Oct 2015.

Gervais, Daniel. 2003. *The TRIPS Agreement: A Drafting History.* 2nd ed. London: Sweet & Maxwell.

Goldstein, Paul. 2001. *International Copyright: Principles, Law and Practice*. Oxford: Oxford University Press.

Hoekman, Bernard M., and Michel M. Kostecki. 2001. *The Political Economy of the World Trading System: The WTO and Beyond*. 2nd ed. Oxford: Oxford University Press.

International Intellectual Property Alliance. 2015. Description of the IIPA. http://www.iipawebsite.com/aboutiipa.html. Accessed 19 Aug 2016.

Jackson, John H. 1997. *The World Trading System: Law and Policy of International Economic Relations*. 2nd ed. Cambridge, MA: The MIT Press.

Jacobson, Harold K., and Edith Brown Weiss. 1998. Assessing the Record and Designing Strategies to Engage Countries. In *Engaging Countries: Strengthening Compliance with International Environmental Accords*, ed. Edith Brown Weiss and Harold K. Jacobson. Cambridge, MA: The MIT Press.

Lehman, Hon. Bruce. 2002. Copyright, Culture and Development: The Role of Intellectual Property and of WIPO in the Cultural Industries. http://iipi.org/wp-content/uploads/2010/07/Beijing_Culture_052202.pdf. Accessed 20 Oct 2015.

Maskus, Keith. 2002. Intellectual Property Rights in the WTO Accession Package: Assessing China's Reforms. *World Bank*. http://siteresources.worldbank.org/INTRANETTRADE/Resources/maskus_tips.pdf. Accessed 20 Oct 2015.

May, Christopher, and Susan K. Sell. 2006. *Intellectual Property Rights: A Critical History*. London: Lynne Rienner Publishers.

Negotiating Group on Trade-Related Aspects of Intellectual Property Rights. 1990a. Communication from Argentina, Brazil, Chile, China, Columbia, Cuba, Egypt, India, Nigeria, Peru, Tanzania and Uruguay. https://www.wto.org/gatt_docs/English/SULPDF/92100147.pdf. Accessed 20 Oct 2015.

———. 1990b. Minutes of Meeting of Negotiating Group of 14–16 May 1990. https://docs.wto.org/gattdocs/q/UR/GNGNG11/21.PDF. Accessed 20 Oct 2015.

Negotiating Group on Trade-Related Aspects of Intellectual Property Rights including Trade in Counterfeit Goods. 1991. Meeting of Negotiating Group of 27 and 28 June 1991- Note by the Secretariat. https://docs.wto.org/gattdocs/q/UR/GNGTRIPS/1.PDF. Accessed 20 Oct 2015.

Reichman, Jerome H. 1996. Enforcing the Enforcement Procedures of the TRIPS Agreement. *Virginia Journal of International Law* 37(2): 335–356.

Richards, Donald G. 2004. *Intellectual Property Rights and Global Capitalism: The Political Economy of the TRIPS Agreement*. Armonk: M. E. Sharpe.

Sell, Susan K. 2003. *Private Power, Public Law: The Globalization of Intellectual Property Rights*. Cambridge: Cambridge University Press.

Stewart, Terence P. 1993. *The GATT Uruguay Round: A Negotiating History (1986–1993)*. Deventer: Kluwer Law and Taxation Publishers.

———. 2004. China's Compliance with World Trade Organization Obligations: A Review of China's First Two Years of Membership. *U.S.-China Economic and Security Review Commission*. http://www.uscc.gov/Research/chinas-compliance-world-trade-organization-obligations-review-chinas-1st-two-years. Accessed 20 Oct 2015.

UNCTAD-ICTSD. 2004. *Resource Book on TRIPS and Development: An Authoritative and Practical Guide to the TRIPS Agreement*. http://www.iprsonline.org/unctadictsd/docs/RB_4.30_update.pdf. Accessed 20 Oct 2015.

WIPO. 2015. What is WIPO? http://www.wipo.int/about-wipo/en/what_is_wipo. html. Accessed 20 Oct 2015.

World Trade Organisation. 1994a. Agreement Establishing the World Trade Organization. http://www.wto.org/english/docs_e/legal_e/04-wto.pdf. Accessed 20 Oct 2015.

———. 1994b. Agreement on Trade-Related Aspects of Intellectual Property Rights. http://www.wto.org/english/docs_e/legal_e/27-trips.pdf. Accessed 20 Oct 2015.

———. 1996. *Technical Cooperation Handbook on Notification Requirements: Agreement on Trade-Related Aspects of Intellectual Property Rights.* WTO Document WT/TC/NOTIF/TRIPS/1. https://www.wto.org/english/tratop_e/trips_e/ tc_notif_trips1_e.doc. Accessed 19 Aug 2016.

———. 1998. India- Patent Protection for Pharmaceutical and Agricultural Chemical Products. WTO Document WT/DS79/R. https://www.wto.org/english/ tratop_e/dispu_e/cases_e/ds79_e.htm. Accessed 20 Oct 2015.

———. 2012. WTO Analytic Index- Guide to WTO Law and Practice. 3rd ed. http:// www.wto.org/english/res_e/booksp_e/analytic_index_e/analytic_index_e.htm. Accessed 20 Oct 2015.

———. 2015a. What is the WTO? http://www.wto.org/english/thewto_e/whatis_e/ whatis_e.htm. Accessed 20 Oct 2015.

———. 2015b. Overview: The TRIPS Agreement. http://www.wto.org/english/ tratop_e/trips_e/intel2b_e.htm#enforcement. Accessed 20 Oct 2015.

———. 2016a. Disputes by Agreement. https://www.wto.org/english/tratop_e/ dispu_e/dispu_agreements_index_e.htm?id=A26. Accessed 19 Aug 2016.

———. 2016b. The WTO and World Intellectual Property Organization. https:// www.wto.org/english/thewto_e/coher_e/wto_wipo_e.htm. Accessed 19 Aug 2016.

———. 2016c. International Intergovernmental Organizations Granted Observer Status to WTO Bodies. http://www.wto.org/english/thewto_e/igo_obs_e. htm#trips. Accessed 19 Aug 2016.

———. 2016d. Frequently Asked Questions About TRIPS in the WTO. http://www. wto.org/english/tratop_e/trips_e/tripfq_e.htm. Accessed 19 Aug 2016.

———. 2016e. Understanding the WTO: Members and Observers. http://www.wto. org/english/thewto_e/whatis_e/tif_e/org6_e.htm. Accessed 19 Aug 2016.

CHAPTER 4

A Framework for Assessing Compliance with the TRIPS Agreement

This project used a combination of research methods to assess the compliance of China's intellectual property (IP) system with the World Trade Organisation (WTO) Agreement on Trade-Related Intellectual Property Rights (TRIPS). These methods included the use of a questionnaire as an initial contact with respondents in late 2005, with follow-up interviews taking place in 2006 face-to-face, via telephone and email. Qualitative data was also gathered from key texts such as the primary legislation to further aid a deeper understanding of the operation of China's post-TRIPS intellectual property system. A further series of detailed semi-structured interviews were carried out in April 2015. This chapter will first outline the choice of these specific methods used before considering ethical considerations as well as key practical issues that were faced during this research such as translation and access and will conclude with an overview of the respondents and data collected.

4.1 Research Strategy and Design

Much of the relevant information regarding IP in China is virtually unattainable due to the illegal nature of IP infringements (Chow 2000, p. 12), the confidential nature of commercial strategies to tackle infringements and the opaque nature of the Chinese legal system in general. In order to overcome this problem, not only were a number of research methods used but also the issue was examined from the viewpoints of a variety of different respondents. These included lawyers, both international and domestic; representatives of multinational or foreign-invested enterprises in China; Chinese companies themselves and the official government view. Therefore, it is hoped that the data obtained can provide a full picture of the IP system in China. Thus, this research study combined different methods to collect qualitative data from a variety of sources, including survey data, detailed semi-structured interviews

© The Author(s) 2017
K. Thomas, *Assessing Intellectual Property Compliance in
Contemporary China*, Palgrave Series in Asia and Pacific Studies,
DOI 10.1007/978-981-10-3072-7_4

and documents. Previous studies of the legal system in China have also followed a similar research approach. For example, an early study of China's compliance with international treaty obligations used a combination of interviews with around 50 respondents and examination of primary source materials to see if they corroborated the respondents' views (Lee 1969, p. 19). Carter's more recent study of China's trademark protection in the 1990s also adopted interviews as the main research method used. A total of 19 respondents were listed, from Europe, China and the US (Carter 1996, pp. 74–6).

Throughout the research process, I also tried to remain reflexive and sensitive to the historical and cultural context of my research. Specifically, there are recognised problems in attempting to study China through the legal system. As early as the 1970s, Jones (1977, p. 226) noted that law was an outstanding example of the difficulties faced by researchers attempting to fit the reality observed on the ground in China into an existing Western framework. More than 20 years later, Lubman (1999, p. 12) continued to acknowledge that "law, of all disciplines that can be used in the West to study China, seems the most difficult for Westerners to use meaningfully because it is so rooted in Western values." Therefore, it was important not to attempt to judge China through the application of Western legal norms and conclude that if China is lacking these norms, the legal system must be a failure. A clear example of this occurred during the 1990s, when China was being pressured by the United States (US) to raise the level of intellectual property protection based on the American notion that the ideal intellectual property system should closely resemble their own (Lubman 1999).

Turning now to the specific research methods used in this project, in late 2005, a short questionnaire was used to make initial contact with the respondents. This questionnaire contained 18 questions, which combined open, closed and scale-type questions. The main aim of the questionnaire was to elicit brief comments about the intellectual property system in China in order to direct the focus of the follow-up interviews and to provide an overview of opinions about the current IP system. In the case of the preliminary questionnaire used in this study, a number of strategies to enhance the response rate were applied (Wilkinson and Birmingham 2003, p. 16). A short cover letter was enclosed with every questionnaire explaining the purpose of the questionnaire and stating that all respondents would receive a summary of the final results. In addition, a stamped, addressed envelope to return the questionnaire was also distributed to every respondent. Finally, the statement of anonymity was strengthened from the first draft, which stated that names of respondents or companies would only be revealed with their permission. The final draft stated that "no names or company names will be used under any circumstances." (See Appendix 1 for a copy of the questionnaire distributed.)

The length of the questionnaire was also considered, particularly observing the standard advice that a survey should take no more than 20 minutes to complete; otherwise, respondents would lose interest (Wilkinson and Birmingham 2003, p. 17). In this study, as most of the target respondents were professionals working in business, the length of the survey was felt to be of even greater significance. Therefore, the number of questions included was limited from the first draft. The questionnaire contained a mixture of closed and open questions, with a number of Likert scale-type questions included to gain further information about the respondents' opinions, whilst still being quick to complete. The scale questions (questions 8, 11, 13 and 15 on the initial questionnaire) all included five or more possible responses, in order to provide more flexibility to the respondent and afford greater accuracy in recording their views on a given subject (Wilkinson and Birmingham 2003, p. 15). Several of these scales do not include a midpoint. For example question 11 asked, "In your opinion, how effective is the current system of IP protection in China?" and offers a six-point scale for respondents to choose from. As there is no midpoint, respondents are forced to choose either a negative (1–3) or positive response (4–6); this technique aims to prevent "questionnaire drift" setting in as the respondent is forced to provide either a positive or negative view of the statement posed (Wilkinson and Birmingham 2003, p. 13). When drafting the questions, I was also mindful of avoiding leading questions and avoiding ambiguous or unclear questions. To give respondents more opportunity to clarify their answer, an "other" option was included for several questions in which the respondent was asked to choose from a list of responses.

The administering of the questionnaires was successful in its primary aim of establishing contact with respondents, and also provided a lot of rich data from the open questions for further analysis. Following the receipt of the completed questionnaires, respondents who had indicated they would be willing to participate in follow-up interviews were contacted and follow-up interviews arranged, either face-to-face or via telephone or email, depending on the respondents' preferences. The follow-up interviews were carried out with a number of respondents and also provided a great deal of rich qualitative data to analyse. Semi-structured interviews were the format chosen for follow-up interviews conducted in mid-2006, rather than structured or open interviews. The same structure and approach was taken to the later round of interviews conducted in 2015. The structure of the interview tended to follow the topics of the survey (recent changes in the IP system, problems they had experienced, reasons for these problems, as well as possible solutions and predictions for the future development of the system), but with the flexibility to include follow-up questions depending on the interviewee's responses.[1] This flexibility provided the opportunity to seek clarification and elaboration on any key points that were not clear in the respondent's answer or that were thought to be particularly interesting. This is one of the recognised advantages of this form of interviews (May 2010, p. 135).

In addition to the initial questionnaire and detailed interviews, the use of documents was clearly necessary in order to assess the post-TRIPS IP system in China. Consequently, a variety of primary legal documents were collected to assist in assessing China's implementation of the TRIPS Agreement and also proved invaluable in examining the drafting of the TRIPS Agreement and the perceived equity and precision of the resulting Agreement. In this study, documents analysed include laws and regulations concerning intellectual property in China and official documents from the WTO or its predecessor, General Agreement on Tariffs and Trade (GATT), such as minutes of key meetings or proposed drafts of the TRIPS Agreement. A wide variety of documents were identified for inclusion, particularly concerning the drafting of the TRIPS Agreement, in order to fairly represent the relative positions of both the developed countries and developing nations. The documentary data was combined with the survey responses and interview transcripts, and the data was then subject to detailed qualitative content analysis.

4.2   Ethical Issues

Although the research methods applied in this study may appear to be relatively uncontroversial, ethical considerations must still play a part in the design and application of the chosen research methods. As the Economic and Social Research Council (ESRC) explains, research is defined broadly and research ethics refer to the moral principles guiding all research, "during the complete lifecycle of a project" (ESRC 2016). Therefore, any relevant ethical considerations must be identified and taken into account in the context of this specific research. Ethical considerations have a long history in social research, and there are various codes of ethics which guide researchers. However, most codes have similar overlapping principles such as informed consent, avoiding deception, ensuring privacy and confidentiality and the accuracy of the data (Christians 2005, pp. 144–5). Consequently, the ESRC ethical code currently in operation will be applied. From January 2015, the ESRC (2015) put in place an updated Research Ethics Framework (REF). This framework sets out what the ESRC and various other funding bodies perceive to be good practice for all social science research. The framework lays down six broad principles which the ESRC expects to be addressed in all social science research. These are: firstly that research participants must participate in a voluntary way, free from any coercion or undue influence; next, that researchers should aim to maximise the benefits of the research and minimise potential harm to participants; thirdly, research participants should be given appropriate information about the purpose, methods and intended uses of the research, what their participation entails and what risks and benefits, if any, are involved; fourthly, participant preferences regarding anonymity and confidentiality should be respected. Research should also be designed, reviewed and undertaken to ensure integrity, quality and transparency; and finally, the independence of research must be clear, and any conflicts of interest or partiality should be explicit (ESRC 2015, p. 4).

These key principles of research ethics must be considered in turn in the context of my research on intellectual property protection in China. The principle of informed consent is highly relevant to this research. "Informed consent entails giving sufficient information about the research and ensuring that there is no explicit or implicit coercion so that prospective participants can make an informed and free decision on their possible involvement" (ESRC 2015, p. 29). This information was provided to all respondents in this study prior to their initial involvement. My position, initially as a postgraduate researcher and later as a foreign scholar, and the aims of this research were explained in both the cover letter and at the top of the questionnaire or start of the interview, and it was made clear to all respondents that they could raise any questions or concerns that they had about their participation in this study. The issue of informed consent is more problematic in this research project as the majority of the respondents were Chinese. It is well recognised that the conventional Western concept of informed consent relies on the "primacy of the individual," which may not exist in other cultural contexts, where the individual may take less precedence to the family or community (Westmarland 2011, p. 143). In the context of China, it is true that individual rights may not take precedence over collective concerns. However, many of the Chinese respondents worked for foreign-invested enterprises or for multinational corporations operating in China, and they have consequently been exposed to concepts of individual rights such as consent and privacy on previous occasions. Therefore, the same wording was used to deal with the issue of informed consent in both the Chinese and English versions of the questionnaire and was handled in broadly the same way at the start of each interview.

The third principle regarding confidentiality and anonymity is a crucial consideration in this study. This ethical principle requires that "individual research participant and group preferences regarding anonymity should be respected and participant requirements concerning the confidential nature of information and personal data should be respected" (ESRC 2015, p. 4). Anonymity was a key concern to many respondents as the issue of IP protection is extremely commercially sensitive. Therefore, assurances of anonymity were given in the initial contact letter/email and reinforced in the questionnaire/interview. Contact details provided by respondents were contained in a separate sheet, which was detached from the survey immediately on receipt of the completed questionnaire. Furthermore, each respondent was assigned a code relating to which group of respondents they belonged to, and this code was used in all documents relating to their individual responses and comments. In this study, this balance between retaining sufficient detail and ensuring that individuals could not be identified was achieved by only providing basic details of the respondent and the type of company they worked for. The location was also occasionally included when this was felt to be significant and where this did not increase the probability of the respondent's identification.

The next principle concerns the need to ensure that participants take part voluntarily and without coercion. This is closely linked to the issue of informed consent. No pressure was exerted on participants who expressed their concern about participating and all respondents were assured that they could choose to withdraw at any time. Indeed, several respondents declined to answer certain questions as they were deemed to be too sensitive regarding the company's IP strategy and this response was not challenged. The principle of avoiding harm to participants was also considered. Harm does not just include physical or psychological harm; it can also include reputational risk as well as risk to a participant's social standing, privacy, personal values or beliefs, their links to family and the wider community, and their position within institutional settings (ESRC 2015, p. 27). Therefore, a further consideration in this study was the possibility of harm to an individual's or company's reputation as a result of comments made. This possibility was minimised by giving clear assurances of anonymity and ensuring that respondents could not be identified in the results, but the possibility of later identification may have inhibited some respondents from giving their true opinions, particularly where these were critical of the current system or where they were relating to situations in which their company's IP was at risk. The final principle is that the researcher should declare any affiliations and potential conflicts of interest. Although this was not directly relevant to my research, respondents were still informed of my initial status as postgraduate researcher and later as an academic and my affiliation with the University of Nottingham. I also explained clearly that the data collected was for research use only.

The handling of personal data followed the standards laid down in the Data Protection Act 1998, despite the fact that data was collected outside the United Kingdom (UK) and thus outside the remit of this legislation. This legislation provides that data must be obtained for a specific purpose and should not be kept for any longer than is necessary for this purpose. Data should also be kept secure from unauthorised access (Information Commissioner's Office 2016). As a result, data collected from respondents was obtained for the specific aims of the research and will be destroyed on completion of the study. Data will also be stored in secure computer files and the use of codes to identify respondents should further protect their personal information.

4.3   Practical Issues

There were various practical issues which arose during this research. The main two practical issues which I faced were the issue of translation and the issue of research access as an "outsider." In terms of translation, careful consideration had to be given to the language used both in the research materials (letter for initial contact, survey and interview question design) and during the interviews themselves. There are three main practical problems that may arise from attempting to translate such materials from one language into another target language (in this case, English to Mandarin Chinese). These are the lack of semantic equivalence across languages, the lack of conceptual equivalence across cultures and the lack of normative equivalence across societies (Behling and Law 2000, pp. 4–5). For example, legal concepts do not necessarily translate into easily understood Chinese categories. One case in point would be the widely discussed concept of the "rule of law," which has different translations in Chinese depending on the usage. For example, 法治 (*fazhi*) translates as "rule of law," but the Constitution uses the phrase 依法治国 (*yifazhiguo*), which has been translated as both ruling the country by law and rule of law (Zheng 1999). This may also be due to a lack of conceptual equivalence across different legal cultures; coming from a Western common law background, it is important not to assume that legal norms applicable in one jurisdiction are applicable in China.

Finally, the lack of normative equivalence in China may relate to certain social conventions. These include the willingness or otherwise to discuss certain topics, the manner in which ideas are expressed and the treatment of strangers (Behling and Law 2000, pp. 5–6). It is important to be aware of all of these potential problems in the Chinese context as the concepts of "face" (*mianzi*) and "networks/relationships" (*guanxi*) may be influential, both in terms of access, but also in terms of the answers given to an outsider. Furthermore, as the majority of the questions in my survey related to attitudes and opinions, it is more likely that these social conventions and norms would play a role in the answers received from respondents. In order to minimise these potential problems, the following steps were performed. With regards to semantic issues, the language used was carefully considered when drafting the original survey in English. This was especially important when considering the wording of attitudinal questions. Key guidelines developed to aid translation were also considered during the drafting process. These guidelines include: using short, simple sentences of less than 16 words; employing the active rather than passive voice; avoiding subjunctives such as "could" or "would" where possible; and avoiding words indicating vagueness such as "possibly" or "probably" where possible (Brislin 1980). With regards to conceptual issues, as stated above, certain legal concepts may be grounded in the Western legal tradition and this was also borne in mind whilst drafting the survey. To minimise these issues, the legal terms used in the primary People's Republic of China (PRC) legislation was used, as this should represent the most familiar IP terms and concepts.

Finally, with regard to solving normative problems, there are recognised problems in China with questions asking for political opinions. This is thought to be a legacy of the Cultural Revolution which has "led to a general pattern of disguising attitudes and feelings" (Behling and Law 2000, p. 42). As a result, assurances of anonymity in this study were strengthened to assure respondents that their identity would not be revealed under any circumstances. Individual names and company affiliations were also not requested in the initial survey, unless the respondent wished to provide them for follow-up contact. This aimed to reassure respondents and decrease any potential reticence on sensitive topics. However, it is still possible that Chinese respondents were less willing to be critical of their legal system and framework of IP protection and again this must be borne in mind during analysis of the responses.

Two Chinese translators were used to confirm semantic equivalence in the survey; their role was also to advise on the wording of the survey with knowledge of the target culture and social norms, in order to minimise normative issues. The issue of striving for semantic and conceptual equivalence was also an issue in the translation of respondents' answers from Chinese to English.

Again, translations were as close to the original text as possible, but did require some interpretation in certain cases. As with the translation of the original research instruments from English into Chinese, Chinese research assistants were asked to check the translation and discuss any phrases or sentences which were particularly problematic in terms of language or context. Consequently, although it was not always possible to check with the respondents as to their intended meaning, mistranslations were hopefully minimised. However, the issue of translation should constantly be borne in mind when reading quotes given, as they may be an interpretation of the respondents' original meaning.

Fieldwork in China has been described as eye-opening but sometimes also deeply frustrating (Thogersen and Heimer 2006, p. 1) and I would certainly agree with that characterisation in my experience. I certainly did experience a number of problems in gaining access to potential research participants. However, in contrast to researchers such as Gladney (2003),[2] I found access as a foreign scholar in 2015 to be much easier than as an overseas student in China, with many doors opened to me when I explained I was a foreign scholar, which had been closed as a postgraduate student. Nevertheless, in common with many other researchers' experiences with research access in China, access to individual participants was easiest through existing social networks (Liang and Lu 2006, p. 163), either previous contacts or friends of friends or through professional social networking tools such as LinkedIn.

The difficulties in gaining research access were aggravated by the sensitive nature of the topic under discussion, namely the protection of intellectual property rights in contemporary China. The difficulties in gaining research access are also linked to concerns about the validity of the resulting data collected; as Chinese interviewees are more likely to treat a researcher as a stranger and be most concerned about not losing face rather than giving truthful answers (Cui 2015, p. 365). On the other hand, my research status as an outsider may also have opened up opportunities[3] in that I was not seen as a commercial rival; so several respondents were very open and honest about their strategies for protecting their IP in China. The range and number of respondents in this research project, although somewhat limited, reflects the common nature of legal research in China, in which small convenience samples are used rather than large randomly selected samples (Liang and Lu 2006, p. 161). Flexibility was key in order to maximise the number of respondents involved in the project; for example, I met with respondents at their location of choice, often a coffee shop or hotel lobby, rather than always at their office.[4] Additionally, I always respected respondents' decision about any recording of the interview, whether audio or written notes were acceptable, and where the interviewee preferred for an interview not to be recorded, I instead wrote up my notes of the interview as soon as possible after it concluded.

As highlighted by previous studies of China's legal system, a variety of perspectives are necessary to avoid judging the system by foreign norms. Consequently, a range of legal and business professionals were targeted. The sampling strategy was purposive in that key companies were targeted for selection and the approach to sampling respondents evolved as the initial responses were received. For example, legal professionals were initially quicker to respond and responses were frequently more detailed than those from other respondents. As a result, an electronic version of my initial questionnaire was added to the university's web pages in order to give other respondents an alternative method of completion if time was a factor for them. This sampling strategy did also incorporate an element of snowball sampling as several respondents suggested further people to contact and occasionally also facilitated the subsequent initial contact.

The respondents in this study consequently could be broadly categorised into three groups: legal professionals working in IP in China, domestic Chinese enterprises concerned with IP rights and foreign enterprises with a presence in China. There may not also be a clear distinction between these groups; for instance, defining a "foreign-invested enterprise" is difficult given the myriad of business structures existing in China. Consequently, in this study, a company was defined as "foreign" if the respondent stated that the headquarters of the company was outside China. The initial questionnaires were largely distributed between November 2005 and May 2006 to all three groups of respondents. The first group of respondents were legal professionals, to whom questionnaires were sent in November 2005 to a variety of both international and local law firms. These firms were selected based on their inclusion in the *Legal500* list of recommended law firms in China. The second group of respondents were Chinese companies with well-known trademarks, selected from the "Well-known Trademark Enterprise Name List" (Ebuywww 2005) and the *China500*.[5] However, only a handful of responses were received from this group. The final group of respondents were foreign-invested enterprises in China. Questionnaires were sent to the members of the Quality Brands Protection Committee (QBPC), which is a group of multinational companies operating in China (QBPC 2016). Again, the number of responses was disappointing. It is possible that confidentiality concerns were a primary cause of non-responses, as indicated by the response of one company, which claimed that they "could not provide details in this respect as your questionnaire proposes, because all information is highly confidential."[6] In addition to the members of the Quality Brands Protection Committee, questionnaires were also sent to a variety of foreign enterprises operating in relevant sectors such as the luxury goods market and in the technology or telecommunications sector in China. These enterprises were selected from the "China Foreign Enterprise Directory," published by the China Economic Review (2006).

Although response to the initial questionnaire remained somewhat disappointing, the vast majority of questionnaire respondents also indicated their willingness to participate in follow-up interviews and indeed several were very enthusiastic about participating in the study. Consequently, during early 2006, a number of face-to-face interviews with respondents in China were conducted to obtain more detailed information on their opinions of the current state of the intellectual property system, ranging from 30 to 80 minutes. Several telephone interviews with respondents in Hong Kong were also completed and more detailed responses to follow-up questions were received from several other respondents who indicated their willingness to participate via email. In April 2015, I returned to China to carry out a number of further interviews in order to update my understanding of the post-TRIPS IP system in China and how it had changed over the past decade. In total, I carried out 18 formal interviews over a two-week period, with several additional informal chats with respondents who did not wish to formally participate in the research project. Some descriptive statistics about both groups of respondents will be presented below.

4.4   OVERVIEW OF DATA AND RESPONDENTS

In total, 49 respondents participated in the initial 2005 stage of the study, with 18 formal interviews carried out in the second phase of research in 2015. In response to some basic questions about their involvement with this topic, all of the respondents in the initial group informed me that they were involved with IP in China and furthermore, all respondents were based in China or Hong Kong. When asked how long they/their company had been working in China, the majority responded that they had been established in China for more than ten years. This affirms that respondents should be knowledgeable about the topic of intellectual property protection in China as all deal with IP and the majority of individuals had also been working in China for many years. This wealth of experience with the IP system in China was mirrored in the backgrounds of the respondents in 2015; of the 18 interviewees, the majority had over ten years of experience working in the IP field in China, with an average of 11 years.

The respondents also represented a mix of nationalities with 29 of the initial group of respondents from China and 20 from other countries, mostly in Europe or North America. In 2015, the majority of the respondents were Chinese with only four foreign interviewees, again representing a mix of other nationalities. The type of enterprise represented in the study also showed a mix with the majority being domestic Chinese enterprises and the rest being foreign-invested enterprises operating in China. Tables 4.1 and 4.2 show the breakdown of both groups of respondents by nationality and the type of enterprise that they work for.

Table 4.1 Number of respondents according to respondent nationality and type of enterprise, 2005–6

Respondent nationality	Type of enterprise	Works for domestic Chinese enterprise	Works for foreign-invested enterprise	Total
Chinese		22	5	27
Foreign		5	17	22
Total		27	22	49

Table 4.2 Number of respondents according to respondent nationality and type of enterprise, 2015

Respondent nationality	Type of enterprise	Works for domestic Chinese enterprise	Works for foreign-invested enterprise	Total
Chinese		10	4	14
Foreign		1	3	4
Total		11	7	18

Table 4.3 Number of respondents according to the goods or services their company offers, 2005–6 and 2015

Type of goods or services offered	Coding	Number of respondents 2005–6	Number of respondents 2015
Legal services	LAW	31	10
Manufacturing	MANU	8	1
Food and beverage	FOOD	3	0
Electronics	ELECT	0	2
Academia	ACAD	0	2
Fashion and luxury goods	LUX	2	1
Services	SERV	2	1
Automobile	AUTO	1	0
Pharmaceutical	PHARMA	1	1
Technology and telecommunications	TECH	1	0
Total		49	18

In addition to a variety of nationalities and enterprise types represented amongst my respondents, a number of different industries were represented. The majority of respondents were from law firms, but this was broadly defined as including trademark and patent agencies, as well as companies offering legal advice under a broader framework of consultancy. The number of respondents is shown in Table 4.3 according to the type of goods or services that their enterprise offers. A further column also indicates how respondents from this type of enterprise were coded to ensure their anonymity.

Therefore, the number of respondents represented a wide variety of nationalities, types of enterprises, and goods and services offered. In addition, the respondents provided a great deal of rich qualitative data overall. Turning to data analysis, the answers given on the questionnaire in response to the open questions were combined with the interview transcripts and notes, as well as documentary data and analysed using the NVivo software to code the answers given, to build a model of TRIPS compliance in post-WTO China. My initial coding framework was extensive and featured 41 potential nodes under which the data was coded. These nodes are shown below:

- Assessing the Current System
  - Comparisons to other systems
  - Experiences with the current system
  - Praise for the current system
  - Problems in the current system
  - Inconsistency
  - Local protectionism
  - Problems with corruption
  - Problems with enforcement
  - Problems with legislation
  - Other problems
- Causes of the current state of the IP system
  - Fundamental factors
  - Attitudes and values
  - Economy
  - Political or institutional
  - Parameters
  - History of IP in China
  - Physical characteristics of China
  - Proximate Factors
  - Administrative capacity
  - Knowledge and Information
  - Leadership
  - Other causes
- Forces for Change
  - Changes observed in the IP system
  - Attitude of leadership
  - Foreign companies and foreign countries
  - Impact of WTO entry
  - Local companies
  - Natural development or "matter of time"
  - Other force for change
  - Administrative changes
- Solutions
  - Awareness
  - Government commitment
  - International cooperation
  - Resources
  - Training
  - Other solutions
  - Predictions for the future of the IP system

Following this initial coding, several of the nodes were then merged to create a more manageable framework for analysis and I then continued this process of reading the data and making decisions about coding categories whilst attempting to move towards a dynamic and comprehensive model of compliance. In terms of presentation of data, a different font will be used for direct quotes from respondents, for ease of identification. In addition, the interview transcripts followed some basic transcription conventions (Silverman 2004, pp. 368–9); the following are the most important which may appear in quotes taken from these transcripts:

( )	parentheses indicates that the words were inaudible, or not clear enough to transcribe, words within the parentheses represent a best estimate of what was said;
[ ]	square brackets indicates overlapping talk, most commonly saying "yeah" or "uh-huh" whilst the respondent was talking;
(( ))	double brackets indicates commentary of other events, such as observing a mobile phone ringing or knocking being audible on the tape;
-	hyphen represents a self-interruption or an abrupt cut-off of what the respondent was saying.

In order to maintain the confidentiality of all respondents, codes were assigned to each respondent which will be used to identify their comments. These codes aim to identify the basic characteristics of the respondents, such as the nature of the enterprise they work for, without revealing their identity or enough details to enable identification by someone knowledgeable in the IP field in China. Consequently, the initial number 05 or 15 indicates whether the respondent was part of the initial or later group of interviewees. Three letter codes were then assigned based on the respondents' enterprise, followed by a two-digit number, and then a "T" if the comments had been translated. For example, 05LAW01T represents the first respondent from a law firm from the original 2005–6 group and that their comments have been translated. It is important to identify which comments are translated in order to maintain transparency of the data, as these comments are not in the respondents' own words.

The framework for assessing overall compliance with the TRIPS Agreement outlined in this chapter will now be applied to the specific context of China's compliance with the TRIPS Agreement since formal accession in December 2001. The next chapter will consider how the substantive IP-related legislation was amended to comply with TRIPS, then Chaps. 6 and 7 will outline respondents' experiences of dealing with China's IP system in both the short and long term.

NOTES

1. See Appendix 2 for interview framework.
2. Perhaps due to the commercial nature of the topic of IP compared to the ethnographic study of minorities studied by Gladney.
3. Similar to those experienced by: Scoggins (2014, p. 394).
4. Again, similar to the experiences of: Scoggins (2014, p. 395).
5. The list of the top 500 Chinese enterprises according to their revenue as produced by the China Enterprise Confederation (2010).
6. Comment from respondent 05FOOD03.

REFERENCES

Behling, Orlando, and Kenneth S. Law. 2000. Translating Questionnaires and Other Research Instruments: Problems and Solutions. In *Quantitative Applications in the Social Sciences*, ed. Michael S. Lewis-Beck. London: Sage Publications.

Brislin, Richard W. 1980. Translation and Content Analysis of Oral and Written Materials. In *Handbook of Cross-Cultural Psychology*, ed. H.C. Triandis and J.W. Berry. Boston: Allyn & Bacon.

Carter, Connie. 1996. *Fighting Fakes in China: The Legal Protection of Trade Marks and Brands in the People's Republic of China*. London: The Intellectual Property Institute.

China Economic Review. (ed.). 2006. *China Foreign Enterprise Directory*. 2nd ed. Hong Kong: China Economic Review Publishing.

China Enterprise Confederation. 2010. Top 500 China Enterprises. http://cec-ceda.org.cn/c500/chinese/ep500.php?id=0. Accessed 20 Aug 2016.

Chow, Daniel. 2000. Counterfeiting in the People's Republic of China. *Washington University Law Quarterly* 78(1): 1–57.

Christians, Clifford G. 2005. Ethics and Politics in Qualitative Research. In *The SAGE Handbook of Qualitative Research*, ed. Norman K. Denzin and Yvonne S. Lincoln. London: SAGE Publications.

Cui, Ke. 2015. The Insider-Outsider Role of a Chinese Researcher Doing Fieldwork in China: The Implications of Cultural Context. *Qualitative Social Work*. 14(3): 356–369.

Ebuywww. 2005. 驰名商标企业名录 (Well-known Trademark Enterprise Name List). ed. Ebuywww (Beijing) Info. Co. Ltd. (北京易拜天地网络技术有限剬司). Beijing: Ebuywww (Beijing) Info. Co. Ltd.

ESRC. 2015. ESRC Framework for Research Ethics 2015. http://www.esrc.ac.uk/files/funding/guidance-for-applicants/esrc-framework-for-research-ethics-2015/. Accessed 21 Nov 2015.

———. 2016. Research Ethics. http://www.esrc.ac.uk/funding/guidance-for-applicants/research-ethics/. Accessed 20 Aug 2016.

Gladney, Dru C. 2003. Lessons (Un)learned: Ten Reflections on Twenty Years of Fieldwork in the People's Republic of China. *Max Planck Institute for Social Anthropology Working Paper* No. 60.

Information Commissioner's Office. 2016. Data Protection Principles. https://ico.org.uk/for-organisations/guide-to-data-protection/data-protection-principles/. Accessed 20 Aug 2016.

Jones, William C. 1977. Understanding Chinese Law: Thought Control in Prewar Japan. *Review of Socialist Law* 3(1): 219–226.

Lee, Luke T. 1969. *China and International Agreements: A Study of Compliance*. Leiden: A. W. Sijthoff.

Liang, Bin, and Hong Lu. 2006. Conducting Fieldwork in China: Observations on Collecting Primary Data Regarding Crime, Law and the Criminal Justice System. *Journal of Contemporary Criminal Justice*. 22(2): 157–172.

Lubman, Stanley. 1999. *Bird in a Cage: Legal Reform in China After Mao*. Stanford: Stanford University Press.

May, Tim. 2010. *Social Research: Issues, Methods and Process*. Maidenhead: Open University Press.

QBPC. 2016. QBPC Introduction. http://www.qbpc.org.cn/view.php?id=2715&cid=43. Accessed 20 Aug 2016.

Scoggins, Suzanne E. 2014. Navigating Fieldwork as an Outsider: Observations from Interviewing Police Officers in China. *PS: Political Science & Politics.* 47(2): 394–397.

Silverman, David, eds. 2004. *Qualitative Research: Theory, Method and Practice.* 2nd ed. London: SAGE Publications.

Thogersen, Stig, and Maria Heimer. 2006. Introduction. In *Doing Fieldwork in China,* ed. Maria Heimer and Stig Thogersen. Copenhagen: NIAS Press.

Westmarland, Louise. 2011. *Researching Crime and Justice: Tales from the Field.* Abingdon: Routledge.

Wilkinson, David, and Peter Birmingham. 2003. *Using Research Instruments: A Guide for Researchers.* London: RoutledgeFalmer.

Zheng, Yongnian. 1999. From Rule By Law to Rule of Law? A Realistic View of China's Legal Development. *China Perspectives* 25: 31–43.

PART 2

Assessing Compliance with the TRIPS Agreement in China

CHAPTER 5

Implementing the TRIPS Agreement in China

5.1   The Impact of the TRIPS Agreement on the IP System in China

In this chapter, China's compliance with the obligations associated with the World Trade Organisation (WTO) Agreement on Trade-Related Intellectual Property Rights (TRIPS) will be discussed. China's implementation of the TRIPS Agreement into domestic intellectual property (IP) legislation will first be introduced, and then the implementation of TRIPS obligations into the enforcement system will be considered. Then, overall compliance with the TRIPS Agreement will be evaluated. Compliance will incorporate both procedural and substantive compliance as well as compliance with the spirit of the treaty. The chapter will conclude by examining how China's TRIPS compliance has been formally challenged through the use of WTO's dispute settlement mechanism since accession in December 2001.

According to research conducted on China's pre-WTO entry compliance with TRIPS, China needed to make substantial changes to the law to comply with the TRIPS norms. Almost 40 substantive TRIPS requirements were identified, of which China was already compliant with less than half (Maskus 2002). Consequently, China needed to take action to comply with the remaining requirements. The actions required to comply with the remaining provisions included the following:

- Removing discrimination to uphold the national treatment principle
- Restricting compulsory licences
- Copyright: introducing rental rights and clarifying/enhancing performer rights and broadcast rights
- Trademarks: establishing protection for well-known marks, clarifying provisions on prior use and ineligible signs

© The Author(s) 2017
K. Thomas, *Assessing Intellectual Property Compliance in Contemporary China*, Palgrave Series in Asia and Pacific Studies, DOI 10.1007/978-981-10-3072-7_5

- Introducing protection for geographical indications
- Patents: clarifying basic exemptions and coverage of plant and animal varieties
- Enforcement: sanctions to be enhanced, particularly preliminary injunctions and seizures, as well as levels of damages
- Ensuring the availability of judicial review

With such a multitude of changes necessary, it is clear that China faced a major legislative task to fully comply with all the TRIPS standards.

From the responses gathered in the initial stage of this research project, it is immediately clear that China's IP system changed dramatically in response to the TRIPS Agreement. On the initial questionnaire dispatched in 2005, respondents were asked if they had noticed any changes in the intellectual property system in China in the past five years. Of the 45 valid responses, 43 stated that they had noticed a change, with only two respondents noticing no change. Furthermore, when asked to characterise this change as positive or negative on a scale of −2 to 2 (with −2 representing strong negative changes and 2 representing strong positive changes), the changes were ranked 1.26 by respondents, which suggests that respondents overall perceived the recent changes observed as positive. Moreover, it is notable that only one respondent judged recent changes to be negative.

However, the influence of the TRIPS Agreement on the framework of intellectual property protection in contemporary China actually predated WTO accession by several years. Despite not being a full member, China did participate in the Uruguay Round of negotiations as an observer and had used the TRIPS Agreement as a model law to improve the IP legislation throughout the 1990s (Yang 2003, p. 139). Moreover, the influence of the TRIPS Agreement on the intellectual property system in China was not limited to substantive changes in the formal laws and regulations. Besides the role of TRIPS as a model for China's legislative improvements of the IP protection system, TRIPS implementation also raised the prospect of using the formal dispute settlement proceedings provided by the WTO to make "an objective determination on the efficacy of enforcement measures" (Taubman 2003, p. 347). This possibility further increased the emphasis on enforcement of substantive rights that was already being stressed by foreign rights-holders and trade partners alike.

Indeed, several respondents did explicitly refer to this function of the WTO, as:

The threat of the WTO dispute settlement procedures[1]

Another respondent felt that:

The dispute resolution mechanism in there probably does have a little bit of fear factor and also (pulling) factor.[2]

Thus, the impact of WTO entry in terms of China's TRIPS commitments was multifaceted. Firstly, the TRIPS Agreement was said to have been influential during formal legal revisions of the 1990s. Secondly, the threat of the dispute resolution mechanism that is part of the WTO framework may also have held a bit of a "fear factor" for China. More importantly, the TRIPS Agreement led directly to wide-ranging legislative changes in intellectual property protection and finally, there were also important changes in the IP enforcement system directly linked to WTO accession. These important legislative changes and changes to the enforcement system made as part of China's attempts to observe its TRIPS obligations, as well as an outline of the resulting post-TRIPS system of protection, will be presented below.

5.1.1   Implementing the TRIPS Agreement in the Formal Legislation

In order to comply with the substantial obligations associated with WTO entry, China undertook a massive overhaul of its intellectual property laws beginning in 1999, before official accession in December 2001. During the critical period from 1999 to 2002, many laws and regulations were considerably amended, while others were introduced for the first time. To illustrate this huge legislative effort, a selection of the major laws and regulations passed during this period are outlined below:

- Copyright Law amended and came into effect 27 October 2001;
- Implementing Regulations of the Copyright Law came into force on 15 September 2002;
- Decisions on Safeguarding of Security on the Internet adopted on 28 December 2000;
- Regulations on Computer Software Protection amended and came into effect 1 January 2002;
- Regulations on Publications came into effect 1 February 2002;
- Regulations on Motion Pictures came into effect 1 February 2002;
- Regulations on Sound and Video Recordings came into effect 1 February 2002;
- Patent Law amended on 25 August 2000 and came into effect 1 July 2001;
- Implementing Regulations of the Patent Law came into force on 1 July 2001;
- Patent Examination Guidelines republished 1 July 2001;
- Layout-Designs of Integrated Circuits Protection Regulations (IC Regulations) came into force on 1 October 2001;
- Implementing Rules of the IC Regulations came into force on 1 October 2001;
- Regulations on Administration of Imports or Exports of Technologies came into force on 1 January 2002;

- Rules on Registration of Technology Import or Export Contracts came into force on 1 January 2002;
- Rules on Technologies prohibited or restricted from importation came into force on 1 January 2002;
- Rules on Technologies prohibited or restricted from exportation came into force on 1 January 2002;
- Trademark Law amended and came into effect 1 December 2001;
- Implementing Regulations of the Trademark Law came into force on 15 September 2002;
- Trademark Examination Guidelines revised 17 October 2002.

In addition to the main period of legislative revision from 1999 to 2002, the process of review and modification in China continued after this time. For example, according to the State Intellectual Property Office (SIPO), in 2003, "a total of 26 regulations and documents, which were not in accordance with the rules of WTO, were revised or cancelled" (SIPO 2003). Amendments were made in the legislation specifically to implement the provisions of the TRIPS Agreement, for example, the provision of rental and broadcast rights for copyright. The TRIPS Agreement provides a right to prohibit rental of computer programs and movies under Article 11; this was implemented by the Copyright Law 2001 revised Article 10, which provided rental rights. The TRIPS Agreement also provides the right to prevent fixation, reproduction or broadcasting for 20 years under Article 14; the amendments to Article 10 of the 2001 Copyright Law included these rights of reproduction, broadcasting and communication.

Other key revisions to implement the TRIPS Agreement included extending the symbols which may be protected as trademarks and codifying the protection for well-known marks. The signs that may be subject to trademark under the TRIPS Agreement include distinguishing names, letters, numerals and colours; this provision was implemented by the revised Trademark Law 2001 Article 8. The TRIPS Agreement also requires protection for well-known marks without registration in the member country. Well-known marks were protected in China prior to the revisions of 1999–2002, but this protection was strengthened and formalised by the inclusion of two new Articles in the revised Trademark Law 2001. Articles 13 and 14 prohibited registration of trademarks which are a reproduction, imitation or translation of a well-known trademark not registered in China and provided criteria for determining whether a trademark is well-known.

The major legislative changes that China undertook in connection with WTO accession were also frequently mentioned by several respondents in the initial group, when asked to comment on recent changes in the intellectual property system that they had observed. It was noticeable that these comments on specific legislative changes were predominantly made by lawyers, whereas respondents from business tended to focus more on changes in enforcement or attitude that they had observed.

For example, when asked to comment on recent changes they had observed in the IP system in China, one legal respondent described:

Revision of the relevant laws and regulations, such as the copyright law, trademark law, patent law and other IP-related laws and regulations.[3]

The connection between the amendments and China's WTO entry was made more explicitly by other respondents:

A series of IP laws and regulations have been amended to fulfil China's commitment to the WTO. IP-related clauses have been added into various laws and regulations accordingly.[4]

Furthermore, the revision of China's IP laws associated with WTO entry was described as a "milestone"[5] and finally, a further respondent also linked the substantive amendments to "the requirements of TRIPS."[6]

Therefore, it is clear from the quantity of amendments carried out, as well as the various respondents' comments, that the legislative changes that China made to comply with the TRIPS Agreement were substantial.

5.1.2 Implementing the TRIPS Agreement in the Enforcement System

In addition to amendments to substantive provisions of the IP legislation, accession to the TRIPS Agreement also led to changes in the enforcement of intellectual property rights in China. The TRIPS Agreement is often said to have added teeth to the previous international intellectual property Conventions, such as the Paris Convention and the Berne Convention, which lacked provisions on enforcement standards (Sun 2001, p. 26). Thus, countries could comply with their previous commitments by merely passing a law, even if the law was not applied in practice. Consequently, "one of the key initiatives of the TRIPS Agreement was to resolve the enforcement issues left by the existing IP protection regime" (Gregory 2003, p. 338). As enforcement provisions of the TRIPS Agreement were deemed to be so crucial by WTO members, it is important to examine some of the specific changes that implementation of the TRIPS Agreement brought to China's post-TRIPS enforcement system, including the availability of judicial review; wider implementation of the national treatment principle; increases in the level of fines; the availability of injunctions; and the use of criminal prosecutions.

One of the main changes that the TRIPS regime brought to the administrative system specifically was the addition of the possibility of judicial review of final administrative decisions. Under TRIPS Article 41(4), "parties to a proceeding shall have an opportunity for review by a judicial authority of final administrative decisions". Previously, no independent review was available for appellants from administrative decisions. The amendments of the specific intellectual property laws undertaken in 2000 and 2001 provided for judicial review of administrative decisions under Articles 33, 49 and 50 of the Trademark Law, Articles 41 and 55 of the Patent Law and Article 55 of the Copyright Law. China was thus in compliance with Article 41(4) as a result of this change. This had a major impact on the enforcement system overall; as all final administrative decisions are now subject to external scrutiny, authorities are thought to be less likely to resort to arbitrary decision-making.

A further aspect of enforcement in which TRIPS implementation had an impact was the level of fines imposed by the administrative authorities or damages awarded by the civil courts. Under Article 41(1) of TRIPS, there is a general obligation that remedies should "constitute a deterrent to further infringements." However, fines did not appear to increase significantly following WTO entry. Despite a significant increase in the average fine in 2003 from 5761 RMB to 7414 RMB, this dropped back in 2004 to 5499 RMB (approximately $820 USD) (Thomas 2007, p. 102). Under the Patent Law 2000, Article 58, the administrative authorities could confiscate any illegal earnings and impose a fine of not more than three times the illegal earnings or not more than RMB 50,000 (approximately $7500 USD). The level of fines for both trademark and copyright infringement were governed by implementing regulations. Article 42 of the Implementing Regulations of the Trademark Law 2001 stated that the fine imposed shall be not more than 20% of the illegal business or not more than two times the profit illegally earned. Article 36 of the Implementing Regulations of the Copyright Law 2001 provided the administrative authority with the power to impose a fine not exceeding three times the amount of the illegal business gains, or a maximum of RMB 100,000 (approximately $15,000 USD). Despite these generous limits for levels of fines imposed for IP infringements, there still appeared to be evidence to suggest that authorities were reluctant to impose high fines and that the financial penalties imposed did not constitute an effective deterrent in line with the TRIPS provision.

From respondents' comments in 2005–6, it is clear that both fines imposed by administrative authorities and damages awarded by the courts were still perceived as too low. This is evident in the high ranking given to inadequate penalties in the initial questionnaire as a significant factor contributing to the problems in the post-TRIPS IP system in China. In terms of damages, it was expressed by different respondents that:

damages for intentional infringements are far from enough.[7]

This issue was expanded on by a foreign lawyer working for a Chinese firm:

You can't get damages here very easily, it's so difficult to prove damages so then they just have, you know, a statutory ceiling on most of the damages.[8]

Therefore, the issue of inadequate damages appeared to be linked to the issue of evidence. This was reflected in the comments of at least four respondents who all emphasised the need for "a reasonable Evidence Law."[9] This problem with evidence was due to the burden of proof, which remained on the plaintiff:

> It's a huge problem anywhere in the world, getting evidence in IP cases, but the way the Chinese system is reliant almost exclusively on documentary evidence and will not draw inferences, put(s) the burden of proof on the plaintiff at all times.[10]

Consequently, the issue of low fines and damages is more complex than it initially appears and simply raising the maximum levels available in the primary legislation may not be sufficient to ameliorate this problem. Furthermore, the issue of penalties may also be linked to the lack of court powers to compel infringers to meet the terms of any orders.

Under Article 44 of the TRIPS Agreement, injunctions should be available "to order a party to desist from an infringement". Prior to WTO entry, China's intellectual property enforcement system was often criticised for non-compliance with this provision; "for many years a glaring omission in the IP enforcement system in China was the lack of preliminary injunctions" (Browning and Wang 2004, p. 39). However, the main intellectual property laws were amended around the time of WTO accession to provide authorities with the power to issue injunctions. In China, preliminary injunctions were first permitted under the Patent Law 2000, Article 61, and subsequently by the amended Trademark Law 2001, Article 57, and the Copyright Law 2001, Article 49. There was some initial doubt about how willing the courts would be to issue preliminary injunctions. In the first year or two after introduction, it was suggested that there were still some teething problems in the new preliminary procedures and that the courts were taking a tough stance on the issuing of these orders (Murphy 2003). However, as these problems were resolved and the courts began to become accustomed to issuing injunctions, pre-trial injunctions were seen as offering a useful alternative to administrative actions. Thus, the introduction of these orders was overwhelmingly seen as a positive step for the IP enforcement system in China (Holder 2002). Long term, it was extremely promising for rights-holders to have more enforcement options to consider. Indeed, the introduction of injunctions to the court system was cited by several respondents as one of the key changes in the post-TRIPS IP system in China. For example, when asked to identify the most significant change, this respondent cited:

> The civil injunction system is introduced to the Chinese legal system.[11]

Another key principle of the TRIPS Agreement is the principle of national treatment under Article 3, "that each member shall accord to the nationals of other members' treatment no less favourable than that it accords to its own nationals with regard to the protection of intellectual property." The formalisation of the national treatment principle into the Chinese legal system did lead to some minor legislative changes. For example, Article 18 of the revised Trademark Law 2001 forced foreign enterprises or individuals applying for registration of a trademark or handling other trademark matters to use a state-approved trademark agent. This was arguably in breach of the national treatment principle as domestic applicants could apply directly to the Trademark Office of the State Administration for Industry and Commerce (SAIC). AICs previously would only accept infringement actions from foreign rights-holders through a trademark agent. Although these restrictions were relaxed under the influence of the TRIPS Agreement, in practice, many foreign rights-holders continued to use the services of an agent to navigate the enforcement process, which inflated the cost of bringing an enforcement action.

A further area where the TRIPS Agreement was predicted to have some impact was on the issue of criminal IP enforcement. Article 61 of the TRIPS Agreement provides that criminal procedures should "be applied at least in cases of wilful trademark counterfeiting or copyright piracy on a commercial scale." It is undeniable that criminal penalties were formally available under China's Criminal Law 1997 for serious trademark counterfeiting (Article 213) or copyright piracy (Article 217). However, the relationship between "serious" in China's Criminal Law and "wilful" in TRIPS was not at all clear. Despite a Supreme People's Court interpretation issued in December 2004 which lowered the thresholds for criminal liability, it was still uncertain that all cases of "wilful" infringement would be classed as "serious". The administrative authorities were supposed to transfer serious infringement cases to be considered for criminal liability under Article 54 of the Trademark Law 2001 and Article 47 of the Copyright Law 2001; in practice, such a transfer was rarely made.

The TRIPS Agreement had a minimal impact on the number of cases transferred to judicial authorities for criminal prosecution in the first three years following WTO accession in December 2001. Despite a notable increase in the overall number of cases transferred (from 59 in 2002 to 96 in 2004), the proportion of cases transferred remained constant at around 1 in 400 cases (Thomas 2007, p. 105). However, the thresholds for criminal liability were revised in late 2004 with the aim of increasing the transfer of cases from administrative to judicial authorities.[12] This important modification in the regulations was explained as follows:

In November 2004, the Supreme People's Court and the Supreme People's Procuratorate promulgated the <<Provisions concerning the handling of criminal cases of IP infringement to address a number of questions concerning the specific application of the law>>. These provisions aim to make the rules more concrete and easier for the judiciary to operate in order to fight against IP infringers.[13]

Indeed, this change towards greater use of criminal enforcement for IP infringements was also noted by a respondent from a foreign-invested enterprise in the manufacturing sector:

The Chinese government strengthens attack on IP criminals.[14]

However, criminal enforcement was still seen as problematic in China despite the revised thresholds for liability:

Criminal thresholds continue to make criminal enforcement difficult.[15]

This may be because bureaucratic rivalries between the administrative and judicial agencies still existed and may have continued to discourage the prompt transfer of cases for criminal prosecution. As the administrative agencies relied directly on revenue from confiscated goods to operate, they were thought to be extremely reluctant to transfer cases for criminal prosecution as they would lose the revenue associated with that case (Chow 2002, p. 217).

5.2 AN INITIAL ASSESSMENT OF CHINA'S OVERALL COMPLIANCE WITH TRIPS OBLIGATIONS

Clearly China took significant steps to implement the obligations of the TRIPS Agreement into both the legislative framework and enforcement systems. However, the implementation of TRIPS obligations into the domestic legislation is not enough to be in full compliance with the Agreement. Therefore, China's consequent compliance with the specific provisions of TRIPS will now be analysed. Overall, China appeared to be in substantive compliance with the majority of its TRIPS obligations. These included, for example, Article 41 of the TRIPS Agreement which provided there should be no unreasonable time limits or delays (Article 41(2)); Chinese provisions stated that cases should be concluded within six months or three months for summary cases. Equally, Article 41(3) of the TRIPS Agreement provided that decisions should be reasoned and in writing. Chinese provisions mandated that judgments should be issued immediately or within ten days and must include reasons for the judgment. However, transparency of such judgments did remain somewhat unclear.

Additionally, there were still a handful of provisions where China's compliance was in doubt. The most significant provisions under scrutiny involved enforcement measures, as these were the primary focus of the TRIPS Agreement. The first of these areas of possible non-compliance was Article 45(1) of the TRIPS Agreement, which expressed the principle that "the judicial authorities shall have the authority to order the infringer to pay the rights holder damages adequate to compensate for the injury the rights holder has suffered." Compliance with this provision is not easy to assess in China. The Trademark Law 2001 Article 56 provided that there were two tests for the amount of compensation awarded: either the profits the infringer has earned or the losses to the rights-holder. Article 48 of the Copyright Law 2001 was similar: it stated that compensation shall be the actual losses suffered or unlawful gains where the actual losses are difficult to calculate. Therefore, although in most cases, the calculation of damages was supposed to be based on the actual losses suffered by the rights-holder, in practice many rights-holders were still complaining about the inadequacy of damages awarded. Thus, this remained a possible area of non-compliance for China.

The second substantive TRIPS provision on enforcement that China potentially did not comply with was the requirement in Article 61 that criminal penalties should be available "at least in cases of wilful trademark counterfeiting or copyright piracy on a commercial scale." Furthermore, "remedies available shall include imprisonment and/or monetary fines sufficient to provide a deterrent." This is another difficult area in which to measure China's compliance. As outlined above, criminal penalties were available under the Criminal Law 1997 for *serious* trademark counterfeiting (Article 213) or copyright piracy (Article 217). Furthermore, imprisonment and fines were both available as remedies. However, the precise linguistic relationship between "serious" in China's Criminal Law and "wilful" in TRIPS was problematic. The other issue of possible non-compliance under Article 61 was whether the penalties provided were sufficient to provide a deterrent.

Assessing China's compliance with TRIPS provisions is clearly not straightforward and Article 64 of TRIPS makes disputes about TRIPS obligations subject to WTO's dispute resolution procedures. Up until 2006, there had been 24 cases brought to the WTO dispute settlement body concerning the TRIPS Agreement, with only four cases dealing with the enforcement provisions in TRIPS. The respondents in these cases were Denmark and Sweden (for failing to make provisional measures available in the context of civil proceedings involving intellectual property rights) and the European Community and Greece (involving the regular broadcast in Greece of copyrighted motion pictures and television programmes without the authorisation of the copyright owners). The complainant in all cases was the US, alleging breach of Article 50 in the case of Denmark and Sweden and breaches of Articles 41 and 61 in the case of Greece. All four cases were eventually resolved through negotiation and the dispute settlement body was notified of the relevant mutually agreed solutions.[16]

These cases demonstrated that it is extremely difficult to establish non-compliance with the TRIPS provisions on enforcement. In all disputes brought to the WTO, it is necessary to show clear evidence of systemic failing, not just anecdotal weaknesses. This procedural difficulty is highlighted by the request made in October 2005 by the US, Japan and Swiss governments for China to provide enforcement data to help them to assess China's TRIPS compliance. This must be borne in mind when considering China's compliance with these provisions. The difficulties in bringing a formal complaint to the WTO are also illustrated by the United States Trade Representative (USTR)'s annual reports to Congress on China's WTO compliance. These reports can offer a useful supplementary source of data regarding China's TRIPS compliance as they are largely based upon reports from foreign rights-holders in China. Indeed, the USTR's reports confirm that despite efforts to implement TRIPS obligations into domestic legislation being "largely satisfactory...IPR enforcement, however, remains ineffective" (USTR 2003, p. 49).[17]

It is noticeable that the tone of these reports grew increasingly bullish in the two or three years immediately following WTO accession, as promised improvements in reducing IP infringements proved unforthcoming. Indeed, this reflects the notion that initial reforms made by China to comply with WTO obligations generally were substantial, but when further, deeper reforms were required in subsequent years, the pace of reform slowed considerably. Furthermore, criticisms of the IP system in China initially focused on the poor enforcement system in general and bemoaned the lack of transparency (in the 2003 and 2004 reports), before focusing on the specific problem of the "chronic underutilization of deterrent criminal remedies" (2006 and 2007 reports). This also reinforces the impression that the US was forced to focus on substantive failings in the IP enforcement system in order to bring a WTO dispute, rather than just rely on anecdotal inadequacies reported by rights-holders.

It is perhaps surprising that China had not been the respondent in a case involving compliance with TRIPS obligations before April 2007, given the publicity surrounding China's poor intellectual property enforcement. However, this indicates that despite the perceived failings in the intellectual property enforcement system in China, it is difficult to compile clear evidence of systemic non-compliance with the TRIPS provisions. Furthermore, the request for consultations of April 2007 made it clear that the complaint referred to specific failings in the system, rather than mere inconsistencies in enforcement. In addition, it has also been suggested that the US refrained from filing a WTO dispute against China earlier than 2007 because the US was hoping that TRIPS would force China to finally fulfil its international IP obligations (Harris 2008, p. 98). However, from 2005, China's compliance with its TRIPS obligations was increasingly under US scrutiny; China was placed on the USTR Priority Watch List in 2005 and a China Enforcement Task Force was also established in February 2006, with the aim of preparing WTO cases against China (Harris 2008, p. 114).

On 10 April 2007, the US circulated two requests for consultations with China. The first of these concerned measures affecting trading rights and distribution services for certain publications and audio-visual entertainment products (World Trade Organisation 2007a). This dispute was not directly connected with China's obligations under the TRIPS Agreement, rather it concerned commitments made in China's Protocol of Accession. However, the second dispute did specifically concern commitments made under the TRIPS Agreement. The second dispute concerned measures affecting the protection and enforcement of intellectual property rights (World Trade Organisation 2007b). Following the circulation of the request for consultations by the United States, several other members also requested to join the consultations. They included Japan, Mexico, Canada and the European Communities. Thus, the issue of protection and enforcement of intellectual property rights in China was clearly of concern to many WTO members, not only the US. China's reaction to the initiation of these WTO complaints was strenuous denial and disappointment that the US had deemed such an action necessary (PRC Ministry of Commerce 2007).

Within the broad complaint about enforcement of intellectual property rights, several separate areas were identified for further consultations. The US and China held consultations specifically concerning these issues on 7–8 June 2007, but although "those consultations provided some helpful clarifications but [they] unfortunately did not resolve the dispute" (World Trade Organisation 2007c, p. 1). One element of the US's initial complaint which was resolved by the consultations concerned the unavailability of criminal procedures and penalties for a person who engaged in either unauthorised reproduction *or* unauthorised distribution of copyrighted works. The existing Criminal Law and associated regulations appeared to subject a person who engaged in *both* unauthorised reproduction *and* distribution to criminal liability, but not only one or the other. This appeared to be inconsistent with TRIPS Articles 41.1 and 61. The consultations resolved the issue of confusion about whether both unauthorised reproduction *and* distribution were necessary for criminal liability to arise, but the other issues remained in dispute. As a result, a panel was appointed to consider the dispute (World Trade Organisation 2007d).

The first element of the complaint heard by the WTO panel was that existing Chinese laws and regulations denied copyright and related rights protection and enforcement to works that had not been authorised for publication or distribution within China. In essence, the US alleged that works were not protected by copyright legislation until they were authorised for publication or distribution after going through a stringent content review process. This appeared to be inconsistent with TRIPS Article 9.1 which obliges members to comply with Articles 1–21 of the Berne Convention (1971); Article 5(1) of the Berne Convention states that copyright granted to foreign authors should not be subject to any formality. Furthermore, if foreign authors were indeed not granted copyright protection prior to approval of their works, this may also be inconsistent with Article 3.1 of the TRIPS Agreement which lays down the national treatment principle. The measure at issue was the first sentence of Article 4 of the PRC Copyright Law 2001, the mutually agreed translation of which was as follows: "Works the publication and/or dissemination of which are prohibited by law shall not be protected by this law" (World Trade Organisation 2009, para. 7.1). China conceded that Article 4(1) denied copyright protection to those works which had not passed the content review but argued that this provision did not remove the copyright from such works. The panel found this measure to be inconsistent with China's obligations under Article 5(1) of the Berne Convention (1971), as incorporated by Article 9.1 of the TRIPS Agreement, and Article 41.1 of the TRIPS Agreement.

The second element of intellectual property enforcement that was subject to consideration by the WTO panel was that the disposal of goods confiscated by the customs authorities, which infringe IP rights, was inconsistent with TRIPS Articles 46 and 59. This is because the Chinese customs regulations appeared to endorse the practice of merely removing the infringing features of the counterfeit products and then allowing then to enter channels of commerce through auction instead of destroying them. TRIPS Article 46 on judicial remedies and Article 59 on customs authorities' remedies make it clear that goods seized should only be destroyed or disposed of outside of the channels of commerce. The measures at issue here were the Customs IPR Regulations in force from 2004, Article 27 of which provided different options for the disposal or destruction of goods seized for infringing trademark, copyright and patent rights upon exportation or importation. The Implementing Measures for the Customs IPR Regulations also entered into force in 2004 and Article 30 further clarified the process for disposal or destruction of such infringing goods.

The US claim was made under Article 59 of the TRIPS Agreement which provides "without prejudice to other rights of action open to the right holder and subject to the right of the defendant to seek review by a judicial authority, competent authorities shall have the authority to order the destruction or disposal of infringing goods in accordance with the principles set out in Article 46. In regard to counterfeit trademark goods, the authorities shall not allow the re-exportation of the infringing goods in an unaltered state or subject them to a different customs procedure, other than in exceptional circumstances." The panel held that this Article should be read as part of section 4 of Part III of the TRIPS Agreement which together sets out procedures for dealing with goods at the border. A key consideration for the panel was the obligation in the first sentence of Article 59 that the competent authorities "shall have the authority" to order certain types of remedies with respect to infringing goods.

The US conceded that this obligation would not require members to make such an order, rather the issue was what decisions Chinese Customs authorities were permitted to make by law. Clearly, China's customs measures, taken together, provided for the authority to order the destruction of infringing goods; the issue was whether destruction could only be ordered in highly limited circumstances. The panel found that the US had failed to establish that China's customs measures were inconsistent with Article 59 of the TRIPS Agreement, as it incorporates principles set out in the first sentence of Article 46 of the TRIPS Agreement (World Trade Organisation 2009, para. 7.395). The first sentence of Article 46 read: "In order to create an effective deterrent to infringement, the judicial authorities shall have the authority to order that goods that they have been found to be infringing be, without compensation of any sort, disposed of outside the channels of commerce in such a manner as to avoid any harm caused to the right holder, or, unless this would be contrary to existing constitutional requirements, destroyed."

On the other hand, China's customs measures were found to be inconsistent with Article 59 of the TRIPS Agreement as it incorporates principles set out in the fourth sentence of Article 46 of the TRIPS Agreement. The fourth sentence of Article 46 states: "In regard to counterfeit trademark goods, the simple removal of the trademark unlawfully affixed shall not be sufficient, other than in exceptional cases, to permit release of the goods into the channels of commerce." China's customs measures were found to be inconsistent with this principle because they allowed for the simple removal of the trademark from counterfeit goods and the subsequent auction of such goods in more than just "exceptional cases."

The third element of the US complaint to the WTO concerned the thresholds in place in China which had to be met before criminal liability for IP infringements could be imposed and that these thresholds for criminal procedures and penalties appeared to be inconsistent with TRIPS Articles 41.1 and 61. The first part of Article 61 provides that "Members shall provide for criminal procedures and penalties to be applied at least in cases of wilful trademark counterfeiting or copyright piracy on a commercial scale." The measures at issue were to be found in China's Criminal Law 1997, Section 7 of Chapter III in Part 2 of which provided for crimes of infringing intellectual property rights in Articles 213–20. These Articles in the Criminal Law were also interpreted by several judicial interpretations which were also considered by the WTO panel. The key question considered by the panel was whether China's thresholds were too high to capture all cases of counterfeiting on a commercial scale as required by the TRIPS Agreement.

The panel concluded that the US failed to establish that China's criminal thresholds were inconsistent with its obligations under the first sentence of Article 61 of the TRIPS Agreement. Subsequent analysis of the panel report suggested that this aspect of the US claim relating to "commercial scale" needed more evidence specific to the Chinese market. The US did provide press articles and notes as evidence about the status of the criminal thresholds in relation to the Chinese marketplace; however, the panel found that these were not reliable evidence (Zhou 2011, p. 154). This must be recognised as putting "rather a heavy evidentiary burden on complainants especially when dealing with opaque markets such as the Chinese market where obtaining reliable information or even convincing people to submit it... may be difficult" (Pauwelyn 2010, p. 415).

Overall, the focus of the United States' submission was on fairly minor procedural aspects of the intellectual property system in China. Several of the grounds for complaint may simply have arisen from imprecise language in the primary legislation, such as the doubt over whether prohibiting illegal reproduction *and* distribution included illegal reproduction *or* distribution only. However, the complaint did confirm the need to identify specific failings in the system rather than merely complaining about inadequate or inconsistent enforcement and thus had important lessons for future WTO disputes relating to members' TRIPS compliance. The immediate impact of the panel report may have been described as largely pyrrhic for the US, but nevertheless a number of commentators also recognised the broader impact beyond the limited legislative changes that China was forced to implement. Indeed, 2007–8 was felt to be an excellent time to file a WTO complaint against China as China was preparing to hold the Beijing 2008 Olympics and was thus seen as relatively vulnerable to external international pressure (Harris 2008, p. 186).

In addition, the US complaint to the WTO was not only aimed at tackling systemic failings in China's enforcement of IP rights, but also aimed to send a signal to other countries perceived as not making serious enough crack down on counterfeiting or piracy, such as Brazil or Ukraine (. 2010, p. 400). Moreover, it was felt that even if the US did not pre. .... claim, there may be "extra-judicial" benefits to bringing the dispute to the WTO (Harris 2008, p. 99), at the very least signalling to China that the US would no longer sit idly by waiting for China's IP enforcement to improve, as well as sending a powerful signal of intent to other countries with weak IP enforcement. Overall, the panel report on the US–China IP dispute is interesting "because it suggests an unexpected degree of flexibility in WTO members' compliance with the TRIPS Agreement" (Gervais 2009, p. 549). In particular, in the part of the US claim relating to the disposal of seized goods, the panel considered that the words "shall have the authority" did not amount to an obligation to exercise power in any particular way (Gervais 2009, p. 550).

In general, as discussed in the previous section, China appeared to be in compliance with the majority of its TRIPS obligations on enforcement. The most significant areas where compliance appeared to be in doubt were the issues of damages and the availability of criminal penalties. Assessing compliance in these areas seems to be dependent on how the wording of the relevant articles is interpreted. The difficulties of identifying non-compliance appear to be confirmed by the 2007 complaint to the WTO Dispute Resolution Body by the United States; criminal thresholds were a target of the complaint as they are fixed and evident, whereas problems of inadequate damages or lack of a deterrent are too imprecise to be the focus of a formal WTO complaint. Consequently, this reflects the problem of judging compliance in general; as a relative concept, distinguishing compliance from non-compliance is a largely subjective process (Chan 2006, p. 66).

The limited victory for the US in its dispute with China over the inadequate enforcement of intellectual property rights also illustrates the wider difficulties experienced with bringing WTO disputes concerning the TRIPS Agreement. Contrary to the expected "fear factor" of dispute settlement through the WTO finally adding teeth to the international IP obligations, the WTO dispute settlement system has only dealt with a handful of TRIPS-related disputes. In 1995, the TRIPS Agreement was seen as revolutionary for introducing the formal dispute settlement mechanism into the field of international intellectual property protection. However, now 20 years have passed since the inauguration of TRIPS; in terms of dispute settlement, it is clear that TRIPS has had relatively little impact, with the predicted flood of disputes failing to materialise. In fact, from 1995 to 2010, the share of claims brought to the WTO dispute settlement body under the TRIPS Agreement was only around 3% of the total; additionally, the expected wave of cases initiated by developed countries against developing members did not arrive. Indeed, there is a sense that such frustrations with the inadequacies of the WTO to enforce the global trade rules, including the TRIPS Agreement, have led to a focus on regional trade agreements, such as the Trans-Pacific Partnership (TPP), instead as the future alternative for global trade negotiations (Bhagwati 2013).

5.3   OUTLINE OF CHINA'S POST-TRIPS INTELLECTUAL PROPERTY SYSTEM

Following the massive overhaul of the intellectual property protection system associated with WTO entry, the post-TRIPS system of protection offered a myriad of choices for rights-holders in China. The system of intellectual property protection has been described as a "triple IP system, comprising legislative guidance, administrative control and judicial enforcement of IP" (Yang and Clarke 2004, p. 14). However, it has also been noted that the lines between the categories may be blurred and "any particular enforcement measure may partake of the characteristics of more than one category" (Clarke 1999, p. 31). Essentially, intellectual property rights-holders had several choices in the method they chose to enforce their rights. Administrative enforcement was often the mechanism chosen, as quick raids of the infringer's premises could often be accomplished (Chow 2000). There were various bodies responsible for the administrative enforcement of intellectual property. "The Trademark Office under the State Administration for Industry and Commerce (SAIC) is responsible for trademarks, the State Intellectual Property Office (SIPO) oversees patent protection, and the National Copyright Administration handles copyright" (Potter and Oksenberg 1999).

Judicial enforcement was also an option to pursue. Judicial enforcement could take two forms: civil litigation or criminal prosecution. Although it was possible to bring private prosecution of offenders, this method of enforcement was subject to a wealth of problems (Simone 1999). Therefore, civil litigation was more popular. "Any individual or organisation can bring a lawsuit to a people's court, such as an Intermediate People's Court. If they do not agree with the judicial verdict of that court, the case can be pursued to a higher court" (Yang and Clarke 2004, p. 20). There are four levels of People's Courts in China: Supreme, Higher, Intermediate and Basic. Specialised intellectual property courts were established at the intermediate level and above from early 1990s. "China's specialized Intellectual Property Courts were first established in Beijing at both the Intermediate and Higher People's Court levels on August 5, 1993" (Kolton 1996, p. 436). Following their introduction, specialised IP courts were rapidly introduced in other areas outside Beijing. Intellectual property disputes were previously heard by civil or economic divisions and the specialised courts were intended to go some way towards countering accusations of poorly trained judicial personnel.

Therefore, there were a host of alternatives available to IP rights-holders in China, but there was still some scepticism about how effective these different channels of enforcement actually were at enforcing intellectual property rights. Respondents' detailed experiences of the post-TRIPS IP system in China will be discussed in Chap. 6, in order to analyse how effective these different channels of enforcement were in practice and to try to establish why an "enforcement gap" was perceived to exist between the laws on paper and in reality.

NOTES

1. Follow-up comments from respondent 05LAW12T.
2. Interview comments with respondent 05LAW01.
3. Questionnaire comments from respondent 05LAW07.
4. Questionnaire comments from respondent 05LAW03.
5. Questionnaire comments from respondent 05LAW18.
6. Questionnaire comments from respondent 05LAW12T.
7. Questionnaire comments from respondent 05LAW28T.
8. Interview comments from respondent 05LAW10.
9. Questionnaire comments from respondent 05LAW18.
10. Interview comments from respondent 05LAW01.
11. Questionnaire comments from respondent 05LAW29T.
12. As noted in questionnaire comments from respondent 05LAW28T; full text of the interpretation taken from: Supreme People's Procuratorate (2004).
13. Follow-up comments from respondent 05LAW29T.
14. Questionnaire comments from respondent 05MANU06.
15. Questionnaire comments from respondent 05LAW01.
16. Details on these cases are available at: World Trade Organisation (2016).
17. The full text of all the Annual Reports to Congress on China's WTO Compliance are available at: www.ustr.gov.

REFERENCES

Bhagwati, Jagdish. 2013. Dawn of a New System. *Finance & Development* 50(4): 8–13.

Browning, Tim, and Carol Wang. 2004. Ten Years of Enforcement in China. *Managing Intellectual Property* 136(Supplement 1): 37–41.

Chan, Gerald. 2006. *China's Compliance in Global Affairs: Trade, Arms Control, Environmental Protection, Human Rights*. Singapore: World Scientific Publishing.

Chow, Daniel. 2000. Counterfeiting in the People's Republic of China. *Washington University Law Quarterly* 78(1): 1–57.

———. 2002. *A Primer on Foreign Investment Enterprises and Protection of Intellectual Property in China*. London: Kluwer Law International.

Clarke, Donald C. 1999. Private Enforcement of Intellectual Property Rights in China. *National Bureau of Asian Research* 10(2): 29–41.

Gervais, Daniel. 2009. China- Measures Affecting the Protection and Enforcement of Intellectual Property Rights WT/DS362/R. *American Journal of International Law* 103(3): 543–555.

Gregory, Angela. 2003. Chinese Trademark Law and the TRIPS Agreement- Confucius Meets the WTO. In *China and the World Trading System: Entering the New Millennium*, ed. Deborah Cass. Cambridge: Cambridge University Press.

Harris, Donald P. 2008. The Honeymoon is Over: Evaluating the US-China WTO Intellectual Property Complaint. *Fordham International Law Journal* 32(1): 96–187.

Holder, Sara. 2002. Preliminary Injunctions for Intellectual Property Infringements in the PRC. *Rouse & Co. International Newsletter.* http://www.iprights.com/publications/articles/article.asp?articleID=163. Accessed 16 Nov 2005.

Kolton, Gregory S. 1996. Copyright Law and the People's Courts in the People's Republic of China: A Review and Critique of China's Intellectual Property Courts. *University of Pennsylvania Journal of International Economic Law* 17(1): 415–460.

Maskus, Keith. 2002. Intellectual Property Rights in the WTO Accession Package: Assessing China's Reforms. *World Bank*. http://siteresources.worldbank.org/INTRANETTRADE/Resources/maskus_tips.pdf. Accessed 20 Oct 2015.

Murphy, Matthew. 2003. Supreme People's Court Widens Litigation Options. *Managing Intellectual Property* 134: 65–67.

Pauwelyn, Joost. 2010. The Dog That Barked but Didn't Bite: 15 Years of Intellectual Property Disputes at the WTO. *Journal of International Dispute Settlement* 1(2): 389–429.

Potter, Pitman B., and Michel Oksenberg. 1999. A Patchwork of IPR Protection. *China Business Review* 26(1): 8–11.

PRC Ministry of Commerce. 2007. 商务部新闻发言人对美方决定将中国知识产权、出版物市场准入问题诉诸WTO表示非常遗憾和强烈不满 (The Ministry of Commerce Spokesman Expresses Great Regret and Extreme Dissatisfaction Over the US Decision to Bring a Dispute to the WTO Over China's IPR). http://www.mofcom.gov.cn/aarticle/ae/ag/200704/20070404552941.html. Accessed 10 Nov 2015.

Simone, Joseph T. 1999. China's IPR Enforcement Mechanisms. *China Business Review* 26(1): 14–16.

SIPO. 2003. White Paper on the Intellectual Property Rights Protection in China in 2003. *State Intellectual Property Office*. http://english.sipo.gov.cn/laws/whitepapers/200804/t20080416_380354.html. Accessed 9 Nov 2015.

Supreme People's Procuratorate. 2004. 高法高检关于办理侵犯知识产权刑事案件具体应用法律若干问题的解释(全文)(Transcript of the Supreme People's Court Interpretation of the Application of the Law to Criminal Cases of IP Infringement (Full Text)). http://www.china.com.cn/chinese/law/734357.htm. Accessed 20 Nov 2015.

Sun, Andy Y. 2001. Reforming the Protection of Intellectual Property: The Case of China and Taiwan in Light of WTO Accession. *Maryland Series in Contemporary Asian Studies* 4.

Taubman, Antony S. 2003. TRIPS Goes East: Chinese Interests and International Trade in Intellectual Property. In *China and the World Trading System: Entering the New Millennium*, ed. Deborah Cass. Cambridge: Cambridge University Press.

Thomas, Kristie. 2007. The Fight Against Piracy: Working Within the Administrative Enforcement System in China. In *Intellectual Property and TRIPS Compliance in China: Chinese and European Perspectives*, ed. Paul Torremans, Hailing Shan, and Johan Erauw. Cheltenham: Edward Elgar Publishing.

USTR. 2003. 2003 Report to Congress On China's WTO Compliance. https://ustr.gov/archive/assets/Document_Library/Reports_Publications/2003/asset_upload_file425_4313.pdf. Accessed 30 Aug 2016.

World Trade Organisation. 2007a. China-Measures Affecting Trading Rights and Distribution Services for Certain Publications and Audiovisual Entertainment Products: Request for Consultations by the United States. WTO Document WT/DS363/1. https://www.wto.org/english/tratop_e/dispu_e/cases_e/ds363_e.htm. Accessed 30 Aug 2016.

———. 2007b. China-Measures Affecting the Protection and Enforcement of Intellectual Property Rights: Request for Consultations by the United States. WTO Document WT/DS362/1. https://www.wto.org/english/tratop_e/dispu_e/cases_e/ds362_e.htm. Accessed 30 Aug 2016.

————. 2007c. China-Measures Affecting the Protection and Enforcement of Intellectual Property Rights: Request for the Establishment of a Panel by the United States. WTO Document WT/DS362/7.

————. 2007d. China-Measures Affecting the Protection and Enforcement of Intellectual Property Rights: Constitution of the Panel Established at the Request of the United States – Note by the Secretariat. WTO Document WT/DS362/8.

————. 2009. China-Measures Affecting the Protection and Enforcement of Intellectual Property Rights: Report of the Panel. WTO Document WT/DS362/R.

————. 2016. Disputes by Agreement. https://www.wto.org/english/tratop_e/dispu_e/dispu_agreements_index_e.htm?id=A26. Accessed 30 Aug 2016.

Yang, Deli. 2003. The Development of Intellectual Property in China. *World Patent Information* 25(2): 131–142.

Yang, Deli, and Peter Clarke. 2004. Review of the Current Intellectual Property System in China. *International Journal of Technology Transfer and Commercialisation* 3(1): 12–37.

Zhou, Weighou. 2011. Pirates Behind an Open Door, and an Ocean Away: US-China WTO Disputes, Intellectual Property Protection, and Market Access. *Temple International and Comparative Law Journal* 25(1): 139–177.

CHAPTER 6

Assessing the Post-TRIPS Intellectual Property System in China in the Short Term: Exploring the Enforcement Gap

As detailed in the previous chapter, the sheer quantity of laws and regulations amended or enacted during the main period of revision from 1999 to 2002 illustrates the significant effort that China undertook to implement the Agreement on Trade-Related Intellectual Property Rights (TRIPS) obligations into domestic legislation. It is also clear that World Trade Organisation (WTO) accession led to major changes in the enforcement system such as the introduction of injunctions and the possibility of judicial review of final administrative decisions and thus, the actual substantive implementation of TRIPS provisions into China's formal intellectual property (IP) system was satisfactory overall. However, full compliance with the TRIPS Agreement is more difficult to assess than mere implementation. Although China appeared to be in substantive compliance with the majority of its TRIPS obligations, compliance was in doubt with several provisions, as illustrated by the 2007 WTO complaint initiated by the United States (US) against China discussed in Chap. 5. This chapter will now turn to the effectiveness of the post-TRIPS intellectual property system in 2005–6 by looking beyond the IP laws on paper. Responses and anecdotes from respondents detailing their experiences with the system in practice will be used to highlight some ineffective features of the IP system and of the enforcement framework in particular.

The responses from users of the IP system at that time will show that although improvements had obviously been made in China's IP system as a result of WTO accession, significant barriers still existed to inhibit effective enforcement. Thus, the chapter will then consider some potential reasons to explain why these barriers still existed by returning to the comprehensive model of compliance outlined in Chap. 2 and applying the country-specific part of the model to China's TRIPS compliance in 2005–6.

© The Author(s) 2017
K. Thomas, *Assessing Intellectual Property Compliance in Contemporary China*, Palgrave Series in Asia and Pacific Studies,
DOI 10.1007/978-981-10-3072-7_6

6.1   The 2005 Intellectual Property System in Action

The questionnaire and follow-up interviews conducted in 2005–6 included discussion of the effectiveness of the system of intellectual property protection in China according to the experiences of respondents (see Appendix 1 for a copy of the questionnaire used in this study). When respondents were asked to rank the system on a scale from 1 to 6, with 1 representing completely ineffective and 6 representing completely effective, the average rank was 3.3. Unsurprisingly, the system was ranked as neither completely ineffective nor completely effective, with a breakdown of the results shown in Table 6.1.

Furthermore, when asked whether the main cause of any remaining problems in the system at that time was poor legislation, poor enforcement, a combination of both, or neither, of the 44 valid responses collected, poor enforcement was overwhelmingly seen as the main cause. Twenty-five respondents selected poor enforcement as the main cause, with only one choosing poor legislation and a further 16 respondents indicated that both poor legislation and poor enforcement were to blame for any remaining obstacles in the IP system in China. Thus, these responses confirm the overall judgement observed in Chap. 5 that while China's IP legislation was much improved as a result of WTO accession, problems still remained, particularly in the enforcement of these laws and regulations at that time.

Respondents were also asked if they had experienced any problems with the IP system. Only two respondents answered no, out of a total of 47 valid responses, clearly showing that the system still had problems to resolve. Those 45 respondents who responded that they had experienced problems with the IP system were then asked to rank those problems. On a scale of 1–6, where 1 represented not at all serious and 6 represented extremely serious, the average rank for the problems experienced was 4.02. Thus, most respondents had experienced considerable problems with the post-TRIPS IP system in China. The responses regarding the severity of the problems experienced are detailed in Fig. 6.1.

Table 6.1 Effectiveness of the IP system as ranked by respondents

Rank	Number of respondents	Percentage of respondents (%)
1	2	4.3
2	6	12.8
3	18	38.3
4	18	38.3
5	3	6.4
6	0	0
Total	47	100

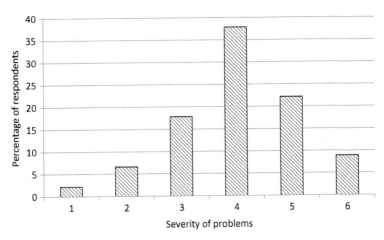

Fig. 6.1 Severity of problems in the 2005 post-TRIPS IP system as ranked by respondents

As the majority of the respondents ranked the problems they had experienced as at least moderately severe, it is clear that there may have been some problems with the overall effectiveness of the post-TRIPS IP system in China at that time.

6.1.1   Respondents' Experiences of the IP System in 2005–6

A few examples of respondents' experiences will now be detailed to evaluate how effective the post-TRIPS IP system was in practice. The first experience comes from a Chinese lawyer based in Guangzhou:

> I acted in the case of a patent infringement dispute. I represented clients in Guangzhou to take quick and effective action. At my request, the court ordered the preservation of evidence and found evidence of violations and the illegal transfer of profits. However, we hadn't yet gone to trial and the invention patent was quickly declared invalid by the patent re-examination board. I took the case to Beijing to appeal the administrative proceeding of the Patent Re-examination Commission. I met two experts in the field of technology patents, who were both very well prepared; I thought with these experts, we would definitely win the case. However, we lost. This is very common, but not normal. We later heard that we lost because our client is a foreign company. But of course we have no evidence of this.[1]

The experiences of this lawyer highlight several points. Firstly, patent disputes were more often resolved through the courts as they were frequently too complicated for administrative personnel to adjudicate, compared to, for example, trademark infringements. Secondly, there was still a perception that foreign and local rights-holders received different treatment, although there was no evidence available of a systemic bias. Finally, there was also a perception that pursuing a case in a different city may result in a different outcome than if the case were pursued in the "home" city. This links to the supposed problem of local protectionism and also highlights the inconsistency that may have existed in enforcement.

The second example of the system in action is taken from a foreign lawyer working for a major law firm in Shanghai:

> I can give you a specific example, (…) to give you an example of the problems we have. We raided a factory in Ningbo? They had counterfeits there, we looked into (searching) their records and found another invoice for the same model numbers, so we sued these people for the damages, when the (…) found (…) suing not just for the damages, but (the issue was) how much were the damages, it was actually quite (tragic), because the court gave us damages for the products that had been seized, which I can actually think theoretically, we shouldn't get damages because they haven't been sold, […] but refused to give us damages for the goods which were shipped out, on the basis that the invoice did not say that the products had the trademark on it.[2]

This second account of the system in action also highlights several problems that may have remained in the 2005 IP system in China. First, it confirms the first respondent's comments regarding different treatment of infringement claims in different cities, echoing the common complaint of local protection-ism. Second and perhaps most important, these comments highlight the per-ception of judicial incompetence, that the judges did not have the training or knowledge to make competent and reasoned decisions. Finally, the problem that damages were awarded for goods not sold, but denied for goods already shipped suggests that the rules regarding evidence were far from satisfactory.

A final example of the system in action comes from a respondent in the services sector:

> One customer who for the 1st time came to China to attend an exhibition had his company name and Chinese website hijacked by a Chinese competitor within 1 month of the exhibition. We already told him in advance this might happen. But as usual they didn't heed our suggestion. For them the battle is already lost before they really could enter the Chinese market.[3]

This third account of the system in action also confirms previous observations as these comments reflect the feelings of frustration that were expressed by several of the respondents. Moreover, they highlight the continued prevalence of the problem of intellectual property infringements at that time and the need for extreme vigilance in seeking to protect IP rights. This would also suggest that the post-TRIPS IP system remained somewhat ineffective as intellectual property infringements were still pervasive and tackling such infringements was a key objective of the whole system.

On the other hand, despite these anecdotes concerning the ineffectiveness of the system in action, there were also several positive comments regarding the operation of the IP system, most notably praise for the system of administrative enforcement. For example, this Chinese lawyer working for a major international law firm stated:

> The big advantages between administrative approaches to judicial proceedings are that administrative measures tend to be more expedited and more cost-effective, then they can take, the agencies themselves, can take initiative in investigating the infringing activities so that saves costs for the client also.[4]

Thus, both the speed of administrative action and the lower costs involved for the rights-holder were stressed as significant advantages of pursuing infringers through administrative enforcement.

Therefore, overall, despite continuing problems in certain aspects of the system, such as perceptions of local protectionism, poor quality of some judicial personnel and inadequate laws regarding evidence, it must be stressed that the 2005 post-TRIPS IP system was not completely ineffective. As the mix of comments from respondents shows, although there were some problematic areas particularly linked to the issues of local protectionism and assessment of damages, the system did also have some strong features, particularly the administrative enforcement system. Thus, the effectiveness of the system in 2005 appeared to be almost satisfactory, reflecting the overall judgement of the effectiveness of the system as reasonably effective, according to most questionnaire responses. Nevertheless, where problems did remain in the 2005 IP system in China, they appeared to lie between the black letter laws on paper which had largely been amended in line with the TRIPS Agreement, and the enforcement of these laws in practice. This "enforcement gap" between the laws on paper and enforcement on the ground will now be explored within the comprehensive model of compliance as outlined in Chap. 2.

6.2   Exploring the Enforcement Gap Using the Comprehensive Model of Compliance

According to the comprehensive model of compliance outlined previously, in addition to the characteristics of the activity involved, the characteristics of the accord and the international environment, there are various country-specific factors which should be considered in analysing China's compliance with the provisions of the TRIPS Agreement. Under this model, these country-specific factors can be divided into three categories: parameters, fundamental factors and proximate factors. It is immediately clear that these categories may not be mutually exclusive and indeed, there is a considerable overlap between some of the factors.

On the questionnaire sent to respondents in 2005, the factors which may have contributed to the state of the IP system in China at that time were

Table 6.2 Factors contributing to the IP system as ranked by respondents

Rank	Factor	Average score
1	Lack of public awareness of IP rights	4.44
2	Local protectionism	4.13
3	Inadequate penalties	3.96
4	Lack of consistency in enforcement	3.8
5	Weak judicial enforcement	3.76
6	Lack of powers to enforce court judgments	3.73
7	Lack of trained and experienced legal personnel	3.71
8	Length of the process	3.24
9	Lack of transparency	3.11
10	Lack of the concept of individual rights in China	3
11	The role of the government in the economy	2.89
12	Over-reliance on public enforcement mechanisms	2.84
13	Lack of a unified agency for dealing with IP	2.76
14	Perception that IP only benefits foreigners	2.42
15	Influence of socialism	1.78
16	Influence of Confucianism	1.09

divided into four broad categories: social and cultural factors, economic factors, political factors and factors specific to the legal system (see Appendix 1 for a copy of the questionnaire used in the 2005 study). Specifically, question 15 listed 16 factors which had been previously cited in the literature as responsible for the state of the modern intellectual property system in China. Respondents were asked to rate the contribution of each of these factors on a scale from 0 to 6, where 0 represented no contribution and 6 signified a major contribution to the IP system in China. The results of question 15 in terms of the respondents' ranking of these factors is summarised in Table 6.2.

These country-specific factors contributing to the state of China's TRIPS compliance in 2005–6, and the "enforcement gap" which was observed, will now be analysed in more detail.

6.2.1   Parameters

The first category of country-specific factors that may have affected China's compliance with its international obligations consists of parameters which include basic characteristics of the country such as the previous behaviour of the country; the history and culture of the country; the physical size of the country; the physical variation within the country and the number of neighbours that the country has. As described above in Chap. 1, the development of Chinese intellectual property law has not followed a smooth and unbroken path. Intellectual property, as a set of exclusive legal rights, was virtually unknown until the final years of the Qing dynasty and its introduction in the early years of the twentieth century was predominantly as a result of Western pressure to reform the legal system and China's concomitant desire to bring extraterritoriality to an end. When the People's Republic of China (PRC) was established in 1949, the entire legal system, including the early intellectual property laws, was overhauled as new socialist laws were launched. In addition, much of the wider legal framework of courts, lawyers and judges was dismantled during the Cultural Revolution. Thus, at the start of the reform and opening-up period in the late 1970s, China faced an awesome task in rebuilding the entire legal system, embracing both substantive laws and regulations, reforming the court system and recruiting the necessary legal personnel.

The establishment of a modern legal system beginning in 1978 also included the need for a modern system of intellectual property protection. Therefore, it could be said that the intellectual property system in China was still less than 30 years old when WTO accession led to the obligation to comply with the TRIPS Agreement. However, no respondent in 2005–6 explicitly referred to intellectual property protection in China prior to the start of the reform period in 1978, although many respondents did consider China's rapid development in the post-1978 period as a key factor in the contemporaneous IP system. For instance, one Chinese respondent explicitly stated that the IP system

Is changing every year since China's reform and opening-up

and that

The success that China has achieved in intellectual property protection in the past 20 years is equivalent to what has been gained by others through several decades or even the efforts of a century. Without knowing this, it is unlikely that you will fully understand the development of IPR in China, or learn the relevant regulations.[5]

The idea that China's previous behaviour in the intellectual property arena only stretched back a short distance was echoed by this respondent:

Don't forget that the country only opened up 30 years ago. So these issues are only a small hick up ((*sic*)).[6]

As a consequence, it would seem that respondents did not feel that China's previous behaviour of protecting intellectual property rights was a significant factor in explaining the "enforcement gap" in the system of protection at that time. Rather, the only mention of the past was to recognise, and indeed praise, China's progress in such a short time span.

The historical influences of Confucianism and socialism are often cited as continuing influences in contemporary Chinese culture and consequently on the post-TRIPS intellectual property system. Confucianism was often cited as the main reason why intellectual property protection was not stronger in China, even to the exclusion of other factors.[7] There are two aspects to the influence that Confucian thought was believed to exert on the concept of intellectual property in China. Firstly, it is contended that Confucianism advocates a belief that "copying another's creative works is not morally bankrupt, a view contrary to Western beliefs" (Kolton 1996, p. 424). This is because copying or imitation is seen as a "noble art," and thus the Chinese were encouraged to become compilers rather than composers (Yu 2002, p. 17). The second aspect of Confucianism that is held to impact upon the modern protection of intellectual property is the emphasis placed on collective rights, over individual rights (Yu 2002, p. 18). It has been suggested that this led to a lack of individual private property rights, which in turn was blamed for the lack of intellectual property enforcement (Endeshaw 1996, p. 37).

However, despite the strong emphasis placed on the influence of Confucianism in the literature, most respondents considered the influence of Confucianism on the modern IP system to be minimal. Out of the 16 factors identified on the questionnaire as potential influences on the IP system in China, Confucianism ranked 16th with an average score of 1.09 suggesting that it played only a minor role, if any, in the twenty-first-century Chinese IP system. In addition, there did not appear to be clear agreement about exactly what Confucianism meant in the context of the intellectual property system. As one respondent commented when questioned about the influence of Confucianism:

> I don't really know about the Confucian part, but I would definitely, for social issues anyway, yeah, they, they have an attitude that yep, copying can be good... Copying is not necessarily bad.
> And the whole idea of, um..., you know, of taking something that works, that you maybe didn't develop yourself and being able to duplicate that and, and, you know, the bottom line here is all about making money... So I don't know so much if it's about Confucianism.[8]

This perception of confusion about exactly what Confucianism meant and whether it necessarily equated to willingness to copy is strengthened by the comments of another respondent who explained the influence of Confucianism as follows:

> The principle generally is, let's say, don't do something radical, just keep quiet, keep everything in the middle, don't go to extremes. Let's say, this is an interpretation of Confucianism in one aspect. So, with the influence of Confucianism over 2000 years, or 2500 years, most of the Chinese people feel the best way to solve conflicts and disputes are not in court.[9]

Thus, these two respondents defined Confucianism quite differently in their interpretation of what it meant for the post-TRIPS intellectual property system in China. The first respondent appeared to be suggesting that Confucianism was linked to "an attitude that copying can be good," whereas the second respondent appeared to be defining Confucianism more in terms of the preference for non-legal resolutions to disputes, rather than linking it to an attitude towards copying.

The second element of history and culture that may have been influential in the context of China was the influence of socialism. The lack of an emphasis on individual rights may also be attributed to the impact of socialism, as the socialist economic system was based on the notion that property belonged to the state, rather than the individual. Furthermore, as intellectuals had been targeted at various times during the PRC's history, especially during the Cultural Revolution, creators and innovators became reluctant to acknowledge their creations (Yu 2002, p. 18). Both Confucianism and socialism were thus seen by many academic observers to have played a major part in the evolution of the post-reform legal system (Jenckes 1997, p. 554).

As discussed in Chap. 1 , it is undeniable that the initial development of intellectual property in the PRC was strongly influenced by socialism, particularly in the years immediately following the establishment of the PRC in 1949. The initial reliance on Soviet legal models in the early 1950s gave way during the 1960s to a more extreme socialist concept of intellectual property whereby all creations and innovations were properties of the state and the individual had no claim over them whatsoever. This view was at its height during the Cultural Revolution, but clearly faded from the legislation and official rhetoric in the years following the beginning of the reform and opening-up period.

Overall, socialism was not considered to be a highly significant influence on the post-TRIPS IP system by the majority of respondents in this study. The influence of socialism was ranked 15th out of the 16 factors on the questionnaire and on the scale of 0–6, scored an average of 1.78. Therefore, it is clear that although it appears that socialism exerted a powerful influence on the intellectual property system in the pre-reform years of the PRC, this influence had diminished by the turn of the twenty-first century. However, there appeared to be some differences of opinion amongst the respondents, with some respondents still attributing much of the ineffectiveness of the post-TRIPS IP system on the continuing influence of socialism. For example, one respondent from a foreign-invested enterprise in China claimed:

Socialism is an important cause of the problem.[10]

On the other hand, most respondents expressed the opinion that the influence of socialism was no longer highly significant:

I don't think socialism can be blamed at all, I think maybe (specifically) it could, but in general I don't think it can be blamed or, you know, said to be a reason for, for the ineffectiveness of the protection of intellectual property here.[11]

Besides this, several respondents mentioned the influence of socialism in the context of the success of the ruling Communist party; for instance,

> At the end of the day, the traditional Communist party is at threat if there is no innovation.[12]

This opinion, that further economic reform and development were essential for the future of Communist party rule and in turn, were dependent on increased innovation supported by an effective intellectual property system, was also expressed by several other respondents. Therefore, although the influence of socialism was not significant in the idealistic way it was in the pre-reform years of the PRC, it could still be argued that socialism was still a significant factor in the 2005–6 IP system as the government attempted to tread the fine line between maintaining China as a communist country and moving further towards a free market economy.

The parameters which may have impacted upon China's compliance with its obligations under the TRIPS Agreement also include basic characteristics of the country such as the size and variation of the country. Clearly China is a huge country, with great variation between the highly developed and industrialised seaboard and the largely rural and underdeveloped western interior. Indeed it has been recognised that "the sheer size of China's landmass inhibits effective monitoring of compliance with Chinese intellectual property laws" (Feder 1996, p. 253). Moreover, there was also an acknowledgement that certain areas of China, notably Beijing and Shanghai, were better at protecting IP than other smaller cities, or inland areas. As a matter of fact, one respondent from a multinational operating in China stated:

> It's much better in some areas of China than others - China is not a single country but more like a series of smaller countries![13]

Consequently, it is difficult to make sweeping generalisations about the entire intellectual property system in China as there were massive variations between major cities such as Beijing and Shanghai and smaller cities or inland areas. This characteristic of China could be classified as one of the primary parameters of significance under the comprehensive model of compliance applied in this study and furthermore, could be said to have just as much effect on the IP system in 2015 as in 2005. In the context of China's physical size and variation, one of the most significant considerations which may influence the operation of the modern intellectual property system is the divide between the central and the local levels of government. As China is so large, many local and provincial governments are physically very far away from the central government in Beijing. Thus, even if the central government shows a strong commitment to the protection of intellectual property rights, "there is some doubt that the central government has enough influence over the local governments to effectuate their cooperation" (Jenckes 1997, p. 569). These problems are not new in China; in fact, "perennial problems" of tensions between central and regional authorities and of cross-cutting bureaucratic lines "had plagued China since the late Ming dynasty" (Spence 1999, p. 498).

These concerns over the ability of local-level governments to strongly enforce intellectual property rights were also voiced by several respondents. For example, this respondent from a multinational enterprise drew a clear distinction between the central government's commitment to IP protection and the reality in many provinces:

> The central government starts to realize the importance of IP protection. It starts to realize a better IP protection mechanism is essential for China to move to higher value added service. However, the municiple ((sic)) do not see it the same way.[14]

A luxury goods manufacturer contradicted this perception by identifying the following as the primary factor in the ineffective enforcement they had experienced:

> Unwillingness from central as well as local authorities.[15]

However, by distinguishing the central and local authorities, this respondent was also implicitly acknowledging that the different levels of government did not always place the same level of emphasis on enforcing IP rights. Therefore, there seemed to be overall agreement amongst various respondents that there may be differences between the policies of the central and local levels of government and that all levels of government need to be fully committed to enforcing intellectual property rights in order for an effective system to be established.

The number of neighbours that a country has is also posited as a factor influencing that country's compliance with their international obligations. In the context of intellectual property obligations, the number of neighbours that China has may have two effects; firstly, in connection with the vast physical size of China, the customs enforcement of IP at China's borders may be a challenge and secondly, China may have used the example of the intellectual property system in neighbouring countries as a model for developing its own.. China has a large number of bordering countries; fourteen countries share land borders with China. As a direct result of this, China has a long border to defend against import and export of goods which may be infringing intellectual property rights. In 2006, the US customs authorities estimated that 81% of all IP-infringing goods seized came from China (US Customs and Border Protection 2007, p. 267) and the Chinese customs authorities themselves declared a total of 1210 infringement cases in 2005, involving goods with a total value of almost 100 million RMB (General Administration of Customs of the People's Republic of China 2006, p. 268). Therefore, exports of goods which infringe IP rights were clearly a significant problem for the customs authorities to tackle.

However, customs enforcement of intellectual property rights was highlighted by several respondents as an area of some improvement in the years leading up to 2005. For instance, one respondent from a multinational company cited, as the key positive change that they had noticed in the IP system in the past few years,

Expanded IPR protection channels (like customs protection).[16]

Furthermore, two legal respondents independently cited key regulations expanding the powers of customs' authorities in IP enforcement as notable improvements that they had recently observed.[17]

In addition to the impact of China's long borders on the protection of intellectual property rights, China's neighbouring countries may also have an impact on the IP system by providing an example for China to follow. Taiwan and Korea, in the 1960s and 1970s, both focused on duplicative imitation of mature technologies from abroad, utilising their highly skilled, but cheap labour force. At this time, lax IP helped to nurture economic development, especially through reverse engineering (Kim 2003, p. 17). In the 1980s and 1990s, both began to lose their comparative advantage in the face of rising labour costs and increased competition from second-tier newly industrialised economies. As a result, both shifted towards more technology-intensive industries (Van Hoesel 1999, pp. 56–7). In this "creative imitation" phase of economic development, intellectual property became more important, for local firms as well as foreign firms. The influence of other countries' IP systems is mentioned in passing by some respondents, who directly compared China's IP system to the development of intellectual property protection in neighbouring countries such as Taiwan, Japan and South Korea. For example, it is implicit in this Chinese respondent's comments that China needed to look at neighbouring countries and their path of economic development:

A lot of people call China a manufacturing base of the world, but it can start from this base and become other things like, uh... to become a base of creating more technology, innovation. We don't say we copy the way or approach from Japan or others, but they do really quite good job in the past 20 years or 40 years. We have to learn something from advanced economy.[18]

This notion that China should look at neighbouring countries and follow their example of economic development was expressed more definitely by this respondent:

You can't (rely on) factories, you've got to (adapt), just look at Taiwan, Korea, even building a domestic market, you need to have innovation to go to the next level. Without it (...), every country in Asia, I mean look at Japan, no matter what you think of it or say, it sits there at the edge of Asia like a shining light in terms of economic development.[19]

Thus, these comments seem to suggest that this role of the neighbouring countries as an example to be applied is more to be desired than one that actually existed at that time.

6.2.2 Fundamental Factors

In addition to basic parameters of the specific country such as the size and history of the country, there are various fundamental factors which, according to the comprehensive model of compliance being applied, may influence China's overall compliance with the TRIPS Agreement. One of the most important categories of fundamental factors in this model of compliance is that of attitudes and values which may have played an especially significant role as much of the post-TRIPS IP system was directly imported from foreign systems. Consequently, the framework they imposed may not have necessarily fitted entrenched societal values (Qu 2002, p. ii). It has been suggested by some observers that intellectual property protection was weak in China due to the lack of a strong belief in individual rights, which was felt to exist in other jurisdictions where IP was more effectively protected. In order to examine this factor in isolation from the concepts of Confucianism and socialism, it was included as a separate factor on the questionnaire. On the whole, it was felt by respondents to be more significant than either Confucianism or socialism, but was still not ranked highly in terms of overall significance. It was scored an average of 3 on the scale of 0–6 and was thus ranked tenth out of the 16 factors overall. However, some respondents did deem the lack of the concept of individual rights to be

> A fundamental factor- for example, most people will not feel guilty for buying pirated CDs.[20]

Another respondent went further in emphasising the significance of individual rights to the functioning of the intellectual property system in China:

> I think that awareness of individual rights is the driving force behind our society's protection of intellectual property rights. Without this, it means that the car does not have enough speed and forward momentum.[21]

It is clear from these comments that the concept of individual rights was regarded as a crucial factor by some respondents. However, there may be a blurring between this emphasis on the concept of individual rights and public awareness of intellectual property rights more generally. This is evident in the quote above from respondent 05LAW29T about the importance of "awareness of individual rights" as the "driving force" behind China's IP protection.

It has rather improbably been claimed that as the concept of intellectual property protection was "unknown to the majority of the Chinese population... many infringers simply do not know that what they are doing is illegal" (Jenckes 1997, p. 556). Although the level of public awareness of intellectual property was nowhere near as low as this comment would suggest, the lack of education regarding intellectual property was still regarded as a major problem (Kolton 1996, p. 456). Overall, respondents highlighted the lack of public awareness of intellectual property rights as the most significant factor in contributing to the IP system in China at that time. On the scale of 0–6, it scored an average of 4.44 and was ranked most significant overall out of the 16 given factors in the questionnaire. Thus, lack of awareness of IP was clearly perceived to be a serious problem in the post-TRIPS IP system and many of the respondents' comments reflected this. For example, a common view expressed was that

> People don't see IPR infringement [as] a disgrace and a very serious problem (the awareness is improving however).[22]

This was echoed by a Chinese respondent, who felt strongly that

> Public awareness of IPR is not yet widespread, which directly leads to frequent infringements. In many places in China, the concept of IPR lacks public support. Infringers do not feel guilty for their wrongdoings.[23]

However, it was noticeable that several of the foreign respondents were sceptical about the true extent of the ignorance of intellectual property rights. One respondent went so far as to call the notion that ineffective IP protection could be attributed to cultural factors:

> Complete crap.[24]

Thus, although a lack of public awareness was emphasised by respondents as the key factor behind the ineffectiveness of the IP system at that time, this view was not unanimous.

A further factor which deserves consideration is the notion that intellectual property protection only benefitted foreigners which may have acted as a disincentive for China to enforce intellectual property rights. As China was seen as having little intellectual property of its own, there was said to be a suspicion that intellectual property protection "only fills the coffers of foreign IPR holders with Chinese funds" (Feder 1996, p. 253). Overall, this factor was not ranked particularly highly by respondents, scoring an average of 2.42 on the scale of 0–6 and ranked 14th out of 16 factors in total. However, there was an interesting contrast between the Chinese and foreign respondents when asked about the significance of this factor. Whilst Chinese respondents only scored this factor with an average of 1.53, foreign respondents scored it with an average of 3.36. Chinese respondents clearly did not consider the perception that IP only benefits foreigners to be of any significance whereas foreign respondents perhaps felt that this perception still affected the operation of the IP system to their detriment. This perception may also be linked to the potential role of domestic Chinese companies to change the IP system in China, a link explicitly made by respondent 05LAW07, who claimed that

Chinese companies' growth is going to gradually change such situation.[25]

A further cultural element that may have affected the operation of the intellectual property system was the influence of *guanxi* or the use of informal networks or relationships to achieve specific aims. *Guanxi* generally refers to "interpersonal connections," but more specifically often carries a more pejorative meaning, especially to foreigners, of the unethical use of someone's authority to obtain political or economic benefit (Fan 2002, p. 546). Although *guanxi* was not explicitly identified by most respondents, there were several references made to "relationships." For instance, one respondent directly attributed his dissatisfaction with the IP system in terms of these "relationships":

> Generally the efficiency is not very uh... satisfying. I couldn't understand the reasons, but sometimes it is because China is a (city), is a society full of relationships. OK? So in some of the cases, like IP cases, we could say the legal enforcement people are also, let's say, indulged with this kind of relationship.[26]

Benefitting from an informal connection with an official could be seen as an initial step on the slippery slope to corruption as another respondent made clear:

> the temptation to corruption is huge and it starts very (simply) I'm sure, (...) a friend who's a private lawyer, you're a judge, he's making a hundred thousand or whatever, and you're making ten or whatever it is, they're going to of course treat you... to dinner and take you out and say don't worry about it (...), but it comes to a very fine line of when it crosses to corruption. If you can't afford a (house) and they say we'll lend you the money, we'll work it out later on, you know, and the Chinese are very good at building relationships in that way.[27]

This further mention of relationships exemplifies the underlying attitude of many respondents that these "relationships" were at the heart of many interactions throughout the legal system, including the IP system, and indeed, many respondents seemed resigned to this fact.

Turning to political and institutional influences on the IP system, a major factor to consider is the role of law in China generally. Despite committing to establishing a rule of law state in a Constitutional amendment in 1999 (Chinese Government Network 2004), there was still evidence to suggest that China followed a rule by law, rather than rule of law system even following WTO accession. A legal system based on rule by law sees law as a means by which the state's policies may be implemented, rather than as an end in itself; "law then becomes a tool of the Party to be used to serve the interests of the people and to attack the enemy" (Peerenboom 2002, p. 10). The implications of this instrumentalist model are that "the line between law and policy in China is often said to be blurred" (Clarke 1999, p. 32), as the law is simply seen as a mechanism for implementing Party policy (Potter 2013). However, respondents in the 2005 phase of the study did not explicitly refer to the overall status of law in China and this characteristic of the legal system may be largely academic rather than a concern to the end-users of the post-TRIPS IP system.

Nevertheless, this blurring between official policy and law may have had multiple influences on the operation of the intellectual property system in China at this time. Firstly, the lack of a clear hierarchy of legislation led to a lack of transparency in the intellectual property system generally. Overall, respondents had mixed feelings about the continuing influence of a lack of transparency on the intellectual property system in China. On a scale of 0–6, lack of transparency scored an average of 3.11 and was ranked ninth out of the 16 suggested influences. There were two noticeable opinions on transparency amongst most respondents' more detailed comments. Several respondents cited greater transparency as one of the improvements they had noticed in the IP system in the past few years, in response to question 10 on the questionnaire. These respondents included one member of the Quality Brands Protection Committee (QBPC), who cited the main change observed as:

More transparency on legislation

and another multinational respondent who simply cited an important change in the IP system as:

Increased transparency.[28]

One of the legal respondents based in Hong Kong gave more detail on the improvements in transparency they had witnessed:

Lack of transparency, I think is OK, I mean, the legal system is getting more transparent especially with the Trademark Office now publishing their internal guidelines, they're making an effort there... It is getting better.[29]

In contrast to those respondents who cited transparency as an area of improvement, other respondents claimed a lack of transparency was still harmful to their interactions with the IP system and that increased transparency would be a considerable improvement. These respondents included a lawyer based in Shanghai who stated that a system of watchdogs would improve the system greatly.[30]

Another Shanghai-based lawyer went further and said that

"I think the biggest thing people don't do and the argument about it is I think there needs to be more openness about these problems," because "transparency in every system improves enforcement."[31]

Consequently, whilst it was generally acknowledged that transparency in terms of the legislative framework was much better following WTO accession in

December 2001, transparency in the implementation of this framework was still alleged to be poor.[32]

The role of law as an instrument for implementing Party policy could also have led to the overall preference for public rather than private enforcement mechanisms. This remained true for the enforcement of intellectual property even after TRIPS implementation, as "IPR enforcement remains largely a government, rather than a private-sector matter" (Potter and Oksenberg 1999, p. 117). For example, in 2004, the number of IP cases dealt with through administrative enforcement totalled 62,997 (with a further 385 criminal cases initiated by the state), with only 8332 cases brought to the civil courts by individual rights-holders (Chinese Government Network 2005). This emphasis on administrative (and criminal sanctions) for IP infringers reinforced the government's central role in enforcement, rather than empowering economic actors to enforce their own rights. Greater use of private enforcement was strongly advocated by several commentators, "because such a system would not rely... on government policy priorities at any given moment" (Clarke 1999, p. 31) and it was hoped that greater consistency could be introduced in the protection of intellectual property.

However, although respondents did raise some problems with the system of criminal enforcement of IP, specifically the thresholds used to decide criminal liability, there was strong praise for the public enforcement mechanisms overall. This was reflected in the results regarding the possible influence of over-reliance on public enforcement mechanisms; this factor was ranked 12th out of the 16 suggested factors on the questionnaire and scored an average of 2.76 overall for its contribution to the IP system, on a scale of 0–6. Thus, the overall preference for criminal and administrative enforcement in the IP system was not seen as a problem by respondents in this study. On the contrary, the operation of the administrative system, particularly the Administration for Industry and Commerce (AIC) responsible for trademark infringements, was expressly commended for swift enforcement actions.[33]

Another consequence of the lack of a clear distinction between government policy and the law may have been a lack of consistency in the implementation of the system of intellectual property protection in China. Enforcement actions were often praised as "waves of coordinated actions, each targeted on specific types of infringement activities."[34] Although this style of IP enforcement followed a typically Chinese model of enforcement of "crackdowns," it was at odds with the basic rule of law concept that laws should be enforced consistently. Symbolic crackdowns were also frequently highlighted in the media when intellectual property protection was under international scrutiny, leading to the suspicion that IP rights were only respected when absolutely necessary for geopolitical reasons (Endeshaw 1996, pp. 44–5).

On the whole, most respondents in this study did show concern about the impact of inconsistency in the IP system. Out of the 16 suggested factors included in the initial survey, lack of consistency was ranked fourth and scored an average of 3.8 on a scale of 0–6. Thus, consistency was clearly of interest to many of the respondents and was frequently expressed in terms of frustration with infringers not being pursued consistently:

> Relevant agencies work hard to achieve something during certain period, and thereafter loose up, and this gives the infringer a misleading signal that after the periodical "fire", their life would become easy.[35]

This concern was echoed by a Chinese lawyer who painted the following picture of IP enforcement in China:

> "You could say that enforcement is mainly focused on those big cities now, for the middle and smaller cities are not very much to feel this enforcement and sometimes we can also feel that enforcement are not become day-to-day work or day-to-day operation, it's just a few times in the year."[36]

Hence, lawyers and business-people alike shared concerns about the impact of inconsistent enforcement of the IP laws and regulations, particularly in terms of strongly enforcing IP rights at certain specified times and not at others. Generally, enforcement problems were widely seen as arising from the transition from a centrally planned to a market economy (Lagerqvist and Riley 1997, p. 3). This was due to the economic system in place before the start of reforms, when "most Chinese enterprises did not heed intellectual property rights because the absence of market competition under a centrally planned economy made the protection of intellectual property rights dispensable" (Tian and Lo 2004).

Despite reforms which had introduced market forces into the Chinese economy, the government still had a significant role to play in economic development with "multiple roles as regulator, entrepreneur, and law enforcer," with the clear potential for conflicts of interest (Chow 2000). With such a large degree of control over the commercial sector, it is little wonder that intellectual property protection concerns took a back seat to the economic aims of the government and thus, economic factors affecting China's TRIPS compliance cannot be ignored. The government's control over the economy "undermines private property rights—especially the intangible kind. This creates economic instability that makes it difficult for innovation by domestic companies to be rewarded, and thus be sustained" (Stevenson-Yang and DeWoskin 2005). Furthermore, as government ownership of the loss-making state sector still dominated the economy, it can hardly be surprising that the government aimed to protect these enterprises at all costs (Endeshaw 1996, p. 151). As one commentator succinctly put it, "the instinct to protect what you own is basic" (Stevenson-Yang and DeWoskin 2005).

Despite these commentators stating that the economic priorities of the central government were to blame for problems in the IP system, opinions amongst respondents in this study regarding the significance of the government's role in the economy were somewhat mixed. Out of the 16 suggested factors on the questionnaire, the role of the government in the economy was ranked eleventh, with an average score of 2.89 on a scale of 0–6. This would suggest that most respondents did not share these concerns. However, more detailed comments from certain respondents did reflect the notion that there was a certain amount of resentment about unequal treatment between state-owned enterprises (SOEs) and private companies. For example, one Chinese lawyer commented:

> The interests of the state and the SOEs are over-protected and over-emphasised, while private rights are usually neglected. If the state or SOEs breach the IPR of an individual, often they will not be severely punished.[37]

These comments reflected the impression of poor enforcement where SOEs were the infringers, but as another respondent notes, unequal treatment may also have applied where an SOE was the injured party:

> There'll be state-owned enterprises that are being killed and yes, they've got more methods for enforcing their IPR; the larger you are, the more close to government if you, if you go to your local police and say, we want to investigate this, it happens.[38]

Thus, it would appear that although government ownership of the economy was not as problematic as suggested by some commentators, a minority of respondents perceived inequalities between state-owned enterprises and private companies, both in terms of infringements by SOEs not being pursued and infringements against SOEs being vigorously confronted.

Local protectionism could also be considered as an economic influence on the implementation of the intellectual property system in China and must be acknowledged as a major issue in the non-enforcement of intellectual property rights at this time (Finder 1999, p. 261). However, local protectionism is a complex issue and thus incorporated elements of political factors as well. Even government officials admitted that "local protectionism is the real culprit" behind problems in the post-TRIPS enforcement system (Duan 1999, p. 217). Local protectionism acted against effective enforcement in various ways, for example, "in most cases, IP owners are required to bring... proceedings in the infringer's home court, rather than in the jurisdiction where counterfeit products have been sold. This significantly increases the risk of bias" (Simone 1999).

In addition to bias in the courts, local protectionism could also be a crucial issue in administrative enforcement. Intellectual property infringement was often an ingrained part of the local economy, as was the case in Yiwu city in Zhejiang province, where the trade in counterfeit goods played such a significant role that "shutting down counterfeiting is functionally equivalent to shutting down the local economy with all of its attendant social and political costs" (Chow 2000). Although Yiwu city represented an extreme example of the reliance of a local economy on IP infringements, there were many other places in China where intellectual property infringements did play a major role in the local economy at that time and enforcement agencies in these areas were therefore extremely reluctant to enforce intellectual property rights, at the expense of their own interests.

On the whole, local protectionism was cited by many respondents as one of the primary problems with the IP system in China in 2005–6. Out of the 16 potential factors presented to respondents in the questionnaire, local protectionism ranked second only to a lack of awareness as an influence on the intellectual property system, with an average score of 4.13 on a scale of 0–6. As the only two factors with average scores above 4, it is clear that both a lack of public awareness of IP rights and local protectionism were major concerns for respondents. Specifically, respondents used the term "local protectionism" to refer to a number of behaviours, including difficulties in initiating cases with local agencies; bias in the enforcement process and trivial penalties for local infringers. As one respondent defined the issue:

> Local protectionism, I think is the code word that people use for all these different types of things.[39]

The significance of local protectionism was also highlighted by these comments from a local lawyer in Guangdong province:

> Local protectionism in the intellectual property protection system has a very negative impact. It undermines justice, not just in individual cases, but in the entire legal system. This has an adverse impact on China: it's prejudicial to the import of foreign advanced technologies into China.[40]

Two respondents both working for multinationals in China commented on the impact of local protectionism that they had experienced. The first respondent commented:

> It is hard to get a good catch, and even when caught, the infringer may not be punished to the severest extent possible.[41]

This shows that local protectionism impacted not only on the infringers that may be targeted, but also the level of penalties awarded. The second respondent from a multinational manufacturer related the experiences of pursuing two Chinese companies for copying their designs:

> Although we stopped the companies no financial compensation or costs were given. This was because we are a foreign company and the two companies were local. In general if legal proceedings are followed outside one's own area, the legal system in another area favours their own.[42]

This frustration with the impact of local protectionism on enforcement efforts was echoed by comments from several of the lawyers who responded. For example, one remarked on the difficulties of pursuing large-scale infringers, in contrast to individual infringers:

> They have whole cities that specialise in car parts... You're talking about a whole city you're fighting or a whole region, then it gets really difficult.[43]

Consequently, it is clear that for these respondents with day-to-day experience of the post-TRIPS Chinese IP system, local protectionism was a major issue.

6.2.3   Proximate Factors

The final category of factors to consider under the detailed model of compliance outlined in Chap. 2 is proximate factors. These factors are specific to the system under analysis and incorporate influences such as the capacity of the existing agencies to implement the system effectively and the role of other organisations in pressurising for or monitoring changes in the system. The legal system in China at this time was basically the product of 25 years of rebuilding, as "decimated by the Cultural Revolution and decades of neglect and abuse, the legal system had to be rebuilt virtually from scratch" (Peerenboom 2002, p. 6). Despite the government swiftly reassembling the rudiments of a legal system (Spence 1999, p. 670), systemic problems in the legal system remained the subject of intense criticism. Resources were one of the problems haunting the legal system, specifically the lack of trained, experienced legal personnel. A lack of lawyers qualified to deal with intellectual property cases had also been identified as one of the major forces preventing full enforcement of intellectual property rights (Endeshaw 1996, p. 38).

Although these problems stemmed partly from the position of the legal system in the Chinese political system as a mere instrument of governance, they could also have been attributed to the professionally underqualified legal personnel administering the law (Chen 2002, p. 8). Clearly, many commentators believed that better-trained lawyers and judges were needed to handle intellectual property cases (Qu 2002, p. 390). In general, respondents concurred that a lack of trained and experienced legal personnel contributed to problems with the intellectual property system in China. This factor was ranked seventh out of 16 potential factors presented to respondents, with an average score of 3.71 on a scale of 0–6 and a concern over the quality of some of the personnel responsible for enforcing the framework of intellectual property laws and regulations was shared by several of the respondents. The following comment is typical of the opinions expressed:

> The government employees' understanding of intellectual property rights is far from proficient.[44]

Accordingly, it is obvious that the knowledge levels of the legal personnel involved in enforcing intellectual property rights were a significant concern to some respondents. Enforcement of intellectual property rights was complicated by the bureaucratic structure of power in China. As the pre-reform command economy had been split into vertical sectors, with separate agencies having full control over their sector, but with few links to other sectors, this still had implications for the bureaucratic structure of power in twenty-first-century China (Mertha 2005). Consequently, there was no unified agency to deal with intellectual property (Potter and Oksenberg 1999), with responsibility spread across several agencies including the State Administration for Industry and Commerce (SAIC or local-level AIC) responsible for trademarks, the National Copyright Administration (NCA) responsible for copyright and the State Intellectual Property Office (SIPO), which was responsible for patents. As a result, there was a considerable lack of communication and coordination, as well as a great deal of rivalry between the various agencies (Simone 1999, pp. 14–6). It was recognised by a couple of respondents that these multiple agencies potentially caused problems in IP enforcement. For instance,

> Concurrence of several IPR enforcement authorities, such as TSBs, AICs, Patent offices, copyright offices and PSB leads to be unefficient ((sic)).[45]

However, the majority of respondents did not agree that a unified bureaucratic structure for the enforcement of IP rights would be an improvement to the existing framework of agencies. For instance, one respondent pointed out:

> It wouldn't be workable to just have one... to have one national uh... type of an agency to deal with it, because it's so diverse you have to break it down and so we do have the copyright, the trademark, the patent, you know, the different organs that deal with it and then under those organs, is generally local, their local counterparts that actually deal with it.[46]

Thus, there was recognition that the issue of intellectual property enforcement was too complex to be handled by only one agency. On the whole, unifying the separate agencies into one overall body responsible for intellectual property was not regarded as a priority by respondents. Out of the 16 factors suggested as factors which contribute to problems in the post-TRIPS IP system in China, the lack of a unified agency was ranked 13th by respondents. On a scale of 0–6, this factor scored an average of 2.76.

Another barrier that had been identified in the enforcement process was the length of the process. It was claimed that courts were often slow in pursuing their claims; local AICs had also been accused of delaying enforcement actions to give infringers enough time to dispose of infringing goods and machinery used to produce counterfeit products. Therefore, according to some observers, there were, on occasion, costly delays in both the civil and administrative enforcement of intellectual property rights. Conversely, the length of the enforcement process was not felt to be a major concern for the majority of respondents. This factor scored an average of 3.24 on a scale of 0–6 representing the contribution it makes to the IP system and ranked eighth out of the 16 potential factors that were presented to respondents on the questionnaire. Although it was recognised by many respondents that

A lot of time and money have to be put into the IP enforcement,[47]

it was also suggested that this may not always be the case and was merely a perception that some rights-holders had:

Foreign rights holders are not willing to litigate in order to protect their rights; firstly, because they think it takes too much time and money and secondly, they don't really believe in China's courts.[48]

Consequently, the length of the process may not actually have acted as a barrier to a rights-holder seeking to uphold their rights, but rather as a perception that may have discouraged some rights-holders from initiating the enforcement process in the first place. As a matter of fact, lawyers with a lot of experience in the field of IP actually commended the speed with which some IP enforcement actions could be concluded. For instance, this Chinese lawyer working for a large international law firm commented on the administrative system of IP enforcement:

One good thing about the administrative approach besides the speediness of resolution will be the fact that you can (seize) the infringing goods or even the tools used to make the infringing goods really quickly and that actually it's a tangible result.[49]

Thus, the length of the enforcement process did not appear to be a major problem in the IP system once an action had been initiated.

A further proximate factor influencing the effectiveness of the post-TRIPS Chinese IP system was the level of penalties awarded against infringers. Even if a plaintiff succeeded in an enforcement action, damages awarded to successful plaintiffs were generally low by Western standards (Clarke 1999, p. 40). Moreover, these paltry damage awards were not always even sufficient to cover the substantial fees, payable by the plaintiff to the intellectual property court in advance (Kolton 1996, p. 451). Fines and compensation awarded through the administrative enforcement system were also criticised as insufficient, as they were not perceived to be high enough to act as a deterrent to infringers. Indeed, inadequate penalties were identified by many respondents as a key area of dissatisfaction with the 2005–6 system of intellectual property protection in China, scoring an average of 3.96 on a scale of 0–6 and also ranking third overall, out of the 16 suggested factors.

It is clear from respondents' comments that there was a certain amount of dissatisfaction with the levels of penalties imposed on infringers, as the following typical comments illustrates. The main problem with the IP system was felt to be the

> Lack of punitive compensation for IP infringement[50];

and

> The power to produce a ruling is too large, while the punishment is not enough to act as a deterrent.[51]

More detail about the effects of inadequate penalties was given by another respondent who explained

> Although they're starting to impose criminal liability, (those) are hard to get and then, civil liability or remedies awarded by administrative agencies, they're minimal... they basically just come out to make an announcement, to me, they don't have a significant deterrent effect... to the infringers.[52]

It is clear from these comments that respondents felt frustrated at the level of penalties awarded against the infringers and appeared to feel that appearances in enforcement were more important than actually deterring infringers. A further consequence of the pre-reform structure of power in China, closely linked to the continuing preference for administrative enforcement of intellectual property rights, was weak judicial enforcement. As the legal system had essentially been constructed only since the late 1970s, it was perhaps inevitable that expertise was still lacking in the judicial system. Overall, respondents did show some concern over the judicial enforcement system; weak judicial enforcement was ranked fifth out of the 16 possible factors contained on the questionnaire, scoring an average of 3.76 on a scale of 0–6. In general, launching a case through the judicial system was perceived as more problematic than pursuing a straightforward claim through administrative agencies. An example of this kind of opinion is illustrated by the following comment:

> I think China's courts lack authority and protection of their power.[53]

Strengthening the judicial system of enforcement was also seen as key by several respondents:

> What they need to do, is put more of a, you know, to develop more their civil court system..., and there, the civil side of it, because that's still fairly weak.[54]

One of the main ways that the weakness in the judicial enforcement system was manifest was in the lack of powers that the courts had to enforce their judgments. Estimates suggested that around 50% of all civil judgments could not be enforced (Li 2002). The primary reason for the non-execution of so many judgments was that the courts had little "weaponry" to back up their commands (Clarke 1999, p. 39). This problem was identified by a number of respondents, all of whom expressed frustration at the inability of the court to enforce judgments made against infringers:

> Ineffective implementation of court decisions is a problem. Fundamentally speaking, it's a general lack of credibility. Debtors evade the enforcement of court judgments. If defendants fail to provide assistance in the implementation, the court very rarely resorts to coercive measures and very rarely brings them to justice.[55]

On the whole, respondents did show concern over the lack of effective powers used to enforce court judgments; this factor scored an average of 3.73 on a scale of 0–6, similar to the score for weak judicial enforcement in general. Out of the 16 suggested factors, it was ranked as sixth most significant by respondents. This overall weakness in the judicial system has even been attributed to a reluctance to create a truly independent judiciary despite an official commitment to this:

> No-one wants to give the court that power because if the courts have power, you're creating an independent judiciary and not completely, but you know, you're creating more-, the more power you give judges, the closer you get to an independent judiciary and that is not what the Communist Party wants. They want a judiciary that resolves disputes, but is still under the control of the Party.[56]

Accordingly, although the weakness of judicial enforcement was usually attributed to the immature nature of the legal system in China, these comments go further and suggest that the judicial system was being deliberately enfeebled for political reasons. Whatever the reason, it is clear that the judicial system of intellectual property enforcement was still problematic.

In addition to China's administrative capacity to deal with intellectual property enforcement, several respondents shared a belief that some IP personnel lacked the knowledge to be able to effectively enforce intellectual property rights. For example, the consequence of judges lacking detailed knowledge of intellectual property was explained as follows:

> If people don't understand IP laws, there's a (price), if you're a judge and you don't understand patent law and there's all this political pressure and stuff around you, you can be convinced pretty easily by someone who says black is white or white is black.[57]

In other words, lacking sufficient knowledge of the legal basis for intellectual property could either have left the judge more open to reaching inconsistent decisions or not reaching the correct decision at all. This lack of knowledge was explained by a different respondent, who attributed the continued lack of expertise to a lack of experienced teachers at university level:

> A lot of them have not historically had the opportunity of receiving training with regard to IP, for example, (university) might offer some IP course, but have those

people teaching those courses had any experience with IP work?... They might only have book learning, so you get professors experienced at teaching, but I don't know how extensive their experience is with regard to IP.[58]

Thus, so-called book learning of intellectual property was distinguished from real-life "experience" and was seen as insufficient to allow for true understanding of the system in action. Furthermore, increasing the knowledge level of personnel involved in intellectual property enforcement was also seen as crucial by several respondents. For example, one respondent claimed it was vital

To keep increasing the quality of personnel from related professions.[59]

This was echoed by another respondent who saw the key to improvement in the IP system as follows:

By improving the allocation of human and material resources, especially human resources, the government can equip the Intellectual Property Office with more personnel who understand intellectual property law, to strengthen the fight against IP infringers as a team.[60]

Consequently, the knowledge levels of personnel involved in the intellectual property system was acknowledged to be a concern for many respondents.

The attitude of the central government in Beijing was also acknowledged as key to the effective enforcement of intellectual property rights in China. Indeed, this was recognised as a key area of change in the years 2001–5 by some respondents. In response to questions regarding changes they had witnessed in the IP system in China in the past few years, one respondent noted:

Attention of the IP right from the government bodies,[61]

and another that

China's leaders emphasize the importance of IPR.[62]

There also appeared to be a strong belief amongst respondents that change in the legal system generally and the intellectual property system more specifically was often driven from the attitudes of the central leadership. For instance, one respondent observed that

And also in the latest (successions) of the leadership, central leadership, they travel a lot overseas; have a lot of exchange with overseas. Uh... this created the internal desire or drive to open China more and logically, how to open, how to protect IP, I think maybe this is one of the aspects.[63]

The logical consequence of this belief that change in the intellectual property system was driven by the leadership is the belief that non-enforcement was also a direct consequence of the policies of the central leadership. Several respondents expressed this idea that the central leadership could have effectively enforced intellectual property rights if it chose to:

> I believe that if, if the central government is taking an interest, then something will happen in the whole country.[64]

Therefore, leadership from the central government was seen as crucial to the effective enforcement of intellectual property rights in China.

The final category of proximate factors that may influence China's compliance with the TRIPs Agreement was the influence of non-governmental organisations (NGOs). Domestic NGOs faced many political and practical barriers at that time; specifically, the political culture in China was said not to be conducive to civil society activism (Lu 2005, p. 6). Moreover, NGOs had more focus on and relevance to other areas of international obligations; for instance, environmental protection was strongly influenced by pressure from both domestic and international NGOs. However, intellectual property did not elicit similar NGO involvement. On the contrary, organisations concerned with intellectual property tended to be commercial groups, often consisting of businesses with strong intellectual property rights. Therefore, the influence of NGOs in the intellectual property arena was based predominantly on pressure from key groups of companies, both domestic and international.

Specifically, the main organisation pressurising for better protection with regard to intellectual property in China was the QBPC. The QBPC is a group of more than 160 multinational companies concerned with counterfeiting in China and their stated aim is "to work cooperatively with the Chinese central and local governments, local industry, and other organisations to make positive contributions to intellectual property protection in the People's Republic of China" (QBPC 2016). Several foreign respondents independently mentioned the QBPC in connection with their views on the intellectual property system in China and this shows that the Committee was well known amongst practitioners in the IP field in China. One respondent from a professional services company stated that the QBPC:

> Have been working very hard in China to make the case for IP and design protection, and to get enforcement.[65]

One lawyer based in Hong Kong mentioned the role of the QBPC in connection with a client who was struggling to stop infringers of their IP:

> What they do now is they join forces with other car makers and spare part makers... through the QBPC.[66]

This respondent went on to explain that through the QBPC, this manufacturer was able to contact other manufacturers of similar products and join together in enforcement actions, thus saving costs. This role of the QBPC as a network for companies to join together to tackle infringements thus seemed to be an important one for some respondents. However, another respondent expressed some frustration at the consistently "positive" approach taken by the QBPC. For example, the QBPC hosted annual award ceremonies where officials were recognised for special achievements in IP enforcement, but this respondent did not agree with this approach, claiming,

> You know you get the QBPC... there have been some people in there talking about blacklists and things like that but (the basic position is) say no, no we can't do that, we have to reward, we should do it by positive encouragement, you know, like best cases and best officials... (and I'm thinking) this sucks, you see the most corrupt officials in the business getting awards for their great cases and stuff, we should be outing them, you know, as crooks.[67]

Accordingly, although the QBPC was praised by some respondents for its role in IP in China, this praise was not universal. It is also noteworthy that the QBPC was only mentioned by foreign respondents and was not commented on by any of the Chinese respondents. Therefore, the QBPC appeared to serve a specific purpose of bringing multinational companies together and raising awareness of IP issues amongst them.

On the contrary, although formal organisations of domestic businesses were limited or invisible in China, the role of Chinese companies in pressing for change in the intellectual property system was recognised as increasingly important. The experience of Taiwan and Korea had been used by several commentators to argue that a combination of external and internal pressure was truly necessary to bring about genuine change in IP protection (Maruyama 1999, p. 167). Consequently, many observers believed that if Chinese private companies possessed more intellectual property, stronger IP protection would be sought and obtained (Endeshaw 1996, p. 79). Indeed, a few optimistic observers claimed to have already witnessed the start of this change towards greater domestic protection for intellectual property (Potter and Oksenberg 1999). More generally, Chinese citizens were beginning to use the courts more and more, instead of the traditional reliance on mediation or administrative agencies. This was also seen as a positive step for the prospects of enhanced enforcement of intellectual property rights (Jenckes 1997, p. 560).

Therefore, the role of Chinese companies was seen as crucial to achieving sustained change in the IP system in China. Although formal organisations of Chinese companies were limited to a few industries, Chinese companies in general were cited by most respondents as one of the key influences on the Chinese legal system. Some respondents asserted that this shift towards greater pressure from domestic companies had already taken place. For example, when discussing recent changes in the IP system in China, one respondent declared that

> Chinese companies are more aware of IP issues and register in mass,[68]

while another stated that

Chinese companies are now suffering from IP problems and are calling for effective protection measures to be available.[69]

Pressure from Chinese companies was also cited by several respondents when discussing the future for the intellectual property system in China and was even described as the "main driver" for change by one respondent.[70] For instance,

> Improved IP protection would mostly benefit foreign companies at present, though it would benefit domestic companies in a long-term view. With the request and demand of IP protection from domestic companies and consumers becoming stronger, the IP protection would be improved more and faster.[71]

Overall, most respondents declared Chinese companies to be a highly significant influence on the IP system in China. As a consequence, although pressure from Chinese companies was seen as critical for the future of the Chinese intellectual property system, the political structure of government in China may have been hindering the impact of their collective voice.

6.3   Summary and Conclusion

In terms of the changes made in response to China's WTO accession and consequent obligation to comply with the TRIPS Agreement, it was found that almost all respondents had noticed a positive change in the IP system in the past five years (2001–6). However, overall, many respondents expressed frustration with seeking to enforce IP rights in the post-TRIPS system, but some respondents were also keen to point out certain strengths of the IP system, particularly in administrative proceedings. On the other hand, respondents reported experiencing local protectionism, judicial incompetence, perceived discrimination against foreign rights-holders and problems with evidence. Thus, the comprehensive model of compliance outlined in Chap. 2 offered a framework for analysing some of the remaining problems in the enforcement of the post-TRIPS IP system.

These various factors influencing compliance with the TRIPS Agreement which were specific to China have been considered under three main headings: basic parameters of China, fundamental factors such as political and institutional factors, and proximate factors such as administrative capacity. Some of the factors identified above were perceived to be more significant than the others. In terms of parameters overall, survey responses indicated that China's previous behaviour and historical and cultural factors were not felt to be major influences, but the size and number of neighbours of China may have had a minor influence on compliance. Therefore, basic parameters should not be ignored in assessing China's compliance, but they were certainly not the most significant influences on the framework of intellectual property protection and enforcement in 2005–6.

134 K. THOMAS

Turning to fundamental factors impacting upon China's TRIPS compliance, several of these factors were identified as crucial contributing factors to the post-TRIPS IP system in China, particularly the lack of awareness of IP rights, local protectionism and a lack of consistency in enforcement, which were all identified as highly significant by respondents. Several proximate factors were also identified as key contributors to the state of the IP system in China at this time. These were, most importantly, the inadequate level of penalties imposed on infringers and the judiciary's lack of strength in dealing with IP issues. In addition, the personnel in the IP system were subject to many comments from respondents, but the focus of these comments was primarily on the low quality of the personnel. Furthermore, more minor proximate factors identified by respondents which may have had an influence included the attitude of the central government leadership and the role played by pressure groups such as the QBPC.

In general, although China had been largely successful in meeting its formal substantive obligations under the TRIPS Agreement, the problem of intellectual property infringements had not diminished by 2005–6 and consequently overall effectiveness was still a problem in the IP system in China. Clearly, additional changes were necessary to fully comply with all the aims of the TRIPS Agreement, including the effective enforcement of IP rights, and this process of further development will be considered in Chap. 7 which focuses on the transformed state of the IP system in 2015.

Notes

1. Follow-up comments from respondent 05LAW29T.
2. Interview comments with respondent 05LAW01.
3. Questionnaire comments from respondent 05SERVICES01.
4. Interview comments from respondent 05LAW05.
5. Questionnaire comments from respondent 05LAW27T.
6. Questionnaire comments from respondent 05SERVICES01.
7. See, for example: Feder (1996, p. 231).
8. Interview with respondent 05LAW10.
9. Interview with respondent 05LAW16.
10. Questionnaire comments from respondent 05SERVICES01.
11. Interview comments from respondent 05LAW10.
12. Interview comments from respondent 05LAW01.
13. Questionnaire comments from respondent 05FOOD02.
14. Questionnaire comments from respondent 05FOOD01.
15. Questionnaire comments from respondent 05FASHION02.
16. Follow-up comments from respondent 05MANU02.
17. Follow-up comments from respondent 05LAW29T and interview with respondent 05LAW05.
18. Interview with respondent 05LAW16.
19. Interview with respondent 05LAW01.
20. Email follow-up correspondence with respondent 05LAW12T.

21. Email follow-up correspondence with respondent 05LAW29T.
22. Questionnaire comments from respondent 05MANU02.
23. Questionnaire comments from respondent 05MANU01T.
24. Interview with respondent 05LAW01.
25. Email follow-up correspondence with respondent 05LAW07.
26. Interview with respondent 05LAW16.
27. Interview with respondent 05LAW01.
28. Questionnaire comments from respondents 05MANU02 and 05FOOD02.
29. Telephone interview with respondent 05LAW31.
30. Interview with respondent 05LAW10.
31. Interview with respondent 05LAW01.
32. This was also reflected in the repeated requests by trading partners such as the US that China produce enforcement statistics for intellectual property protection (Barraclough 2006).
33. For example, interview comments from respondent 05LAW05.
34. Duan (1999, p. 217). As Director-General of the Office of Intellectual Property Executive Conference of the State Council (1994–8), Duan's statement can be seen as reflecting the official government's view of enforcement at this time.
35. Email follow-up comments from respondent 05MANU02.
36. Interview with respondent 05LAW16.
37. Questionnaire comments from respondent 05LAW15T.
38. Interview comments from respondent 05LAW01.
39. Interview with respondent 05LAW01.
40. Follow-up comments from respondent 05LAW29T.
41. Email follow-up comments from respondent 05MANU02.
42. Questionnaire comments from respondent 05MANU03.
43. Telephone interview with respondent 05LAW31.
44. Follow-up comments from respondent 05LAW12T.
45. Questionnaire comments from respondent 05MANU08.
46. Interview with respondent 05LAW10.
47. Follow-up comments from respondent 05LAW07.
48. Follow-up comments from respondent 05LAW12T.
49. Interview with respondent 05LAW05.
50. Questionnaire comments from respondent 05LAW03.
51. Questionnaire comments from respondent 05LAW13T.
52. Interview with respondent 05LAW05.
53. Follow-up comments from respondent 05LAW29T.
54. Interview with respondent 05LAW10.
55. Follow-up comments from respondent 05LAW29T.
56. Interview with respondent 05LAW01.
57. Interview with respondent 05LAW01.
58. Interview with respondent 05LAW05.
59. Questionnaire comments from respondent 05LAW30T.
60. Follow-up comments from respondent 05LAW29T.
61. Questionnaire comments from respondent 05MANU05.
62. Questionnaire comments from respondent 05LAW12T.
63. Interview with respondent 05LAW16.
64. Telephone interview with respondent 05LAW31.
65. Questionnaire comments from respondent 05SERVICES02.

66. Telephone interview with respondent 05LAW31.
67. Interview with respondent 05LAW01.
68. Questionnaire comments from respondent 05SERVICES01.
69. Questionnaire comments from respondent 05SERVICES02.
70. Questionnaire comments from respondent 05LAW06.
71. Questionnaire comments from respondent 05LAW07.

REFERENCES

Barraclough, Emma. 2006. China Urged to Provide IP Enforcement Data. *Managing Intellectual Property*.

Chen, Jianfu. 2002. Implementation of Law in China: An Introduction. In *Implementation of Law in the People's Republic of China*, ed. Jianfu Chen, Yuwen Li, and Jan Michel Otto, 1–21. Dordrecht: Kluwer Law International.

Chinese Government Network. 2004. 中华人民共和国宪法 (Constitution of the PRC). http://www.gov.cn/gongbao/content/2004/content_62714.htm. Accessed 30 Aug 2015.

———. 2005. 《中国知识产权保护的新进展》白皮书发布 (China White Paper on New Progress in IPR Protection Published). http://www.gov.cn/xwfb/2005-04/21/content_321.htm. Accessed 13 Sept 2015.

Chow, Daniel. 2000. Counterfeiting in the People's Republic of China. *Washington University Law Quarterly* 78(1): 1–57.

Clarke, Donald C. 1999. Private Enforcement of Intellectual Property Rights in China. *National Bureau of Asian Research* 10(2): 29–41.

Duan, Ruichun. 1999. China's Intellectual Property Rights Protection Towards the 21st Century. *Duke Journal of Comparative and International Law* 9(1): 215–218.

Endeshaw, Assafa. 1996. *Intellectual Property in China: The Roots of the Problem of Enforcement*. Singapore: Acumen Publishing.

Fan, Ying. 2002. Questionning Guanxi: Definition, Classification and Implications. *International Business Review* 11: 543–561.

Feder, Gregory S. 1996. Enforcement of Intellectual Property Rights in China: You Can Lead a Horse to Water but You Can't Make It Drink. *Virginia Journal of International Law* 37(1): 223–254.

Finder, Susan. 1999. The Protection of Intellectual Property Rights Through the Courts. In *Chinese Intellectual Law and Practice*, ed. Mark A. Cohen, A. Elizabeth Bang, and Stephanie J. Mitchell, 255–268. London: Kluwer Law International.

General Administration of Customs of the People's Republic of China. 2006. Statistics for China Customs IPR Seizures. http://www1.customs.gov.cn/Portals/191/IPR/2005figure1.doc. Accessed 20 Nov 2006.

Jenckes, Kenyon S. 1997. Protection of Foreign Copyrights in China: The Intellectual Property Courts and Alternative Avenues of Protection. *South California Interdisciplinary Law Journal* 5: 551–571.

Kim, Linsu. 2003. *Technology Transfer and IPRs: The Korean Experience*. UNCTAD-ICTSD Project on IPRs and Sustainable Development.

Kolton, Gregory S. 1996. Copyright Law and the People's Courts in the People's Republic of China: A Review and Critique of China's Intellectual Property Courts. *University of Pennsylvania Journal of International Economic Law* 17(1): 415–460.

Lagerqvist, Thomas, and Mary L. Riley. 1997. How to Protect Intellectual Property Rights in China. In *Protecting Intellectual Property Rights in China*, ed. M.L. Riley, A.S.F. Lee, T. Lagerqvist, and S. Liu. Hong Kong: Sweet & Maxwell Asia.

Li, Yahong. 2002. Pushing for Greater Protection: The Trend Toward Greater Protection of Intellectual Property in the Chinese Software Industry and the Implications for Rule of Law in China. *University of Pennsylvania Journal of International Economic Law* 23(4): 637–661.

Lu, Yiyi. 2005. The Growth of Civil Society in China: Key Challenges for NGOs. *Chatham House Briefing Paper*. http://www.chathamhouse.org.uk/pdf/research/asia/China.pdf. Accessed 2 Feb 2005.

Maruyama, Warren H. 1999. U.S.-China IPR Negotiations: Trade, Intellectual Property and the Rule of Law in a Global Economy. In *Chinese Intellectual Property Law and Practice*, ed. Mark A. Cohen, A. Elizabeth Bang, and Stephanie J. Mitchell. London: Kluwer Law International.

Mertha, Andrew C. 2005. *The Politics of Piracy: Intellectual Property in Contemporary China*. London: Cornell University Press.

Peerenboom, Randall. 2002. *China's Long March Toward Rule of Law*. Cambridge: Cambridge University Press.

Potter, Pitman B. 2013. *China's Legal System*. Cambridge: Polity Press.

Potter, Pitman B., and Michel Oksenberg. 1999. A Patchwork of IPR Protection. *China Business Review* 26(1): 8–11.

QBPC. 2016. QBPC Introduction. http://www.qbpc.org.cn/view.php?id=2715&cid=43. Accessed 20 Aug 2016.

Qu, Sanqiang. 2002. *Copyright in China*. Beijing: Foreign Languages Press.

Simone, Joseph T. 1999. China's IPR Enforcement Mechanisms. *China Business Review* 26(1): 14–16.

Spence, Jonathan D. 1999. *The Search for Modern China*. 2nd ed. New York: W. W. Norton & Co.

Stevenson-Yang, Anne, and Ken DeWoskin. 2005. China Destroys the IP Paradigm. *Far Eastern Economic Review* 168(3): 9–18.

Tian, Xiaowen, and Vai Io Lo. 2004. *Law & Investment in China: The Legal and Business Environments After China's WTO Accession*. London: RoutledgeCurzon.

US Customs and Border Protection. 2007. Seizure Statistics for Intellectual Property Rights. http://www.cbp.gov/xp/cgov/import/commercial_enforcement/ipr/seizure/. Accessed 18 Jan 2007.

Van Hoesel, Roger. 1999. *New Multinational Enterprises from Korea and Taiwan: Beyond Export-Led Growth*. London: Routledge.

Yu, Peter. 2002. The Second Coming of Intellectual Property Rights in China. *Occasional Papers in Intellectual Property* from Benjamin N. Cardozo School of Law, Yeshiva University Number 11.

CHAPTER 7

Assessing the Post-TRIPS Intellectual Property System in China in the Long Term: Adapting to Local Conditions

7.1   THE 2015 INTELLECTUAL PROPERTY SYSTEM IN ACTION: CHANGES OBSERVED FROM 2005

The previous chapter showed that although improvements had obviously been made in China's intellectual property (IP) system as a result of World Trade Organisation (WTO) accession, significant barriers still existed to inhibit effective enforcement. Specifically, the effectiveness of the 2005 system was examined by looking beyond the laws on paper and instead detailing experiences from respondents dealing with the IP system on a day-to-day basis. Chapter 6 concluded that there remained a significant "enforcement gap" between the substantive laws and the enforcement practices experienced on the ground. This chapter will now bring this analysis up to date by using the experiences of a variety of respondents in 2015 to consider how China's IP system has adapted to the WTO Agreement on Trade-Related Intellectual Property Rights (TRIPS) in the longer term.

It is clear to even a casual observer of China's legal system that a number of sweeping changes have been made in the field of intellectual property since the TRIPS Agreement was initially implemented in the early years of the twenty-first century. In the decade from roughly 2005–15, not only were a number of legislative changes promulgated, but significant changes were also made to the enforcement framework in China. These changes were mirrored by noteworthy shifts in both the attitude towards and awareness of IP in wider Chinese society as well as a substantial increase in the number of domestic Chinese rights-holders influencing the operation and effectiveness of the wider IP system. Such changes will be outlined in this first section. In terms of the overall changes observed in China's post-TRIPS intellectual property system in the long term, it is clear that steady progress has continued to be made since the implementation of TRIPS standards into domestic legislation in the few years immediately

© The Author(s) 2017
K. Thomas, *Assessing Intellectual Property Compliance in
Contemporary China*, Palgrave Series in Asia and Pacific Studies,
DOI 10.1007/978-981-10-3072-7_7

following formal accession in December 2001. Several respondents in the 2015 stage of the project had been working within the Chinese IP system for many years and overall, respondents were overwhelmingly positive about the changes they had witnessed over that time in the IP system in China. Although many still acknowledged that problems still existed, it was nevertheless undeniable to the majority of respondents that huge advances had been made in both IP protection and enforcement. Respondents often characterised changes they had observed as a series of incremental improvements rather than great leaps forward. For example,

> From a professional point of view it's incremental changes, yeah. So every time it changes a little bit, it's not like an overhaul of the whole system, it's not like that.[1]

These positive incremental changes are evident in both the substantive legislation and in enforcement practices on the ground, as well as wider changes in Chinese society. These changes will now be broadly outlined before the Jacobson and Brown Weiss (1998) comprehensive model of compliance is applied to China's long-term compliance with the TRIPS Agreement.

7.1.1   Legislative Changes

In terms of the IP-related legislation, all of the major laws were subject to at least one change or amendment during this period from 2005 to 2015. The PRC Trademark Law was amended on 30 August 2013, with the updated version taking effect from 1 May 2014.[2] The newly amended law aimed to streamline the trademark registration procedures and to strengthen the legal protection of trademarks in China, as well as clarifying minor uncertainties such as whether OEM (Original Equipment Manufacturers) in China making goods solely for export to foreign markets may nevertheless be infringing the trademark of the Chinese rights-holder. Another key change is the raising and tightening of the threshold for well-known trademarks in China as a result of the perception that the status of well-known trademark was previously too easily granted:

> This is quite a substantial change and actually creates some panic to the trademark owners.[3]

In addition, the revised law also prohibits the use of the phrase "well-known trademark" on promotional materials such as packaging and advertising. This prohibition aims at restoring the status of well-known trademark as a purely legal one instead of the marketing tool it had become to many domestic Chinese companies (Tan and Cui 2014).

One respondent suggested that the latest amendments to the Trademark Law were at least partly motivated by "fixing the TRIPS compliance gap."[4] For example, the amended provisions dealing with cancellation of a registered trademark for non-use consecutively for three years appears to directly parallel the relevant provision in Article 19 of the TRIPS Agreement with regards to whether a justifiable reason has to be given to explain the non-use of the trademark. However, it was also acknowledged by the same respondent that there were still some areas of the amended Trademark Law which may potentially fall short of full TRIPS compliance. For instance, paragraph 2 of Article 60 allows a seller of infringing goods to claim that they were not knowingly selling counterfeit products and escape from punishment. Providing that such sellers can produce a contract with a supplier, they will merely be ordered by the Administration for Industry and Commerce (AIC) to stop selling the infringing goods. However, producing such a contract and claiming lack of knowledge of infringement seems a low hurdle for a counterfeiter to meet to avoid any penalties and thus this provision has clear scope for abuse and provides a "very big loophole."[5]

Similarly, the PRC Copyright Law was amended by a Decision of the Standing Committee of the National People's Congress (NPC) on 26 February 2010, with the changes coming into effect on 1 April 2010.[6] These changes made to the Copyright Law in 2010 were minor, with the key change being the amendment of Article 4, following the WTO dispute with the United States (US) about whether works awaiting content review or failing content review would still be subject to protection under the Copyright Law. Consequently, the 2010 revisions were aimed primarily to give effect to the WTO dispute settlement body's ruling in case DS362 (World Trade Organisation 2010). In this dispute, the panel had ruled that China's failure to protect copyright in prohibited works (in other words, that are banned because of their illegal content) was inconsistent with TRIPS Article 9.1, as well as with TRIPS Article 41.1, as the copyright in such prohibited works could not be enforced (World Trade Organisation 2009). Consequently, the 2010 amendment to China's Copyright Law made it clear that works awaiting or denied approval would still be subject to copyright protection. The amended Article 4 now states: "Copyright holders shall not violate the Constitution or laws or jeopardise public interests when exercising their copyright. The State shall supervise and administer the publication and dissemination of works in accordance with the law." Accordingly, the state is reserving the power to only approve works following a stringent content review process; however, such works should still be able to claim protection under the amended Copyright Law.

Further amendments to the Copyright Law have also been drafted and released for comment on 6 June 2014, although they have not yet been finally passed into legislation (PRC Legislative Affairs Office of the State Council 2014). Nevertheless, the 2014 draft amendments are of interest because they propose wider reaching changes than the minor amendment made in 2010. The 2014 draft amendments would increase the damages available for infringement as well as increasing enforcement powers. The categories of works to which copyright may apply would also be expanded under the amendments to include "works of applied art" and "three-dimensional works." The protection period for photographic works would also be extended to the life of the creator plus 50 years which would bring such works in line with the period of protection offered to other copyrighted works. There may be a potential extension to the fair use exceptions under which copyright infringements are permissible by the addition of "other circumstances" to the list of exceptions; however, this vague category would very much depend on how it was applied in practice.

Finally, the draft amendments also deal with safe harbours for internet service providers (ISPs); new provisions on copyright licensing; and employee rights to copyrighted works created during their employment and would confirm the principle that the contract between employer and employee is paramount for the allocation of such rights. It is clear that by both increasing damages for infringement and broadening the potential categories of works which may be subject to copyright, the draft amendments to the PRC Copyright Law would continue to improve the copyright environment for rights-holders. This shift is echoed by several respondents who also noted significant changes in the copyright field: "in copyright, for copyright it has improved a lot, a lot. You see more and more people using the genuine Microsoft software."[7]

> I think that the most prominent changes are in the copyright area... I think more people are thinking that it is okay and it is reasonable for me to pay the authors for their effort to create those films, TV shows and books. And the IP as a whole in those areas, entertainment, film industry, it is just booming and people are more respecting those efforts.[8]

However, as the draft amendments have not yet been finalised and passed into legislation, it is too early to say how the amended Copyright Law might further shape the creative industries in China.[9]

Turning to patent protection, the PRC Patent Law was amended for the third time in late 2008, with the amended law coming into force on 1 October 2009,[10] following the unofficial but perceptible pattern previously established of reviewing the patent law every eight years. The Implementing Regulations for the Patent Law were also consequently amended and entered into force from 1 February 2010. The amendments show that the substantive law in China is still closely connected to the TRIPS Agreement; one of the key changes to the patent law was concerned with compulsory licensing which had been the subject of a 2005 protocol amending the TRIPS Agreement to take account of public health concerns in developing countries (World Trade Organisation 2005). In order to implement this Protocol into domestic law, Article 50 was added to the Patent Law enabling the process of compulsory licensing for pharmaceuticals (State Intellectual Property Office of the PRC 2010).[11]

On the other hand, the 2008 revision to the PRC Patent Law also illustrates the adaptation of the formal law to local domestic conditions; the revision process was initiated in 2005 with the first draft amendments released in August 2006 for comments. Thus, the revision process was not rushed and could be seen as attempting to respond to the feedback from relevant stakeholders in

the IP system. This responsiveness to rights-holders' concerns was ap
by several respondents, for example: respondent 15PHARMA01 discusseu …
latest proposed amendments and stated that "last week I just attended a seminar organised by the Chinese Patent Office to talk about it because they just
published the draft amendment to the patent law. So they had the seminar to
listen to the comments from companies." However, the same respondent tem-
pers the positive view of the frequent interaction between rights-holders and
law-makers by relaying their experiences of trying to get trade secrets removed
from employee compulsory remuneration regulations; it took several rounds of
comments and amendments before this specific suggestion was heeded.

In addition, the amendments to the Patent Law overall were widely viewed
by external commentators as the first in China which were led through domestic demands rather than in response to external pressure from trading partners
or in response to international legal obligations, such as those arising from
WTO accession (Yang and Yen 2009). As a result, there was a wide degree
of satisfaction with the patent-related legislation amongst respondents with
one commenting that the system was now "very close to European practice
in terms of acquiring IP rights."[12] Thus, all of the major IP-related legislation
has been amended over the past decade and the majority of these revisions
have been driven by the desire to better adapt the law to domestic conditions,
although some minor amendments have also been motivated by closer compliance with provisions of the TRIPS Agreement.

7.1.2 Changes in Enforcement

Compared to the systematic updating of the substantive IP legislation, the
enforcement options available to rights-holders in China have not undergone
such significant changes, as the main IP agencies remain essentially unchanged
in terms of bureaucratic structure, with the State Administration of Industry
and Commerce (SAIC) responsible for trademark registration and enforcement;
the General Administration of Customs the body responsible for enforcement
of IP at the border; whilst copyright is still dealt with by the National Copyright
Administration (under the General Administration of Press and Publication).
Finally, the State Intellectual Property Office (SIPO) remains the body responsible for patent registration and enforcement. However, a noticeable recent
change which was discussed by several interviewees was the establishment of
several specialist IP courts in Beijing, Shanghai and Guangzhou from late 2014
onwards. Prior to the establishment of these three specialised courts, there
already existed, from the mid-1990s onwards, specific intellectual property tribunals in many courts: by the end of 2013, such specific intellectual property
tribunals numbered around 410 (Li 2016, p. 304). Consequently, there was
already a recognised need to concentrate skilled and experienced personnel
into specialised IP fora for the purposes of dispute resolution. However, the
more recent establishment of these three specialist courts in Beijing, Shanghai

and Guangzhou was intended to funnel this expertise into regional centres and indeed, has been extremely positively received by rights-holders generally.

Several respondents independently mentioned these newly established specialist IP courts as a welcome positive development in the framework of IP protection in China. Indeed, recent statistics suggest that these courts are already proving popular amongst rights-holders, with the 2015 Supreme People's Court Work Report, issued 13 March 2016, reporting that these specialist courts concluded 9872 cases in 2015 alone (Supreme People's Court of the PRC 2016a). However, despite the relative success of these three pilot intellectual property courts, some commentators are also critical that there remains no central national appeal court for IP-related cases which "would greatly improve the judicial protection of intellectual property rights" by ensuring greater consistency (Li 2016, p. 317). Respondent 15LAW02 also expressed concern about the heavy workload for these specialist judges as case volumes increase and also that the quality of judgments issued may subsequently be compromised. Thus, it is to be hoped that resources provided to these specialist courts, in terms of the number of judges appointed, can keep pace with the continual growth in the number of IP-related civil cases filed, as clearly these courts are well regarded by respondents overall.

In terms of foreign rights-holders bringing litigation against infringers, there was a clear belief a decade ago that the foreign party would be disadvantaged by a perceived bias against foreign rights-holders. However, more than one respondent in 2015 referenced the high success rate of foreign companies bringing cases before Chinese courts, "probably because they're more prepared and they're spending more money."[13]Another respondent reported specifically on their analysis of win rates in patent infringement cases: "comparing the ratio for foreign patentee and domestic patentee to win the case, almost the same... maybe 70[%], maybe 72[%], only 2% difference, quite low, yeah."[14] This narrowing of the gap between foreign and domestic rights-holders is a significant shift from 2005 and should boost the confidence of all rights-holders that the courts can offer a viable option for enforcing their intellectual property. Nevertheless, the vast majority of civil litigation related to IP heard by the Chinese courts involves a Chinese plaintiff and a Chinese defendant, with one respondent 15LAW01 estimating that 95% of cases are between Chinese parties; thus, foreign rights-holders are largely absent. On the other hand, when foreign rights-holders do bring civil litigation against infringers, experiences from the 2015 respondents suggests that they should feel quite confident about the perceived equity and fairness in the civil litigation process.

Conversely, there can still be a certain degree of reluctance on the part of major multinational corporations (MNCs) to bring civil litigation in China if their IP rights are infringed which may be as a result of the low levels of damages typically awarded or due to difficulties in obtaining sufficient evidence of infringements. One respondent from a large MNC operating in China for several years admitted that their company has deliberately never brought civil litigation in China to tackle IP infringements; not only was it thought to have

potentially negative consequences for the company's reputatic
in China, but it was also thought to be impossible to catch ⌐
ultimately responsible for the infringements rather than the "small n ,
cally caught red-handed in the infringing factory or warehouse. Thus, their 11
enforcement strategy instead focused on building relations with key administrative enforcement agencies such as the local AICs.

A further significant enforcement issue which appears to have persisted
since the initial research project began in 2005, which may also hamper rights-
holders in tackling infringers in court, is the issue of inadequate damages. One
respondent from the pharmaceutical sector estimated average compensation
across the whole IP litigation field at only around 80,000 RMB per case.[15]
Indeed, respondents mentioned damages as not just insufficient to act as a
deterrent:

> The penalties often aren't there at the level that will really put that person in jail
> or make them pay... sometimes it's just the cost of doing business, people pay the
> fine, open up a new shop next week.[16]

They also discussed the damages as insufficient to even cover the costs of
bringing an action against the infringer:

> So it still remains that some trademark owners cannot cover their legal costs with
> the damages. Actually one of our clients complained about this recently.[17]

Therefore, although there have been some high-profile damage awards
recently[18] with large amounts being awarded to rights-holders, the impression
remains that the typical award of damages is insufficient to fully compensate
rights-holders for the infringement. This issue of low damages was also highlighted as a major concern in 2005 and arguably little progress has been made
in this area in the past decade. Another frustration which remains with the
contemporary system of IP protection is with difficulties in gathering evidence
of potential infringements. For example, if a patent is granted covering a manufacturing process, it is difficult to access a potential infringer's factory to gather
evidence![19] However, it could be argued that such frustrations are not unique
to China and arise more from the nature of IP infringements being an opaque
activity.[20]

In contrast to civil enforcement by the courts, criminal enforcement was cited
by several respondents as a potentially positive means of pursuing infringers
which was used frustratingly infrequently, with one respondent's own estimates
suggesting only 2% of raids result in a transfer to criminal liability.[21] This low
rate of transfer from administrative agencies to criminal liability is also reflected
in the official statistics which showed only 2684 concluded criminal IP cases
in 2007 compared to more than 100,000 cases dealt with through administrative sanctions and 17,395 civil IP cases handled by the local courts (Liu
2010, p. 141). Nevertheless, the past decade has seen a rapid criminalisation

of IP infringements witnessed in both the expansion of criminal IP offences in the substantive law and the rapid and consistent rise of transfers from administrative agencies to criminal courts (Liu 2010, p. 153). This increase in the criminalisation of IP infringers is welcomed by respondents, amongst whom there was a clear consensus that criminal liability for infringers was seen as a more effective deterrent compared to facing administrative or civil consequences because "criminal action is mostly effective in China. The infringer, they don't care about the economic fine but they do care about their personal safety issues."[22] As a result, there was an unmistakeable desire for the threshold at which criminal liability can be imposed to be further lowered and the rate of transfer from administrative to criminal liability to continue to increase.

An interesting issue in the enforcement of intellectual property rights in general is the question of who is seen to be the "victim" of IP infringements? Rights-holders would clearly say that they are the victims as it is their exclusive rights which are being breached and as such, they should play a key role in the prosecution of any infringers. On the other hand, enforcement authorities now more commonly perceive the "victim" to be the public, for example, innocent individual consumers who may be deceived or even harmed by counterfeit goods. This increased focus on the rights of individual consumers reflects the consumer "revolution" said to have taken place in China since the reform and opening-up era began in 1978 (Wu 2014). Prior to 1978, the notion of individual consumer choice and corresponding consumer rights were completely unknown in China as the socialist economy was directed by the state and relied on collective production and distribution. However, as China began to transition to a socialist market economy throughout the 1980s, the role of the individual consumer in selecting from a range of goods and services rose to prominence. Nevertheless, the focus on individual consumers as the true "victim" of IP infringements does push rights-holders out of the enforcement process. Although this sidelining in the enforcement process may be a source of considerable frustration for rights-holders, the countervailing focus on the public as the victim could actually be seen as a significant prompt for the improved enforcement environment. As enforcing intellectual property rights becomes more aligned with the central government policy focus on improving rights for individual consumers, IP enforcement should continue to become more and more consistent.

However, despite clear changes and improvements in the domestic enforcement environment, the export of counterfeit products from China to major trading partners such as the US and the European Union (EU) continues to be a concern. China continues to be the origin of 80% of counterfeit goods detected at the EU's borders according to the Report on EU Customs Enforcement of Intellectual Property Rights 2014 (European Commission 2015). Furthermore, United States Trade Representative (USTR) annual reports on China's WTO compliance still show concerns about the IP system in China; for example, the 2015 report highlighted "serious problems with intellectual property rights enforcement in China, including in the area of trade secrets" as a particular area of concern (United States Trade Representative 2015, p. 4). As a result, although respondents were positive about the changes they had witnessed in the IP enforcement system in China, enforcement practices remain far from perfect, with issues such as the evidentiary burden on plaintiffs or the level of damages routinely awarded persisting from ten years earlier.

In terms of enforcement, the changes that China made have evidently increased formal compliance with the TRIPS Agreement, for example, an increase in the availability of criminal liability by lowering the quantitative threshold for liability. However, there is little evidence that the improvements in the IP enforcement environment in China were primarily motivated by the desire to increase compliance with the TRIPS Agreement. Rather, the changes in enforcement of IP rights witnessed over the past decade have been largely driven by domestic demands. Thus, both legislative and enforcement changes, although undeniably resulting in positive improvements for rights-holders, have not been primarily driven by compliance with the TRIPS Agreement.

7.1.3   Changes in Domestic Chinese Rights-Holders

Alongside changes in the legislation and enforcement aspects of the IP system, there has also been a noteworthy proliferation in domestic Chinese registrations for IP, particularly patents. It is irrefutable that patent filings by Chinese companies have increased significantly, with the number of domestic Chinese patent applications for inventions more than doubling in the past five years according to data from the SIPO (State Council of the PRC 2016). However, there is some scepticism about whether this so-called patent "explosion" can really be held to be a proxy for Chinese innovation. In other words, some commentators argue that the rise in patent filings reflects more low-quality applications rather than high-quality innovations. In addition, some analysis suggests that the majority of the increase, particularly in overseas filings by Chinese companies, can be largely attributed to a very small number of large companies, predominantly in the information and communications technology (ICT) sector (Eberhardt et al. 2011).

One reason for the sharp rise in patent filings in the twenty-first century is the incentives provided by the government in order to encourage innovation. A recent study carried out by the EU Chamber of Commerce in China found over ten national-level quantitative patent targets, with a further 150 provincial- or municipal-level quantitative patent targets (Prud'homme 2012). Furthermore, several respondents independently mentioned the substantial effect of government incentives or subsidies on local Chinese companies' behaviour in the IP field; for example,

> Lots of Chinese domestic companies are trying to harness the IPR protection to protect their brand and technologies as well. And this is mostly motivated or incentivised by the Chinese government to promote a very creative environment

for those companies. For example, a company that applied for a patent, invention patent, and it is awarded, they'd be eligible to receive tax reduction.[23]

However, there remains significant and widespread doubts about the quality of the patents filed as a result of such governmental incentives (Prud'homme 2012). This doubt about a consequent rise in the quality of patents filed was echoed by one respondent from the pharmaceutical sector who specifically noted that "if we look at the chemistry or the pharma or the biotech, actually I haven't seen the big change on the quality side."[24] Nevertheless, even if we accept that the quality of Chinese filings falls behind the quantity of the filings, some of the patents filed are still of extremely high quality.

> In terms of quality, it will take time. But we should be aware. If we have the quantity accumulated, definitely the quality will come. That's my view.[25]

> There are quality issues in China, definitely, but in the midst of this tsunami of IP coming out of China there are some very valuable gems, and the West really needs to wake up to what is happening.[26]

In addition, one respondent working closely with start-up companies in Beijing noted that such governmental incentives were still useful for initiating an innovative mentality, even if they initially only led to a glut of low-quality filings:

> Of course, it's facilitating innovation because people need that incentive to at least start filing. Even if it's not the quality, even if it's you know, there's no promise, even if they do not want to commercialise it.[27]

On the other hand, although respondents were broadly in agreement that domestic Chinese enterprises were not yet fully exploiting their intellectual property, several examples of top Chinese enterprises leading the way in terms of recognition of their IP rights were identified and discussed without prompting, such as ZTE, Huawei and Alibaba. Such leading companies, predominantly in the technology sector, were perceived as sharing similar concerns about IP enforcement with foreign rights-holders from MNCs: "all those already international companies, they share the same view as us because they are facing the very same problems as we are facing."[28] Additionally, other examples were given of Chinese companies commercially exploiting their registered IP to unprecedented levels. For instance, in March 2014, Tralin Paper secured financing of 7.9 billion RMB from a syndicate led by China Development Bank by using their substantial IP portfolio as collateral (Chinapaper.net 2014). This was seen as a hugely significant step forward in the wider recognition of IP in a commercial setting in that even if the value of the IP was vastly overestimated, "the fact that they chose intellectual property as the window dressing shows IP has really arrived in China."[29]

The role of domestic rights-holders in further developing an effective system of IP rules in China is undeniable; there is still felt to be "a clear dissonance between formal IP law 'in books' and actual IP norms in practice in China," which can be reduced by policy-makers motivated by such domestic innovation (Bruun and Zhang 2016, pp. 60–1). The role of domestic Chinese rights-holders as essential to sustain long-term reforms in the IP system was also recognised by respondents in the 2005 phase of the study. For example, this international lawyer highlighted: "Things are improving and will continue to improve, with the main driver being the Chinese companies' desire to be IP creators and licensors and not just IP users and licensees."[30] In other words, domestic innovation is key to tackling the "enforcement gap" identified in 2005 and analysed in Chap. 6. Consequently, as domestic rights-holders become not only more numerous but also more reliant on their own IP for continued future growth, the central government cannot ignore their demands for an improved IP system. Overall, it is clear that a number of changes have been made in the legislation relevant to IP registration and enforcement as well as slight improvements in the enforcement mechanisms as well. The number of domestic IP rights-holders has also surged in the past decade and these changes have all led to an improved and more effective intellectual property system overall. The next section will attempt to consider some reasons for these positive changes by applying the comprehensive model of compliance proposed by Jacobson and Brown Weiss (1998).

7.2 Factors Contributing to the Current State of the IP System: Explaining the Changes from 2005 to 2015

7.2.1 Parameters

In terms of the existing comprehensive model of compliance which has already been applied to the state of the post-TRIPS IP system in 2005–6, the IP system in 2015 could still be judged as being affected by many similar factors. The first category of country-specific factors that may have continued to affect China's compliance with its international obligations consists of parameters which include basic characteristics of the country such as the previous behaviour of the country; the history and culture of the country; the physical size of the country; the physical variation within the country; and the number of neighbours that the country has. As in 2005, those factors classed as parameters were not identified by respondents as very significant apart from the vast size of China which was felt to continue to contribute to problems in implementing the formal IP legislation:

There is some issues or problems or challenges, it's more in implementation phase because China is so big (*sic*).[31]

In addition, the vast size of China was also thought to be at least partly responsible for evident inconsistencies in the enforcement of IP rights across the country. For example, there was some consensus amongst respondents that the state of IP protection in developed cities such as Beijing, Shanghai and Guangzhou was commendable. However, other areas were not perceived as being so strict about cracking down on IP infringements:

> So in some inner lands, such as Guizhou or in Tibet or in Xinjiang, those areas, the IP system is not as professional as in the east coast of China.[32]

This pattern of uneven enforcement seems to have changed little in the past decade and closely echoes remarks made by respondents in 2005 and reported in Chap. 6.

In terms of the previous behaviour relating to IP infringements, as in 2005–6, respondents infrequently referred to China's pre-reform legal system as influential upon the contemporary system. Only one respondent raised the issue of the short history of the modern Chinese legal system as an explanation for the state of the contemporary IP system:

> The general people, the public, do not have a strong sense on law as western countries because we have a special culture over 2,000 years of old system. So we only have maybe two decades or three decades' years of the legal system.[33]

The changes discussed by respondents in the most recent phase of the study were almost all focused on the past five to ten years, suggesting that the pace of rapid developments seen in the IP system in China in that time makes the previous system which existed prior to WTO accession in December 2001 almost irrelevant. Turning to cultural values such as the influence of Confucianism or socialism upon the modern system, respondents in 2015 were if anything even more dismissive than those respondents a decade earlier, with only one respondent independently mentioning either of these concepts:

> It's difficult for Western people to understand why Chinese do not respect IP too much. My personal view is because before the 1980s everything belongs to the country, everything belongs to the Communist Party. So at that time I still remember when I was a kid we always tried to take something from the factory my father was working at, take something back to home without anyone noticing.[34]

This supports the notion that although cultural values are often identified in the academic literature as continuing to play a significant role in the modern intellectual property system in China, the majority of respondents dealing with the system day-to-day do not recognise either Confucianism or socialism as major influences. Again, this is a significant departure from much of the academic literature which attributes any inefficiencies in the current Chinese IP system to the deep-rooted and persistent values of collective rights and shared ownership (Alford 1996).

7.2.2   *Fundamental Factors*

Moving to fundamental factors, the most significant in 2005 were found to be the lack of awareness of IP rights, local protectionism and a lack of consistency in enforcement. These factors were broadly still at issue in 2015, although significant progress appears to have been made in all three areas. In particular, a noticeable improvement from 2005 was the increase of awareness of IP rights generally in China:

> For the public side, for normal people they have more understanding of the IP system. Or I believe today if you asked the normal people, at least they heard of patent or IP but ten years ago there only were a few people who heard of these kind of words. So this could be some improvement.[35]

In the 2005 study, respondents to the questionnaire were asked to choose from a list of possible improvements to the IP system those improvements that they felt would make the most significant difference to the current system of protection. Unsurprisingly, given that a lack of public awareness was selected as the most significant contributory factor to the system in 2005, campaigns for greater public awareness were highlighted by most respondents to the 2005 questionnaire as the most important potential improvement that they wished to see.[36]

Consequently, it is clear that there was a need for awareness of IP rights to be significantly improved and such an increase in awareness was clearly perceived by respondents in the 2015 phase of the study both amongst the general public and amongst domestic Chinese enterprises, who "when they are talking about IP they are quite positive because they can see the benefit from it."[37] This recognition by domestic companies of the importance of IP for future sustained economic growth was recognised as a key change from just ten years earlier when IP rights were often ignored by local Chinese businesses in the pursuit of short-term profits. Awareness through education in schools was also mentioned by one respondent who mentioned that their child of around 10 or 11 years "drew a picture of how to play a game like chess, kind of chess, how to play, have some rules how to play, and write a lot on the picture. And [they] said 'It's designed by me, and the other person cannot copy the design of me, so the copyright belong to me."[38] Consequently, this respondent was optimistic that by inculcating knowledge and awareness of individual intellectual property rights from such a young age that, in time, respect for IP would naturally become more widespread and ingrained within Chinese society.

However, although such an increase in awareness was widely applauded by respondents, a note of caution was sounded by several who distinguished between awareness of the key words or concepts associated with IP such as "patent" or "'trademark" and awareness of the full potential or commercial value of such concepts. This was perceived to be a problem within the general public: "a taxi driver would know what intellectual property is, what copyright is, but they just don't (care)."³⁹ Perhaps more worryingly, this lack of full understanding of the nature and value of intellectual property rights was also recognised within domestic Chinese rights-holders:

> The major purpose is to get a [letters] patent, to get the certificate maybe for owners or for advertisements or for maybe to tell their clients 'Oh, we have patents'. But nowadays, a small percentage of Chinese companies realise the real value of patents.⁴⁰

In other words, many domestic companies are perceived as seeking to register their intellectual property rights (IPR) not as part of a wider IP strategy, but rather just to "attract the consumers, to attract the investor."⁴¹ This perception was also mirrored by my personal experiences attending a trade fair in Shanghai in March 2015 at which numerous local small- and medium-sized enterprises (SMEs) were using the number of registered patents and trademarks that they held in their promotional material as some kind of "trophy" or signal that they were a successful and ambitious company. However, there was little corresponding sense of awareness of such IP as strategic tools to further develop and expand their business. Thus, increased awareness, both amongst the general public and amongst local businesses, was widely recognised and praised by many respondents, but there was still a lingering sense that many Chinese rights-holders still did not either truly value or seek to fully exploit their IP.

The second significant fundamental factor, local protectionism, was also independently mentioned by some respondents as still a persistent and major concern preventing rights-holders from effective enforcement across the whole of China. For example, 15LUX01 highlighted problems experienced in Guangdong province as a regional economy focused on the manufacture of cosmetic products and fast-moving consumer goods: "the local government, they want to protect the economy, you know... the local development is their priority." Local protectionism was also experienced through inconsistent levels of transparency demonstrated by local AICs, with some issuing detailed notifications following a raid whilst others did not. Equally, another respondent from a multinational electronics company highlighted local protectionism as the biggest challenge facing companies operating in China:

> [The biggest] challenge is how to convince not the central officials, central government but more important is local officials, why it is important for their local economy rather than ... they are not talking about the whole of China but they are talking about my province, my city, my employment, my tax, my GDP.⁴²

Local protectionism is also frequently recognised by external commentators as the primary obstacle to effective IP enforcement in contemporary China (Mercurio 2012). Nevertheless, local protectionism was also identified as an area in which noticeable improvement had been made over the past 10 to 12 years:

I think local protectionism is getting less and less influential on the whole system; okay? So ten years ago, see ten years ago you see, if you are a foreign company, probably ten years ago is a little bit better, let's say 12 years ago; 12 years ago if a foreign company is suing you know, a Chinese company, then it is very likely ... of course the local court tends to protect the Chinese company, particularly in those medium-sized cities or small cities.[43]

In addition, as stated above, both Beijing and Shanghai were praised as cities where local protectionism was no longer a concern and where the relevant administrative authorities were thought to act more professionally and transparently than in other less prosperous provinces, often located in the Western or inland regions of China. For example, in terms of judicial expertise and consistency, one respondent reported that "judges, especially in Beijing and Shanghai... is very experienced. They have very high level, very experienced. And they can provide quite deep comments on the merits of the case."[44]

Closely linked to the issue of local protectionism is the problem of inconsistent enforcement. Again, respondents report such inconsistency manifesting in higher levels of administrative enforcement in some more developed regions with lower levels of administrative enforcement in less developed inland areas. However, inconsistent enforcement is also experienced in judicial enforcement: "all IP judges realise that we are on the same law, one law in China, we need you know more consistent judgment to be made in different ... by different courts,"[45] as well as in dealings with customs enforcement, with some customs officials involving trademark owners to a greater extent than others when, for example, verifying the seized goods as counterfeit.[46]

The wider issue of inconsistency within judicial decision-making has also been addressed through the introduction of the Guiding Cases System in 2010.[47] Although not formally binding, People's Courts at all levels are now required to refer to relevant Guiding Cases when adjudicating similar cases according to Article 7 of the 2010 Provisions of the Supreme People's Court concerning Case Guidance Work (Supreme People's Court of the PRC 2010). As of July 2016, the Supreme People's Court (SPC) has issued 64 guiding cases in 13 batches (Supreme People's Court of the PRC 2016b). However, the SPC was slow to begin to select cases relating to intellectual property issues as Guiding Cases. The first IP-related Guiding Case (No. 20) involving a patent infringement dispute was only issued in late 2013. However, despite a slow start, "the SPC's confidence in providing guidance in intellectual property and unfair competition through GCs seems to have grown" (Gechlik 2015). Consequently, since then, a further nine Guiding Cases have been issued which deal with issues broadly related to intellectual property rights, including patent infringement, copyright, trademark and unfair competition.[48] However, there is still some scepticism about the significance of the Guiding Cases on judicial practice and it is likely that some degree of inconsistency will continue to exist in judicial decision-making for the foreseeable future.

7.2.3   Proximate Factors

The final category of factors to consider under the detailed model of compliance outlined above in Chap. 2 is proximate factors. Such factors are specific to the system under analysis and incorporate influences such as the capacity of the existing agencies to implement the system effectively and the role of other organisations in pressurising for or monitoring changes in the system. In terms of the quality of the personnel involved in the operation of the intellectual property system in China, respondents seemed less concerned about the knowledge levels of the relevant personnel. On the other hand, the workload of key personnel such as judges was a concern for several respondents: "The cases are driving up, the volume is driving up. It made the judges crazy and probably they have to like decide two cases in a day."[49]

"And they have a quite high criteria for IP judges you know, your Beijing IP Court in total they only have 25 judges, IP judges. Every judge … if I'm a judge, I have a judge assistant, I have a team. Each team has to handle you know, 150 cases a year. So this is a very heavy burden."[50] In other words, although this respondent clearly believes that the judges deciding IP cases are well qualified and experienced, they still expressed fears that the pressure of the workload may have a detrimental effect on the quality and consistency of the judgments being made. Specifically, respondent 15LAW03 observed that although judges are very experienced, their heavy workload has a direct effect on the number of appeals allowed:

> Because it is easy to maintain a decision, but it will be quite complicated to revoke a decision. So you must provide detailed analysis of why you consider it is wrong; otherwise the panels do not agree to it. But if you maintain a decision, it's very easy.

Consequently, although respondents seemed to agree that judges were on the whole highly competent, nevertheless there remained some serious concerns that the steady annual increases in cases filed with the courts placed objectionable pressure on those judges to deal with cases quickly.

On the other hand, respondents did occasionally express some disquiet about other personnel working within the contemporary Chinese IP system. In particular, some respondents in the field of patents felt that it was difficult to find people with both the necessary technical background as well as knowledge of IP and the strategic awareness of how best to exploit such IP: "And that kind of expertise, just from a human resource perspective, is very, very difficult to find."[51] This particular shortage was also noted by respondent 15LAW03, who noted: "Such patent attorneys which can match the demand from those hi-tech companies are very few, they're difficult to find." In addition, respondent 15LUX01 also identified that AICs may lack enough resources "to really investigate" and find out who the real bosses are behind the wide-scale infringements. Thus, the knowledge levels of the relevant personnel within the IP system which had been a significant concern in 2005 was much less of a concern in 2015, with the exception of high-quality patent attorneys whose numbers may not be in keeping abreast with the increasing volume of high-tech companies in China. On the other hand, there are still some suspicions that the administrative capacity of key agencies such as the AIC could be further enhanced with additional resources dedicated to tackling IP infringements.

The final category of proximate factors that may influence China's long-term compliance with the TRIPs Agreement is the influence of non-governmental organisations (NGOs). However, organisations concerned with intellectual property tend to be commercial groups, often consisting of businesses with strong intellectual property rights. Therefore, the influence of NGOs in the intellectual property arena in China remains predominantly based on pressure from key groups of companies, both domestic and international. As in 2005, the main organisation pressurising for better protection with regard to intellectual property in China is the Quality Brands Protection Committee (QBPC 2016). Although equivalent bodies for Chinese enterprises are beginning to emerge, these are not viewed "as effective and powerful as the brand protection committees of foreign companies, no, no."[52] Again reflecting the position from a decade earlier, a number of respondents recognised the important role that QBPC plays in helping to shape China's IP system: "Certainly the QBPC plays many important roles in these changes. As long as there is a law going to be publicised, we always provide a kind of position paper trying to voice our concerns."[53]

In addition to involvement in legislative amendments, the QBPC is also seen as playing an important role in providing training to key personnel within the IP system. For example, "QBPC has a custom committee you know, they also arrange a lot of the training programmes with the key local custom officers and they invite members to present their brands for locals, so that local custom officials can be familiarised with their brands."[54] However, one noticeable change from the role of QBPC in 2005 is the alignment between QBPC's interests and the interests of domestic (particularly large) Chinese companies: "I think now, even in the QBPC, for a lot of the things we also aligned with kind of the Chinese companies, so we can give the same voice."[55] This represents a shift from 2005 when the role of QBPC was only mentioned by a few foreign respondents; in 2015 the QBPC was discussed by a wide variety of respondents in the context of how change can be made in the IP system.

Overall, there were some evident changes in the significance of proximate factors affecting the current IP system in China. Respondents seemed less concerned about the knowledge levels of relevant personnel than a decade earlier, but on the other hand, the workload of key personnel such as judges was a concern for several respondents and there are still some fears that the administrative capacity of key agencies such as the AIC could be further enhanced with additional resources dedicated to tackling IP infringements. The QBPC remains an important positive influence both on the formal legislation and on improving the enforcement environment on the ground, but its goals are now more closely aligned to those of domestic Chinese companies. There are also other factors which emerged from discussions with respondents which fall outside of these categories and which will now be considered.

7.2.4   Other Factors

Compared to the 2005–6 interviews, it was noticeable that WTO accession and the TRIPS Agreement and consequent compliance were not mentioned and discussed as frequently. However, seven respondents did independently mention either the WTO or the TRIPS Agreement in the context of China's IP system, but usually as a historic "milestone"[56] in the ongoing revisions of China's formal IP legislation and also to distinguish from subsequent revisions. Indeed, one respondent went so far as to claim that China's IP-related laws are "totally compliant with the requirement of TRIPS and the legislation is no problem."[57] This was certainly not a unanimous view; however, the enforcement gap which was identified in the first stage of the research project and outlined in Chap. 6 has undoubtedly lessened, as both the legislation and enforcement environment continue to improve.

Technology has been a surprisingly significant contributor to the IP system in China as technological developments have necessitated shifts in business models. For example, the growth of online retailing has been stratospheric, with domestic companies such as Alibaba becoming influential players in the Chinese market. This is certainly not a unique trend experienced solely by China, but has nevertheless played an important role in recent changes to the Chinese IP system. However, the downside of technological innovations in the Chinese economy is that rights-holders may then experience more difficulties in enforcing their IP:

> But now we are facing online, that's even more difficult because the online platform will enable all those people called big fish who are hidden further below, it's almost invisible. And we're also, to be frank, we're closing thousands of online shops every month but they are not our true enemy because they are not manufacturers, they only have individual or small shops selling fake goods, sometimes intentionally and sometimes they are also being cheated, they don't know, they don't have knowledge to tell. So we have to do this, we have to educate them and make them pay some price and so they learn.[58]

Generally, some of the factors which had been identified in 2005 as critical factors affecting the effectiveness of the IP system in China, such as local protectionism, inadequate damages and inconsistent enforcement, were still prominent in 2015. On the other hand, clear changes had been made in other areas, with the administrative capacity of key personnel within the IP system much less of a concern than previously. Finally, factors such as technological changes also emerged as influences on the Chinese IP system which had not existed a decade earlier.

7.3 Exploring the Process of Change

The process of how the post-TRIPS IP system has changed over the past decade will now be considered—have these changes been top-down or bottom-up? What have been the key drivers behind the continual incremental improvements observed in the IP system in China? Overall, the importance of central government commitment is widely seen as the most critical driving force behind the changes made in the Chinese IP system:

> It's mainly driving internally; it's mainly driving from the Chinese government itself. We have to give credit, especially in Beijing, our central government if you talk to high-level, ministry-level; they really have a very good understanding of long-term vision why IP is important.[59]

The emphasis by respondents in this research project on the key role of the central government as a driver for change in the intellectual property system is also reflected in the academic literature. For example, Crookes (2010) contrasts IP regime evolution in China and India and concludes that while market-driven development is key in India, state-sponsored initiatives are still the most important driver of change in the Chinese IP system.

Indeed, the significance of stronger commitment from the central government was also recognised by respondents in the 2005 study, who selected this factor as the second most significant improvement that they would like to see in the IP system in China.[60] The role of the government (and the potential for increased focus on tackling IP issues) was explicitly discussed by several respondents in 2005, particularly in the context of improving enforcement efforts nationwide: "I believe that if, if the central government is taking an interest, then something will happen in the whole country."[61] Thus, the shift in official governmental policy towards greater emphasis on strengthening intellectual property rights was not only identified as crucial by respondents in 2005 but was also recognised as the most significant driver behind improvements witnessed over the past decade by respondents in 2015.

Furthermore, the strong level of central government commitment is closely linked to economic policy goals of diversifying the economy away from low-end manufacturing for export towards more high-tech innovation:

> And actually in my personal opinion, the Chinese government wants to encourage inventions, especially in the recent two years. The Chinese economy experienced dramatic change in these years, it's quite difficult for real estates and the finance, all met big problems. So the government want to encourage innovations to change the structure of the economy.[62]

Therefore, the renewed emphasis on intellectual property rights by central government policy-making reflects the official goal of increasing innovation in the economy. For example, the National IPR Strategy released in 2008 not only contained detailed and extensive proposals of potential improvements and amendments for the Chinese IP system, but also "represented an intention from the top political entity to narrow the gap between law and norms" (Bruun and Zhang 2016, p. 61). More recently, China's 13th five-year plan was approved in late October 2015 and the communiqué issued at the time suggested a shift in emphasis from focusing on solely economic development to more balanced and sustainable development in the future. Analysts at Barclays assessed the frequency of some key terms in the past four five-year plans and noted that mentions of "innovation" had intensified from 26 mentions in the 10th five-year plan, to 31 in the 11th five-year plan, 49 in the 12th five-year plan and 71 in the most recent 13th five-year plan (Moshinsky 2015), underlining the increased focus of the central government on increasing innovation in the economy.

In addition, there is a clear policy link at the central government level between an increased focus on strengthening intellectual property rights and enhancing economic development: "now we want to climb to the upper level of the manufacture chain, we want to encourage the local brands to establish their own brand."[63] However, this increased focus on IP is not just linked to the economic goal of moving from "Made in China" to "Created in China" (Keane 2006), but also reflects the growing role of the consumer in the Chinese economy. In other words, as China's emerging middle class continues to grow, such discerning individual consumers will demand higher quality non-counterfeited products (Li 2010); as this respondent observed: "the general public being richer and more able to afford the real products."[64] It is apparent from any casual visit to the main cities of China that "several years ago a lot of people thought they could buy pirated copies of CDs on the street, and now it is very difficult to see this"[65] and indeed my own observations from visiting China over the past few years suggest that such blatant selling of fake goods is nowhere near as commonplace as it once was.

In addition to the critical role of individual consumers, the role of domestic Chinese rights-holders was widely seen to be of increasing importance as a pressure for improvement within the IP system as a whole because the government is seen as more likely to listen and respond to Chinese enterprises than foreign rights-holders. Indeed, some respondents felt that if they represented a MNC in China or international organisation, then their point of view would be dismissed or ignored without due consideration:

When the foreign companies, when we are talking with the government, the government always says ah, you are representing the foreign voice ((laughs)).[66]

Whereas it was recognised as key particularly for foreign rights-holders to align their own interests with domestic Chinese rights-holders in order to assert more influence over governmental policy in the IP arena:

They do listen to the local companies' requests and demands. So we want to leverage that.[67]

A further influence on the process of change in the IP system in China is the time needed for legal transplants to be embedded into the local legal culture. This was certainly recognised by several respondents, not only at a macro level:

> Improvement can be made every day, step by step. No reform can be done overnight. So I think we need to be patient. Every legal reform needs to be reliant on your economic reality. China is a developing country, the step cannot be as big as the UK or US.[68]

In other words, there remained some sympathy with the notion that had been more frequently expressed in 2005 that developing an effective IP system from scratch is a long process and cannot be achieved in the short term. However, there was also some cynicism about this notion that an effective IP system in China is just a matter of being patient for several decades while China "catches up" with one respondent labelling it "not a good excuse."[69]

Closely linked to the notion that further improvements in the Chinese IP environment are just a natural progression as a matter of time is the proposition that a generational shift needs to take place before greater respect for IP can be embedded both into the Chinese business world and also into Chinese society. As one respondent noted:

> One of the challenges is the current generation of executives in many of the companies, especially in the manufacturing sectors, are people that... you know guys in their fifties and sixties and even maybe late forties that grew up at a time when IP really didn't matter. So they're used to this vision where you get things by stealing, you get things by copying, you don't have to worry about IP, no need to spend money on a patent search. So the old guard are still kind of resisting what the young guard recognises as essential, and what the government also recognises as essential. So there's some slow learning there that might take another decade.[70]

Therefore, it might well be necessary to wait until the next generation of business leaders take charge to see a real shift in the attitudes of many Chinese enterprises. Equally, it could be informative to look at the next generation of business leaders emerging in China; many millennials are focused on creating their own start-ups focused on short-term returns and primarily within the Chinese market; so despite having a much better understanding of the nature and value of IP, they may not require a detailed IP strategy in order to achieve their business goals. As reported by 15SERVICES01: "for the Chinese market, because of the sheer size you know, everyone is talking about capturing market share; you can still do that even without any innovation or very minimal innovation." Consequently, although many Chinese companies are beginning to become more aware of the potential value of their IP, there are still domestic enterprises for whom IP is still not a priority in their business strategy.

Moving now from considering internal pressure, to analysing pressure from outside of China, there appears to have been a shift in perception of the potential of external pressure to further shape the inner workings of the IP system in

China. In 2005, many respondents felt that greater international cooperation and collaboration would be a significant step to improve the IP system in China at that time. Greater international cooperation was suggested by respondents in 2005 as the third most significant improvement that they wished to see in the IP system in China and was stressed as potentially benefitting the IP system in various ways, through moulding the attitude of the government, through improving the expertise of the personnel and through providing positive incentives for consistently enforcing IP laws and regulations: "In addition, the government may promote cooperation both nationally and internationally, to keep increasing the quality of personnel from related professions, and thus to ensure that the relevant laws and regulations are implemented smoothly."[71]

However, the potential for greater international cooperation was also explicitly contrasted with the perceived confrontational attitude taken by some key trading partners such as the US: "Instead of criticizing only, maybe more efforts should be devoted to the countries working together constructively to tackle the problem which will ultimately benefit everyone."[72] Therefore, in 2005, respondents indicated that greater cooperation from international partners or organisations had the potential to stimulate further improvements in the Chinese IP system rather than just provoke resentment. Consequently, there has been a rise in such cooperation programmes, often with a particular focus on knowledge exchange and capacity-building amongst relevant personnel.[73] In addition, such technical assistance programmes are also viewed politically as effective soft power mechanisms (Crookes 2014). Conversely, such programmes have also been criticised as only effective at influencing national-level policy and having no effect on local or regional enforcement which is where problems may remain (Wyzycka and Hasmath 2016).

On the other hand, respondents in 2015 seemed to draw a distinction between the external pressure to improve IP which had previously been exerted on the Chinese government by foreign governments (particularly the US) and the contemporary IP system which is much more affected by domestic stakeholders and interests: "I think in the past we can say we protect China for the IP because pressure from foreign brands, foreign government, foreign brand owners but now they need us to protect because of the request of Chinese companies you know."[74] This disconnect between the external pressure from foreign governments to raise the level of intellectual property protection as opposed to the internal pressure to focus on local economic development is also identified by a respondent from the pharmaceutical industry who noted: "I'd say ten years ago when we talked about IP protection, normally the international community will say ah, this, but for the local government and domestic companies, they say ah, something different, we are in the two directions."[75] This emphasis on the increasingly powerful role of domestic Chinese companies as key stakeholders in the Chinese IP system is echoed by a number of respondents and summed up by respondent 15LAW01 who divided the changes in the IP system in China into three distinct phases. The first two phases (in response to pressure from the US government in the early to mid-1990s and in response to WTO accession at the start of the twenty-first century) were "all because of the outside pressure." In contrast, the latest legislative changes and changes to the enforcement process have not been impelled by demands from external governments or organisations: "And the third one, which is quite interesting, is purely from inside, there's no outside pressure."[76]

Thus, the process of China's IP system adapting to local conditions over the past decade and more has resulted from a combination of increased commitment from central government to move towards an innovation-based economy; a surge in domestic rights-holders who are also increasingly pressuring for more effective protection of their valuable intellectual property; the natural internalisation of the transplanted norms in the post-TRIPS legislation over time; and the shift in external pressure from coercion towards cooperation.

7.4   Summary and Conclusion

In terms of the overall changes observed in China's post-TRIPS intellectual property system in the long-term, it is clear that steady progress has continued to be made since the implementation of TRIPS standards into domestic legislation in the few years immediately following formal accession in December 2001. Furthermore, it is clear to even a casual observer of China's legal system that not only were a number of legislative changes promulgated in the decade between 2005 and 2015, but significant changes were also made to the enforcement framework in China. These changes were mirrored by noteworthy shifts in both the attitude and awareness of IP in wider Chinese society as well as a substantial increase in the number of domestic Chinese rights-holders influencing the operation and effectiveness of the wider IP system.

In terms of the IP-related legislation, all of the major laws were subject to at least one change or amendment during this period from 2005 to 2015, but enforcement options open to rights-holders in China remain essentially unchanged as the main IP agencies have not changed in terms of bureaucratic structure over the past decade. Nevertheless, the specialist IP courts established in Beijing, Shanghai and Guangdong in late 2014 have been pinpointed as a very positive initiative for the effectiveness of the IP system. The perception of bias against foreign rights-holders which existed in 2005 is no longer relevant as win rates for foreign and domestic plaintiffs are now virtually identical. However, inadequate damages still deter some rights-holders from pursuing enforcement through the civil courts. Criminal enforcement has grown in use over the past decade but more cases could potentially be transferred to criminal liability in order to increase the deterrent effect to future infringers.

Alongside changes in the legislation and enforcement aspects of the IP system, there has also been a noteworthy proliferation in domestic Chinese registrations for IP, particularly patents, although some respondents were sceptical about the quality of some of the filings and also about the ability of domestic enterprises to fully exploit their IP. Overall, it is clear the changes made in the legislation relevant to IP, the improvements in the enforcement mechanisms, as well as the surge in the number of domestic IP rights-holders in the past decade have all led to an improved and more effective intellectual property system in China. By applying the comprehensive model of compliance proposed by Jacobson and Brown Weiss (1998), the state of the IP system in 2015 can be explained by key parameters, fundamental factors and proximate factors. As in 2005, those factors classed as parameters were not identified by respondents as very significant, apart from the vast size of China which was felt to contribute to problems in consistent implementation across the country and cultural values such as Confucianism and socialism which were not felt to be significant factors in the current system. In terms of fundamental factors, the three most significant factors were awareness of IP rights, local protectionism and a lack of consistency in enforcement. These factors had all been pinpointed in 2005 as key to the effectiveness of China's IP system and although some progress had been made in the intervening decade, these factors remained of concern to respondents in 2015.

There were also some evident changes in the significance of proximate factors affecting the current IP system in China. Respondents seemed less concerned about the knowledge levels of relevant personnel, but the workload of key personnel such as judges was a concern for several respondents. The QBPC remains an important positive influence according to many respondents, but some concerns linger over the resourcing of key agencies such as the AIC. Finally, the process of China's IP system adapting to local conditions over the past decade and longer has largely resulted from a combination of increased commitment from the central government to move towards an innovation-based economy and a surge in domestic rights-holders who are also increasingly pressuring for more effective protection of their valuable intellectual property. The transplanted norms in the post-TRIPS legislation have also been naturally internalised over time and external pressure has also shifted from coercion towards cooperation. Overall, China's IP system has adapted to the TRIPS Agreement in the longer term through a series of incremental changes and improvements and Chap. 8 will consider how these improvements can be sustained and deepened over time.

Notes

1. Interview comments from respondent 15LAW01.
2. For both English and Chinese versions of the PRC Trademark Law, see: WIPO (2015a).
3. Interview comments from respondent 15LAW10.
4. Interview comments from respondent 15LUX01.
5. Interview comments from respondent 15LUX01.
6. For both English and Chinese versions of the PRC Copyright Law, see: WIPO (2015b).
7. Interview comments from respondent 15ELECT02.
8. Interview comments from respondent 15LAW08.

9. For background on the relationship between copyright and the creative industries in China, see Montgomery (2010), especially Chap. 6.
10. For both English and Chinese versions of the PRC Patent Law, see: WIPO (2015c).
11. Although to date no compulsory licenses have been issued.
12. Interview comments from respondent 15LAW01.
13. Interview comments from respondent 15MANU01.
14. Interview comments from respondent 15LAW03.
15. Equivalent to approximately $12,000 USD.
16. Interview comments from respondent 15MANU01.
17. Interview comments from respondent 15LAW10.
18. For example, in December 2014, Nuoyakate was ordered by the Beijing IP court to pay the unprecedented statutory maximum damages of RMB 3 million (nearly USD $450,000) for trademark infringement and unfair competition.
19. Interview comments from respondent 15PHARMA01.
20. As discussed in Chap. 3.
21. Interview comments from respondent 15LAW05.
22. Interview comments from respondent 15LUX01.
23. Interview comments from respondent 15LAW08.
24. Interview comments from respondent 15PHARMA01.
25. Interview comments from respondent 15LAW09.
26. Interview comments from respondent 15MANU01.
27. Interview comments from respondent 15SERVICES01.
28. Interview comments from respondent 15ELECT01.
29. Interview comments from respondent 15MANU01.
30. Questionnaire comments from respondent 05LAW06.
31. Interview comments from respondent 15ELECT01.
32. Interview comments from respondent 15LAW08.
33. Interview comments from respondent 15LAW03.
34. Interview comments from respondent 15ELECT02.
35. Interview comments from respondent 15PHARMA01.
36. With 33 respondents selecting campaigns for greater public awareness as the potential improvement which they felt would make a significant difference to the IP system.
37. Interview comments from respondent 15PHARMA01.
38. Interview comments from respondent 15ACAD02.
39. Interview comments from respondent 15LAW01.
40. Interview comments from respondent 15LAW03.
41. Interview comments from respondent 15ELECT02.
42. Interview comments from respondent 15ELECT01.
43. Interview comments from respondent 15LAW04.
44. Interview comments from respondent 15LAW03.
45. Interview comments from respondent 15LAW02.
46. Interview comments from respondent 15LAW10.
47. For an introduction to the historical context and technical workings of the guiding cases system, see: Yu and Gurgel (2012).
48. Guiding Cases No. 29, 30, 45, 46, 47, 48, 49, 55 and 58.
49. Interview comments from respondent 15LAW08.
50. Interview comments from respondent 15LAW02.

51. Interview comments from respondent 15LAW06.
52. Interview comments from respondent 15LAW03.
53. Interview comments from respondent 15LUX01.
54. Interview comments from respondent 15LAW02.
55. Interview comments from respondent 15PHARMA02.
56. Interview comments from respondent 15ELECT02.
57. Interview comments from respondent 15LAW03.
58. Interview comments from respondent 15ELECT01.
59. Interview comments from respondent 15ELECT01.
60. With 21 respondents selecting stronger commitment from central government as the potential improvement which they felt would make a significant difference to the IP system.
61. Interview comments from respondent 05LAW31.
62. Interview comments from respondent 15LAW03.
63. Interview comments from respondent 15LAW10.
64. Interview comments from respondent 15LAW06.
65. Interview comments from respondent 15ACAD02.
66. Interview comments from respondent 15PHARMA01.
67. Interview comments from respondent 15LUX01.
68. Interview comments from respondent 15LAW02.
69. Interview comments from respondent 15PHARMA01.
70. Interview comments from respondent 15MANU01.
71. Questionnaire comments from respondent 05LAW30T.
72. Questionnaire comments from respondent 05LAW05.
73. For example, IP Key "is a platform for cooperation and acts as bridge between EU and Chinese agencies in order to create an IP landscape that benefits both Chinese and EU Industry operating in China" (IP Key 2016).
74. Interview comments from respondent 15LAW02.
75. Interview comments from respondent 15PHARMA01.
76. Interview comments from respondent 15LAW01.

References

Alford, William P. 1996. *To Steal a Book Is an Elegant Offense: Intellectual Property Law in Chinese Civilization*. Stanford: Stanford University Press.

Bruun, Niklas, and Liguo Zhang. 2016. Legal Transplant of Intellectual Property Rights in China: Norm Taker or Norm Maker? In *Governance of Intellectual Property Rights in China and Europe*, ed. Nari Lee, Niklas Bruun, and Mingde Li. Cheltenham: Edward Elgar.

Chinapaper.net. 2014. 泉林纸业知识产权质押融资创国内最高 (Tralin Paper's IP Financing is Domestic High). http://www.chinapaper.net/news/show-7442.html. Accessed 19 Aug 2016.

Crookes, Paul Irwin. 2010. *Intellectual Property Regime Evolution in China and India: Technological, Political and Social Drivers of Change*. Leiden: Brill.

———. 2014. EU Soft Power with China: Technical Assistance in the Field of Intellectual Property Rights. *European Foreign Affairs Review* 19(3/1): 77–96.

Eberhardt, Markus. et al. 2011. Is the Dragon Learning to Fly? An Analysis of the Chinese Patent Explosion. University of Nottingham Research Paper. http://dx.doi.org/10.2139/ssrn.196596. Accessed 19 Aug 2016.

European Commission. 2015. Report on EU Customs Enforcement of Intellectual Property Rights: Results at the EU Border 2014. http://ec.europa.eu/taxation_customs/resources/documents/customs/customs_controls/counterfeit_piracy/statistics/2015_ipr_statistics.pdf. Accessed 19 Aug 2016.

Gechlik, Mei. 2015. Guiding Cases Analytics- Issue 4. Stanford Law School's China Guiding Cases Project. https://cgc.law.stanford.edu/guiding-cases-analytics/issue-4/. Accessed 19 Aug 2016.

IP Key. 2016. About IP Key. http://www.ipkey.org/en/about-ip-key. Accessed 2 Sept 2016.

Jacobson, Harold K., and Edith Brown Weiss. 1998. Assessing the Record and Designing Strategies to Engage Countries. In *Engaging Countries: Strengthening Compliance with International Environmental Accords*, ed. Edith Brown Weiss and Harold K. Jacobson. Cambridge, MA: The MIT Press.

Keane, Michael. 2006. From Made in China to Created in China. *International Journal of Cultural Studies* 9(3): 285–296.

Li, Cheng, ed. 2010. China's Emerging Middle Class: Beyond Economic Transformation. Washington, DC: Brookings Institution Press.

Li, Mingde. 2016. Special Intellectual Property Courts in China. In *Governance of Intellectual Property Rights in China and Europe*, ed. Nari Lee, Niklas Bruun, and Mingde Li. Cheltenham: Edward Elgar.

Liu, Haiyan. 2010. The Criminal Enforcement of Intellectual Property Rights in China: Recent Developments and Implications. *Asian Criminology* 5: 137–156.

Mercurio, Bryan. 2012. The Protection and Enforcement of Intellectual Property in China Since Accession to the WTO: Progress and Retreat. *China Perspectives* 1: 23–28.

Montgomery, Lucy. 2010. *China's Creative Industries: Copyright, Social Network Markets and the Business of Culture in a Digital Age*. Cheltenham: Edward Elgar.

Moshinsky, Ben. 2015. Here's Why China Mentioned the Word 'Innovation' 71 Times After a Meeting to Decide Its 5-Year Plan. Business Insider UK. http://uk.businessinsider.com/chinese-government-said-innovation-71-times-after-a-meeting-to-decide-its-5-year-plan-2015-11?r=US&IR=T. Accessed 19 Aug 2016.

PRC Legislative Affairs Office of the State Council. 2014. 国务院法制办室关于制布《中华人民共和国著作权法(修订草案送审稿)》制开征求意见的通知 (Legislative Affairs Office of the State Council Releases Draft of Copyright Law for Public Comment). http://www.chinalaw.gov.cn/article/cazjgg/201406/20140600396188.shtml. Accessed 31 Aug 2016.

Prud'homme, Dan. 2012. Dulling the Cutting-Edge: How Patent-Related Policies and Practices Hamper Innovation in China. EU Chamber of Commerce in China. http://www.europeanchamber.com.cn/en/publications-archive/14/Dulling_the_Cutting_Edge_How_Patent_Related_Policies_and_Practices_Hamper_Innovation. Accessed 19 Aug 2016.

QBPC. 2016. QBPC Introduction. http://www.qbpc.org.cn/view.php?id=2715&cid=43. Accessed 20 Aug 2016.

State Council of the PRC. 2016. China Continues to Top Patent Application List. http://english.gov.cn/state_council/ministries/2016/01/14/content_281475271944980.htm. Accessed 15 Aug 2016.

State Intellectual Property Office of the PRC. 2010. General Introduction to the Third Revision of the Patent Law of the People's Republic of China and its Implementing Regulations. http://english.sipo.gov.cn/laws/lawsregulations/201012/t20101210_553631.html. Accessed 25 Nov 2015.

Supreme People's Court of the PRC. 2010. 最高人民法院关于案例指导工作的规定 (Provisions of the Supreme People's Court Concerning Work on Case Guidance). Stanford Law School's China Guiding Cases Project. https://cgc.law.stanford.edu/wp-content/uploads/sites/2/2015/08/guiding-cases-rules-20101126-english.pdf. Accessed 19 Aug 2016.

———. 2016a. 最高人民法院工作报告 (Supreme People's Court Work Report). http://www.court.gov.cn/zixun-xiangqing-17712.html. Accessed 19 Aug 2016.

———. 2016b. 指导案例 (Guiding Cases). http://www.court.gov.cn/shenpan-gengduo-77.html. Accessed 19 Aug 2016.

Tan, Rachel and Hatty Cui. 2014. Unlocking China's Well-Known Trademark Myth. *China Law & Practice*.

United States Trade Representative. 2015. 2015 Report to Congress on China's WTO Compliance. https://ustr.gov/sites/default/files/2015-Report-to-Congress-China-WTO-Compliance.pdf. Accessed 19 Aug 2016.

WIPO. 2015a. Trademark Law of the People's Republic of China. http://www.wipo.int/wipolex/en/details.jsp?id=13198. Accessed 11 Dec 2015.

———. 2015b. Copyright Law of the People's Republic of China. http://www.wipo.int/wipolex/en/details.jsp?id=6062. Accessed 11 Dec 2015.

———. 2015c. Patent Law of the People's Republic of China. http://www.wipo.int/wipolex/en/details.jsp?id=5484. Accessed 11 Dec 2015.

World Trade Organisation. 2005. Amendment of the TRIPS Agreement. WTO Document WT/L/641. https://www.wto.org/english/tratop_e/trips_e/wtl641_e.htm. Accessed 19 Aug 2016.

———. 2009. China- Measures Affecting the Protection and Enforcement of Intellectual Property Rights- Report of the Panel. WTO Document WT/DS362/R.

———. 2010. China- Measures Affecting the Protection and Enforcement of Intellectual Property Rights- Status Report by China- Addendum. WTO Document WT/DS362/14/Add.2.

Wu, Yanrui. 2014. China's Consumer Revolution. In *The Oxford Companion to the Economics of China*, ed. Shenggen Fan, Ravi Kanbur, Shangjin Wei, and Xiaobo Zhang. Oxford: Oxford University Press.

Wyzycka, Natalia and Reza Hasmath. 2016. The Impact of the European Union's Policy Towards China's Intellectual Property Regime. *International Political Science Review*: 1–14.

Yang, Wei-Ning, and Andrew Y. Yen. 2009. The Dragon Gets New IP Claws: The Latest Amendments to the Chinese Patent Law. *Intellectual Property & Technology Law Journal* 21(5): 18–27.

Yu, Ping, and Seth Gurgel. 2012. Stare Decisis in China? The Newly Enacted Guiding Cases System. In *Reading the Legal Case: Cross-Currents Between Law and the Humanities*, ed. Marco Wan. Abingdon: Routledge.

CHAPTER 8

Implications and Conclusions

This study has examined the state of the intellectual property (IP) system in modern China through the lens of compliance with the World Trade Organisation (WTO) Agreement on Trade-Related Intellectual Property Rights (TRIPS) which China agreed upon accession to the WTO in December 2001. This chapter will first summarise the contents of the preceding chapters before discussing the dynamic process of increasing compliance which emerges from this study. I will then consider the wider implications of the study—for theories of compliance; for the WTO; for China's trading partners; for the Chinese government; and for rights-holders seeking to protect their IP in China. Finally, I will offer some concluding thoughts on the significance of this study and the possible future for the Chinese intellectual property system.

8.1 SUMMARY OF PRECEDING CHAPTERS

Chapter 1 outlined the development of intellectual property protection in China and in the international system more generally in order to highlight the importance of the TRIPS Agreement for international IP protection. This chapter also explained why compliance theory is potentially a useful tool with which to analyse the development of IP rights in contemporary China, compared to previous studies of the legal system in China. Finally, this chapter concluded with the key research questions that this study aimed to address. These key questions related to the characteristics of the TRIPS Agreement itself that may affect a WTO member's compliance; the impact of WTO accession and TRIPS obligations on the IP system in China; China's subsequent compliance with TRIPS commitments; and any outstanding areas of non-compliance and why and how they can be resolved.

© The Author(s) 2017
K. Thomas, *Assessing Intellectual Property Compliance in Contemporary China*, Palgrave Series in Asia and Pacific Studies,
DOI 10.1007/978-981-10-3072-7_8

Consequently, Chap. 2 outlined the key concepts and theories of compliance that were applied in this study and also examined previous work on compliance in China. The chapter concluded that previous studies into China's compliance with its international commitments have focused solely on China without examining the characteristics of the obligations themselves. Equally, previous studies of compliance have predominantly focused on the specific international accord to the exclusion of country-specific factors affecting compliance. Therefore, it was argued that these two approaches should be combined into a more comprehensive approach to compliance by applying the inclusive model of compliance proposed by Jacobson and Brown Weiss (1998a). This comprehensive model of compliance was thus applied to the context of China's compliance with the TRIPS Agreement in the subsequent chapters.

Chapter 3 examined the non-country-specific factors influencing compliance with the TRIPS Agreement. The most significant factors were found to be the perceived inequity and imprecision of TRIPS obligations, which arose due both to the drafting history of TRIPS and the nature of the TRIPS Agreement as a minimum standards agreement. The TRIPS Agreement was also found to have other minor characteristics influencing compliance such as the burden of notifications and the lack of sufficient incentives and cooperation which act against full compliance and the role of the TRIPS Council and WTO dispute resolution body which act to encourage compliance. In terms of other non-country-specific factors outside of the TRIPS Agreement, the international environment and the nature of IP infringements as an activity were also considered in this chapter. As a global activity, the sheer number of countries and actors involved in infringements, as well as the short-term financial rewards from piracy, all discourage active implementation of TRIPS commitments. In addition, there is a lack of consensus in global opinion and even resentment towards certain developed countries and multinational corporations (MNCs) over the push for stronger international IP protection which hinders the subsequent adoption of higher universal standards of IP.

Chapter 4 then outlined the framework which I chose to use to assess compliance with the TRIPS Agreement and also introduced the specific research methods that were used in this study. A qualitative research strategy was designed which combined different methods of data collection: an initial questionnaire, detailed interviews and primary documentary data. The collected data was then codified and analysed in two main phases: 2005–6 and 2015. Details of the respondents who participated in the study were also broadly outlined in Chap. 4 and relevant ethical and practical issues, such as translation and linguistic equivalence, involved in conducting fieldwork in China were also considered.

In Chap. 5, China's implementation of the TRIPS Agreement into domestic IP legislation and the implementation of TRIPS obligations into the domestic enforcement system were both considered. The chapter closed by examining how China's TRIPS compliance has been formally challenged through use of the WTO's dispute settlement mechanism focusing on the dispute initiated by the United States (US) in 2007 concerning enforcement measures in China and their compliance with TRIPS provisions. Overall, the chapter found that despite far-reaching legislative changes and amendments to implement TRIPS into domestic legislation, particularly during the period 1999–2002, full compliance with the TRIPS Agreement was still in doubt in a few limited areas. Furthermore, the effectiveness of the post-TRIPS system was still criticised by a number of respondents who had experienced the system in action.

The experiences of the respondents in 2005–6 were consequently considered in more detail in Chap. 6 which considered the operation of the post-TRIPS IP system at that time and attempted to explain the "enforcement gap" which was observed to exist between the comprehensive laws on paper and the lax enforcement practices witnessed on the ground. This enforcement gap was analysed using the China-specific factors under the categories taken directly from the comprehensive Jacobson and Brown Weiss (1998a) model of compliance, namely the headings of parameters, fundamental factors and proximate factors. Parameters such as previous behaviour and historical factors were not found to be significant influences on the 2005 post-TRIPS IP system, despite the emphasis by many previous commentators on cultural values such as Confucianism and socialism as primarily responsible for the current system. In contrast, several fundamental factors were held to be highly significant by respondents including the lack of awareness of IP rights, local protectionism and a lack of consistency in enforcement. Finally, several proximate factors were also identified as key contributors to the 2005 framework of IP protection in China. The most important of these were the inadequate penalties imposed on infringers of IP rights and the lack of effective powers exercised by the judiciary. Furthermore, the quality of personnel in the IP system was also an issue of concern for many respondents.

Chapter 7 then reported on the more recent changes made to the IP system. In the decade from roughly 2005–2015, not only were a number of legislative changes promulgated, but significant changes were also made to the enforcement framework in China. These changes were mirrored by noteworthy shifts in both the attitude and awareness of IP in wider Chinese society as well as a substantial increase in the number of domestic Chinese rights-holders influencing the operation and effectiveness of the wider IP system. Then, factors contributing to the current state of the IP system were considered under the same headings as in Chap. 6 of parameters, fundamental factors and proximate factors, before the wider process of change was discussed. Respondents in 2015 concurred with the findings from a decade earlier that parameters such as previous behaviour and cultural values were not primary influences on the current IP system. Similarly, the key fundamental factors of lack of awareness, local protectionism, and inconsistent enforcement were still highlighted as significant contributory factors in the current IP system, although some improvements were noted in each of these areas. In terms of proximate factors considered in 2015, progress was also noted in the quality of the personnel within the IP system with particular praise for the introduction in late 2014 of the specialist IP courts. Nevertheless, concerns about inadequate damages still persisted from a decade earlier.

8.2   TOWARDS A DYNAMIC MODEL OF COMPLIANCE

8.2.1   Analysing IP in China Using Theories of Compliance

In general, it is widely recognised that operationalising compliance is problematic as there is a need to differentiate between implementation, compliance and effectiveness (Jacobson and Brown Weiss 1998b, p. 4). This is confirmed by preliminary analysis of China's compliance with the TRIPS Agreement. Although the majority of TRIPS obligations were swiftly implemented into China's formal domestic legislation, there was still some uncertainty about whether this constituted full compliance. Furthermore, China may be fully complying with its TRIPS commitments, but the IP system may be ineffective at tackling the underlying problem of infringements. Thus, the issue may not be one of China's compliance, but rather one of the efficacies of the TRIPS Agreement in combating the problem it was designed to resolve. In addition, wider issues than merely China's TRIPS compliance are involved in analysis of the current IP system in China.

The comprehensive model of compliance applied in this study was initially formulated to account for compliance with international environmental accords (Jacobson and Brown Weiss 1998a). Thus, it is important to consider to what extent this model may be applicable to international intellectual property agreements, specifically the TRIPS Agreement. Clearly, there are differences in the significance of some key factors. For example, pressure from non-governmental organisations (NGOs) was considered crucial to increased compliance in the environmental arena, but NGOs are not as influential in the IP field. In addition, it is difficult to analyse all factors within the rigid framework of the existing model as many categories or key factors overlap. For example, the lack of consistency in enforcement was considered as a political/institutional factor, but could also be seen as attributable to a lack of administrative capacity in the enforcement system, or to a lack of training amongst the relevant personnel. Similarly, although respondents in this study did not consider cultural factors to be significant, attitudes and values did play a part, and it is difficult to distinguish between the direct cultural influences of Confucianism and socialism and their indirect influence on contemporary values in Chinese society.

Therefore, can the basic structure of the existing model of compliance, incorporating both non-country- and country-specific factors, as well as consideration of implementation, compliance and effectiveness as separate components remain valid for the context of compliance with the TRIPS Agreement, specifically in China? It is contended in this study that the basic structure of the model *is* applicable to analysis of compliance with international IP agreements, but that several modifications of the key factors are necessary to reflect the different context of compliance. The distinct elements of the model of compliance will be reviewed below in order to outline the specific refinements necessary for the existing model.

8.2.2   Non-Country-Specific Factors Affecting Compliance

As discussed in Chap. 3, there are a variety of factors which are not specific to China which may influence compliance with the TRIPS Agreement. The non-country-specific factors influencing TRIPS compliance included within the model are those relating to the specific activity of intellectual property infringements; the characteristics of the TRIPS Agreement itself, including both substantive and procedural provisions; and the international environment, including the role of NGOs and the media. In terms of the characteristics of the activity involved, based on analysis of compliance with environmental agreements, it was previously proposed that the number of actors, the number of countries and any economic incentives involved would all have a significant effect on TRIPS compliance. However, the characteristics of IP infringements are markedly different from environmental actions, and thus the characteristics of the activity involved may play a different role in the model of compliance. Specifically, as IP piracy and counterfeiting are global activities, there are both a large number of actors and countries involved in the activity. In addition, economic incentives actually encourage some infringements, as there may be short-term economic gains from IP infringements. Thus, although IP infringements have different characteristics compared to environmental damage, the specific characteristics involved support the notion that the fewer countries and actors involved in an activity, the easier it may be to encourage compliance with international agreements regulating that activity.

The international environment was one of the most significant influences on compliance with international environmental accords, in contrast to its role in the IP context, where the international environment plays a minimal part. The sole feature of the international environment that was found to play a significant role in TRIPS compliance was the number of countries involved in the WTO process, and thus obliged to comply with the provisions of the TRIPS Agreement. As more and more countries have joined this regime, it could be argued that the TRIPS Agreement has gained momentum towards compliance. Consequently, the international environment may play a minor, yet positive role in encouraging compliance with the TRIPS Agreement.

The most significant non-country-specific factors which were shown to influence compliance with the TRIPS Agreement are those associated with the TRIPS Agreement itself. As discussed in Chap. 3, the drafting history of the Agreement gave rise to a certain degree of resentment amongst developing countries that the TRIPS framework favours developed country members. This perceived inequity in the TRIPS Agreement makes it less likely that all members, especially those from developing economies, will be inclined to push for full compliance. The nature of the TRIPS Agreement as a minimum standards agreement also has the unavoidable consequence that the substantive provisions contained within the Agreement lack precision. This imprecision also discourages full compliance from all members.

The perceived inequity and imprecision of the TRIPS Agreement are the most significant non-country-specific factors influencing TRIPS compliance, but there are other minor factors associated with the TRIPS Agreement also affecting compliance. For example, the burden of fulfilling TRIPS' notification obligations and a lack of sufficient cooperation and rewards from developed country members both act as a disincentive to compliance. However, it should also be recognised that there are several features of the TRIPS Agreement and the framework associated with the WTO that can offer positive enticements towards compliance. For instance, the Council for TRIPS established by the TRIPS Agreement is recognised as playing an important role in monitoring and encouraging compliance and the WTO dispute resolution process is also an asset of the WTO framework; by encouraging countries to join the multilateral forum of the WTO, they can avoid unilateral actions by powerful trade partners.

Overall, there are various factors influencing compliance with the TRIPS Agreement which are not specific to China. Although the characteristics of IP infringements are unique, in general, they play a similar role in compliance as in other activities governed by international agreements. In contrast, the international environment is much less significant in the context of international intellectual property, perhaps because of the lack of global consensus about the importance of IP protection and the relationship between IP and economic development.

8.2.3   Country-Specific Factors Affecting Compliance

In addition to the factors affecting TRIPS compliance which are not specific to China, Chaps. 6 and 7 illustrated the factors related to China specifically that have influenced overall compliance with the TRIPS Agreement in both the short term and long term. The basic parameters of China, such as the country's vast size, could be considered as significant factors influencing compliance with the TRIPS Agreement. However, in contrast with previous studies, historical and cultural factors, such as the continuing influence of Confucianism on societal values, were largely dismissed by respondents in both phases of this study as being not significant influences on the current IP system in China. China's previous behaviour in the IP field was also not perceived to be a significant indicator of present-day compliance. In fact, the only parameter which was consistently found to have a noticeable effect on China's TRIPS compliance was its size. China's sheer size has obvious implications for the enforcement of intellectual property rights; of particular concern is the division that exists between central and local levels of government in China. Therefore, although China's size is a major influence on the current IP system, overall the parameters are not highly significant in the model of China's compliance with the TRIPS Agreement.

In contrast to parameters, there were found to be several fundamental factors which are of prime importance for China's TRIPS compliance. Fundamental factors were considered under the headings of attitudes and values, political and institutional factors and economic factors. In terms of attitudes and values, although the cultural influences of Confucianism and socialism were largely rejected as strong influences on the contemporary IP system, the attitudes and values amongst the public in China were seen as important by respondents in this study. In fact, a lack of awareness of IP rights was highlighted as the most significant influence on the current IP system by respondents in 2005 and also proved to be very significant a decade later. Although awareness of IP had improved between 2005 and 2015 amongst both the general public and amongst domestic Chinese enterprises, there was still felt to be room for improvements in terms of awareness of the full strategic potential of IP. Overall, attitudes and values in China are more significant influences on the development of the IP system and corresponding TRIPS compliance than the cultural factors which are often blamed by external commentators. However, other fundamental factors could also be considered to be significant overall.

Political and institutional factors are major contributors to the development of the current IP system in China. The main political and institutional factor which contributes to the state of the current IP system in China is the lack of consistency in enforcement, as noted in both 2005 and 2015. Frustration was expressed by many respondents at inconsistent enforcement of IP rights, although many respondents also praised the administrative enforcement system. Turning to economic factors, local protectionism was one of the most significant factors identified by respondents in both 2005 and 2015. Some improvements were noted by 2015, with some big cities felt to operate effective enforcement mechanisms, although some inland regions were still thought to suffer from tendencies towards local protectionism. Finally, proximate factors also play a crucial role in influencing the compliance of China's current IP system with the TRIPS Agreement. Clearly the most significant aspect of proximate factors analysed in this study was the administrative capacity within the IP system. Specifically, the level of penalties imposed on infringers was seen as inadequate by many respondents in both 2005 and 2015.

8.2.4   *The Dynamic Process of Changing Compliance*

The preceding sections summarised the most significant factors identified both by the documentary data and from respondents' comments as influences on China's current IP system and consequent compliance with the TRIPS Agreement. However, a list of these factors alone is not particularly illuminating as to how China's TRIPS compliance has developed over the past 15 years since WTO accession or how it may continue to change in the future. Therefore, it is necessary to turn to these dynamic processes to understand both the existing compliance with the TRIPS Agreement and possible changes that could increase China's compliance. The dynamic process of change in compliance over time relates to the two aspects of *intention* to comply and *capacity* to comply. These two perspectives can be changed both by internal changes in the country, such as changes in leadership, and by external pressure, for example, offers of financial or technical assistance.

In order to describe these dynamic processes of interaction between the factors affecting compliance and China's intention and capacity to comply, it is necessary to first consider: which factors that have been identified as significant for compliance are fixed and which can most easily be manipulated? Which of these factors affect China's intention to comply? And which affect China's capacity to comply? It is immediately apparent that several of the factors identified above as significant for China's compliance with TRIPS are either fixed or are not easily modified. For example, although the precision of the obligations contained within the TRIPS Agreement was identified as one of the prime characteristics of the Agreement that influenced compliance, these obligations are fixed and could not easily be changed to increase compliance. Similarly, the characteristics associated with the international environment are also fixed or difficult to manipulate. For example, the short-term economic rewards associated with intellectual property infringements are long-standing, but could not be easily minimised to discourage IP infringements.

On the other hand, of the factors identified above as significant influences on China's compliance with the TRIPS Agreement, there are several factors which may potentially be shaped more readily. It is essential to focus on these factors if China's compliance with the TRIPS Agreement is to be maintained and improved further, rather than waste efforts on attempting to manipulate factors which are fixed or of little consequence. Some of the factors under scrutiny influence China's intention to comply with the TRIPS Agreement and others affect China's capacity to comply. There are five key factors which most influence China's intention to comply with the TRIPS Agreement. First, continuing to increase awareness of IP rights can assist in tackling the problem of a lack of awareness of the full strategic potential of intellectual property amongst domestic rights-holders, as well as increasing public understanding of how IP can support and nurture China's future economic development. This in turn can increase intention to comply by facilitating the acceptance of the imported norms by society in general, similar to the process of internalisation as described by Koh (1996).

The second factor which can strongly influence intention to comply in China is that of pressure applied to the government. It is undeniable that external pressure from trading partners or international organisations such as the World Intellectual Property Organisation (WIPO) can encourage or maintain government commitment to fully comply with the TRIPS Agreement. However, it has also been recognised by many respondents that external pressure can create resentment in China if too heavily imposed. Therefore, although it is important to maintain pressure on the Chinese government, it is also important not to overuse this mechanism for change. Indeed, spreading the use of external pressure to include cooperative initiatives or those focused at local- or provincial-level governments should be promoted. As there is a recognised gap between central and local levels of government, pressure applied to the central leadership in Beijing can only achieve so much before creating resentment and consequently, attention should be shifted to lower levels of government which play such a crucial role in IP enforcement, as well as shifting to initiatives aimed at increasing the competency of key personnel in the IP system through targeted training.

The third crucial factor affecting China's intention to comply involves the role of domestic Chinese enterprises in supporting sustained improvements in the IP system. Almost all respondents in both phases of the study independently raised the issue of domestic rights-holders as one which would be essential for future improvements in the current IP system. Therefore, as domestic Chinese enterprises continue to increase their innovative activity, their role as IP rights-holders in China will continue to increase in importance and may act as a tipping point for effective enforcement of existing laws and regulations. Fourthly, although NGOs in general play a minor role in the issue of intellectual property rights globally, they can have a slightly positive effect on intention to comply with the TRIPS Agreement in China. Organisations representing MNCs in China such as the Quality Brands Protection Committee (QBPC) should maintain their role of supporting IP rights and can thus help to maintain the necessary intention to comply, particularly by joining forces with organisations representing domestic companies. Finally, many respondents highlighted inadequate penalties for infringers as one of their main frustrations with the current system. Increasing the statutory levels of penalties which can be imposed and clarifying guidance on calculating damages should significantly increase intention to comply as it would act as a stronger deterrent to infringers by minimising short-term economic gains from infringements.

In addition to these five key factors which influence China's intention to comply with the TRIPS Agreement, there are also three crucial factors which impact upon China's capacity to comply. Firstly, most respondents highlighted the key issue of sufficient numbers of well-trained and experienced personnel in the IP system as a key concern for effective enforcement. According to respondents' comments in 2005, the number of personnel was not so much of an issue as the quality of the personnel involved in IP enforcement. Thus, improving the standard of personnel in the IP system between 2005 and 2015 increased China's capacity to fully implement its TRIPS commitments. Nevertheless, in 2015, the workload of key personnel such as specialist IP judges remained a concern for several respondents and there were still some fears that the administrative capacity of key agencies such as the Administration of Industry and Commerce (AIC) could be further enhanced with additional resources dedicated to tackling IP infringements.

Secondly, although some commentators had previously called for a unified IP agency to oversee the operation of the IP system in China, this notion was rejected by respondents in both 2005 and 2015 as impractical. However, it was recognised that there is a certain amount of overlap and bureaucratic competition between the relevant agencies and thus, the system could be streamlined to simplify the bureaucratic structure of IP enforcement and to encourage greater cooperation and specifically case transfer between the different IP agencies, with transfer of infringers to face criminal liability of particular interest. Finally,

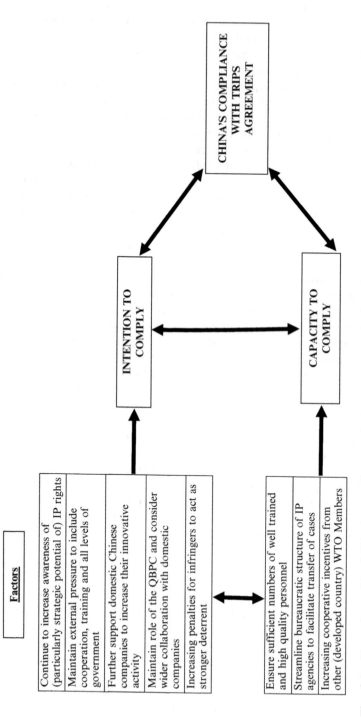

Fig. 8.1 Dynamic model of China's compliance with the TRIPS agreement and key influences on China's intention and capacity to comply

at the international level, there is some disquiet from developing country WTO members that developed country members are not living up to their promises to provide technical cooperation and technology transfers under the TRIPS Agreement. Increasing incentives such as facilitating further technology transfers and cooperation from key developed country members may also have a positive influence on China's overall TRIPS compliance.

Overall, there are various key factors which should be the focus for future improvements in China's TRIPS compliance as highlighted above. These factors influence China's intention and capacity to comply, which in turn impact upon overall compliance with the TRIPS Agreement. This dynamic model of compliance for continuing and future reforms of China's IP system is represented in Fig. 8.1 and will form the basis for the implications and policy recommendations arising from this study which will be outlined in the following section. The factors are divided into factors influencing China's intention and capacity to comply, but these factors are interactive and this should be borne in mind when considering the operation of this model of compliance.

8.3   IMPLICATIONS OF THE STUDY

8.3.1   Implications for Theories of Compliance

There is an obvious need to move beyond traditional competing theories of compliance which focus on one aspect to the exclusion of other significant factors. For example, following Franck's concept of compliance as arising from legitimacy and fairness in the rules would lead to the conclusion that China chooses whether or not to comply with the TRIPS Agreement on the basis of TRIPS obligations alone (Franck 1995). Equally, taking a more neo-realist stance would lead to the conclusion that China chooses whether or not to comply based primarily on any possible sanctions that may be imposed for non-compliance (Neuhold 1999). Clearly, these limited approaches are insufficient to fully explain TRIPS compliance in China, and thus a more comprehensive approach is necessary. Such a comprehensive approach would move beyond the role of the state, which is the preoccupation of traditional theories of compliance, but without discounting the state as a key actor altogether in favour of a more bottom-up approach, as recent liberal theory does (Slaughter 2000). The state still plays a major role in compliance with international obligations, particularly in China, and in the field of IP, the role of the state is considerably more important than that of individuals or NGOs. Consequently, an inclusive model of compliance should incorporate features from several pre-existing theories of compliance to offer a more complete tool with which to analyse compliance with international obligations. This has proved to be the most useful approach to follow in assessing TRIPS compliance in contemporary China and it is proposed that this approach is also applicable to other international agreements and in other states.

Equally, this study has implications for the study of the development of law in China. Previous studies of law in China have tended to focus on one key concept of legal development to the exclusion of other concepts and theories. Concepts such as legal legitimation and transplantation, and selective adaptation alone, are insufficient to fully appreciate the complex and dynamic processes of legal development in China. It is undeniable that China's development of modern IP laws has not been solely "a passive process of accepting Western rules; rather it is a dynamic process" (Bruun and Zhang 2016, p. 44). Thus, one could argue that an approach solely focused on the reception of legal transplants into Chinese law is limited and needs to be expanded to incorporate consideration of the other categories of influential factors used in this study. Consequently, it is proposed that the revised and dynamic model of compliance outlined in the previous section is applicable not only to compliance with other areas of international law, but also to other aspects of law within China.

8.3.2   *Implications for the WTO*

Under the Doha Round of negotiations negotiated by WTO members from 2001 onwards, and also known as the Doha Development Agenda, as the stated focus is intended to be upon improving trading conditions for developing countries, certain revisions to the TRIPS Agreement were scheduled for discussion (World Trade Organisation 2016). The only IP issue that is definitely part of the Doha negotiations is the development of a multilateral register for the geographical indications for wines and spirits. Additionally, other current prominent issues under debate include increasing technology transfer to least-developed countries and the issue of "non-violation" complaints, that is disputes involving the loss of an expected benefit even though the TRIPS Agreement has not actually been violated, as well as the relationship between TRIPS and biodiversity and traditional knowledge (Taubman, Wager and Watal 2012). Although the latest round of trade negotiations appears to have stalled, it is crucial at this juncture to urge the WTO to consider the perceived equity in TRIPS obligations in any revisions that may be negotiated. Clearly, the existing TRIPS Agreement suffers from a perception that it favours developed country members over the interests of developing country members and any future negotiations may offer the ideal opportunity to right this perception. Negotiators of the potentially updated TRIPS Agreement should also consider the precision of the obligations when drafting the revisions and amendments to the 1994 Agreement in order to increase compliance.

However, although ideally the updated TRIPS Agreement would be perceived to be equitable to all members, regardless of their stage of development, and the substantive obligations would be completely precise, in practice, this is unlikely to be achieved. There is a perceptible tension between the internationalisation versus the indigenisation of IP laws, as such rules clearly need to be adapted to local conditions but also need to comply with international standards. As a result, there is very little policy space within which IP standards can be flexed to fit the conditions in each specific WTO member (Ruse-Kahn 2011, p. 33). Unfortunately, the nature of the WTO as an international trading system means that it encompasses many issues, not just that of intellectual property. Therefore, TRIPS negotiations are part of a larger game of give-and-take between members and cannot be considered in isolation, and it would thus be highly improbable for major changes to be made to the TRIPS Agreement in isolation. In addition, although the role of the Council for TRIPS has largely been a positive one in encouraging compliance with the TRIPS Agreement, the Council could further pressure developed country members to increase cooperation and technical assistance under Article 67 and to fully comply with Article 68, regarding technology transfers to less-developed country members. These steps would further boost the available incentives for compliance.

In addition, when negotiating China's accession protocol, China's preferred designation as a developing rather than developed country was a contentious issue. However, following WTO accession, China does not wish to be labelled as a developing country due to the implications for cases of alleged anti-dumping. As a result, the WTO needs to consider establishing a clear definition or workable criteria for designating new members as developed or developing countries consistently in order to avoid such wrangles in the future. The final implication for the WTO concerns the dispute settlement process. This process seems generally satisfactory as, contrary to concerns prior to China's accession in 2001, the process has not been swamped by China-related disputes. In fact, the dispute settlement process has offered a useful alternative to the threat of unilateral sanctions by trading partners such as the US, which were prevalent in the 1990s. The dispute settlement process could thus be used to encourage non-members to join the WTO framework of protection as a way to avoid such unilateral pressure.

8.3.3   Implications for Trading Partners

The implications outlined above for the WTO also link closely to the implications for China's powerful trading partners such as the US and the EU. Firstly, it is clear from the 2007 WTO dispute initiated by the US against China regarding TRIPS enforcement that it can be difficult to collate enough evidence to bring a dispute to the WTO dispute settlement body. As emphasised by the Panel Report, anecdotal weaknesses in the enforcement system are insufficient to initiate an action; the complainant must have clear evidence of systemic failures. Therefore, this reinforces the idea that compliance is difficult to assess objectively and that a more comprehensive model of TRIPS compliance is necessary to understand the complex processes of compliance in different countries.

The second and arguably more important implication for key trading partners of China is that the policy of denouncing the Chinese government in an effort to force stronger IP enforcement is unlikely to succeed. External pressure from the United States Trade Representative (USTR) and their Section 301 mechanism of identifying countries annually seen as IP offenders is unlikely to produce sustained improvements in the enforcement system without corresponding internal changes. This is because external pressure may optimistically increase central government intention to comply, but without any essential improvements in the capacity to comply. Indeed, pursuing external pressure may not even increase intention to comply and instead may only result in resentment.

A more productive long-term strategy to improve TRIPS compliance and IP enforcement in China would be to continue to work with Chinese rights-holders, legal personnel and judges to improve their capacity to enforce IP effectively. Such initiatives have increased in both number and scope since China's WTO accession, but it is important to stress that this type of cooperative activity should remain the focus for trading partners seeking to influence China's IP system in the future. Ultimately, without domestic rights-holders to pressure for IP protection, the system cannot effectively operate to protect IP in the long term. Turning to the wider implications for global IP protection, as shown in Chap. 3, the broad membership of the WTO was found to act as a positive influence on the likelihood of TRIPS compliance; it could thus be argued that key trading partners should encourage remaining non-members to accede to the WTO in order to increase this effect.

8.3.4   *Implications for the Chinese Government*

Many respondents in this study recognised that the central government in Beijing is strongly committed to enforcing IP rights effectively in China. It is crucial that the Chinese government is praised for this and encouraged to maintain this level of commitment to IP development in the future. However, although the central government may have the intention to fully comply with the TRIPS Agreement, there are issues of capacity that prevent full compliance. It must be borne in mind that many of the factors necessary for the operation of an effective IP system lie outside of the IP system itself: for example, "a consciousness of legal rights, respect for the rule of law, an effective and independent judiciary, a well-functioning innovation and competition system, basic infrastructure, established business practices and a critical mass of local stakeholders" (Yu 2016, p. 40). Consequently, there is a need to look beyond the IP system when considering the wider process of reform in China. Additionally, this broader perspective reflects the implication for trading partners that external pressure is unlikely to make a difference to the overall implementation and effectiveness of the IP system in the absence of progress in the other areas.

On the other hand, despite these issues of capacity which may not be easily resolved, there are minor changes that the government can make to improve the effectiveness of the current IP system. Two general issues which emerged from respondents' comments on IP enforcement are a lack of consistency and a lack of transparency. Thus, the government could elude complaints about inconsistency by avoiding enforcing IP in "crackdown" campaigns, for example, annual enforcement campaigns which are renowned for taking place around the World

Consumer Rights Day held each year in March. With regard to transparency, although transparency of the relevant laws and regulations is now cited by respondents as much improved, transparency concerning enforcement actions is still subject to some criticism. Therefore, the government could further improve transparency by making available detailed enforcement statistics. This could also help in the fight against local protectionism; if local enforcement statistics show a markedly low level of fines, for example, there may be reason to suspect some low-level corruption in that area. Further, increased transparency around enforcement actions would also alleviate complaints from rights-holders that they are excluded from the enforcement process.

There are also a few minor substantive amendments that the government could consider making to the existing legislation. As discussed in Chap. 7, perhaps the most pressing of these would be improving the civil procedure rules and shifting the burden of proof to the respondent when calculating damages. Finally, the role of Chinese enterprises is key to sustaining improvements in the IP system in the future. For example, the current restrictive rules governing the formation and operation of NGOs in China could be relaxed to encourage Chinese enterprises to join together to cooperate on IP issues. This would also support the stated aim of developing innovation in contemporary China. At this juncture, it is undeniable that the Chinese government has recognised that the previous approach to economic development of relying on low-end manufacturing at the same time as attempting to develop an innovative high-tech sector is ultimately unsustainable. As the flood of recent news stories concerning inferior quality Chinese products shows,[1] the label "Made in China" is highly vulnerable to downgrading and consequently, efforts are increasingly being made to regulate compliance with quality regulations. The Chinese government appears to have realised that prioritising innovative enterprises over protecting imitative manufacturing enterprises is a better strategy for continued economic growth as seen through both official rhetoric as well as in substantive policies such as offering financial incentives for patent filings. It is clear that the stronger commitment from the central government in China has been a primary factor in driving forward the improvements which have been witnessed in the IP system over the past few years. It is to be hoped that not only does the central government maintain such levels of commitment but also that similar levels of commitment can spread to provincial and local levels of government as the benefits of stronger IP for economic development begin to be more widely experienced.

8.3.5   Implications for Rights-Holders

The consistent message from respondents seems to be that although the current system of protection is not perfect, it is still effective enough to offer some protection against infringements. The key is for rights-holders to seek to engage with the system instead of criticising from the outside. Thus, rights-holders should be encouraged to initially register their IP rights in China and if infringements subsequently arise, then infringers should be pursued through the various mechanisms offered. A further implication for rights-holders in China is to consider their collective position. In order to pressurise for future improvements in the IP system, rights-holders should support the formation of pressure groups or industry associations for Chinese companies, either independently or in cooperation with foreign groups. Thus, there may be scope, for example, for the QBPC to work with domestic holders of well-known trademarks to campaign together for more effective IP protection.

From respondents' comments in 2015, it is clear that there is somewhat of a divergence in strategies employed by rights-holders particularly from MNCs in China with some continuing to rely on administrative enforcement by local level branches of the AIC and to build cooperative relationships with key AIC personnel. Others have largely abandoned administrative enforcement as an effective strategy to tackle counterfeiting in the long term due to a belief that such raids will only ever catch the small infringers, not the "big fish" or bosses who quickly move on to new premises with new frontmen. Indeed, such large-scale infringers often see administrative fines or seized goods as just a cost of doing business rather than as an effective deterrent.

Consequently, some rights-holders are pressing for greater numbers of transfers from administrative to criminal liability as the penal system is justifiably believed to hold more of a "fear factor" for potential infringers. On the other hand, other rights-holders are instead shifting their focus from counterfeiting to product liability. By focusing on the safety and efficacy of products, rather than infringement of their individual proprietary rights, the focus of the enforcement can thus be shifted to consumer protection which may be more likely to receive full support from relevant authorities. A further concern for rights-holders in China to ponder is: how can success be measured in the fight against IP infringements? Does more raids carried out, more fines imposed, more infringers caught equal a more successful IP strategy or less? It is clear that there needs to be a shift in many companies from seeing IP enforcement as an isolated activity, to a cross-departmental approach in which IP-related information from all around the company from design, manufacturing, sales, after-sales, and so on can be captured. This again emphasises that small-scale raids can be ineffective as an enforcement mechanism; on the contrary, there is a clear need to gain intelligence about the entire supply chain in order to effectively protect IP. There is also a distinct message from respondents that there is significant scope for many domestic rights-holders, particularly those from small- and medium-sized enterprises (SMEs), to realise the full monetary and strategic potential of their proprietary intellectual property.

8.4   Concluding Thoughts

This study had several intriguing or unexpected findings; for example, contrary to several previous studies and many observers of China's legal system, cultural influences such as Confucianism and socialism were not found to be major influences on the current IP system. In addition, a lack of transparency had previously been cited as a major flaw in the current system, whereas respondents in this study, particularly in 2005, actually identified transparency as a key improvement they had recently witnessed. As a consequence, enhanced transparency in the legislative framework could be said to be one of the crucial fundamental changes brought about as a direct result of WTO accession. However, transparency in enforcement actions could still be further enhanced and thus, this could be an area for potential future progress.

Other surprising findings included the discussion of the bureaucratic structure of IP agencies by respondents. It had previously been suggested that a unified IP agency could streamline the enforcement process and minimise bureaucratic rivalries. However, respondents recognised this to be impractical as not only is IP such a broad field, but China is also a huge country to administer from one central agency. Finally, it must be recognised that many respondents were keen to point out a more balanced picture of the IP system in China, as many critiques of the current system by external commentators only criticise the remaining flaws without praising the progress China has already made. On the contrary, the majority of respondents in both 2005 and 2015 were optimistic about the prospect for future improvements.

Clearly, this study has raised some important questions for the study of compliance with international agreements, both in China and within the WTO international trading system. In terms of implications for theory, this study suggests that previous studies of legal development in China have largely overlooked the significance of the specific international obligations, whilst existing theories of compliance have mostly focused on the specific obligations rather than characteristics of the specific country involved. Therefore, it has been argued that by combining the strengths of these previous studies, a more inclusive approach can produce a more comprehensive and valid model of compliance, applicable to the specific context of China's TRIPS compliance. The comprehensive model of compliance described in this study was applied to the specific context of assessing China's compliance with the TRIPS Agreement. In order to test the reliability of this amended model, further research could apply this model to the context of China's compliance with other international agreements such as environmental accords or arms control treaties. Alternatively, the model could be applied to TRIPS compliance but in other WTO member countries. This may be a useful tool of analysis in more recently acceded WTO members such as Vietnam or Russia; as they also have to comply with TRIPS immediately upon accession, efforts regarding TRIPS implementation, compliance and effectiveness are crucial.

Turning to policy implications, this study also has significance for various sectors, including the WTO/TRIPS framework itself, China, key trading partners such as the US and individual rights-holders themselves. The WTO needs to recognise that future reforms to the international trading system should consider the consequences for compliance of broad trade-related negotiations; namely that members may agree to certain obligations in order to achieve concessions in another area, but subsequent compliance may be harder to achieve than in negotiations over a single issue. This study has also demonstrated that the fairness and precision of the obligations are highly significant factors for compliance. In terms of implications for China, it is undeniable that China must be praised for the substantial reform efforts to date; these demonstrate that China will strive to fulfil international obligations as a responsible member of the world order, in addition to confirming the central government's recognition of the importance of IP for future economic development. As well as minor legislative amendments, the Chinese government should be encouraged to move away from the irregular crackdown approach to IP enforcement and to continue to strengthen both consistency and transparency in enforcement, in order to attempt to confront the deeply ingrained problem of local protectionism.

Ultimately, sustained changes to the intellectual property system need internal pressure to succeed and thus, domestic rights-holders should be supported in their efforts to monitor and improve the existing system. Overall, China has already made substantial improvements to the system of IP protection and respondents participating in this study remain optimistic about the prospect of future improvements. A cooperative approach from external stakeholders focusing on building capacity, particularly in the enforcement framework, and within all levels of government would also be conducive to encouraging long-term sustained improvements in the IP system. If cooperative efforts could be focused on improving China's capacity to fully comply with TRIPS, then this long-term process of reform may be hastened.

From reflecting on the two stages of the project carried out a decade apart, it seems clear that the dominant theme in 2005 was the immediate impact of WTO entry and the subsequent legislative changes that were made to attempt to comply with the TRIPS Agreement. On the other hand, the dominant theme emerging from the interviews carried out in 2015 was the key role of the government in encouraging and stimulating innovation and of domestic rights-holders in pressuring for more effective IP protection and enforcement. It is undeniable that sweeping changes had been made to the IP system in China in the intervening decade, and I am confident that significant progress will continue to be made in the future as domestic innovation continues to grow.

Note

1. See, for example, BBC (2007).

References

BBC. 2007. 'Brand China' at Risk after Toy Recall. http://news.bbc.co.uk/1/hi/business/6948274.stm. Accessed 14 Sept 2007.

Bruun, Niklas, and Liguo Zhang. 2016. Legal Transplant of Intellectual Property Rights in China: Norm Taker or Norm Maker? In *Governance of Intellectual Property Rights in China and Europe*, ed. Nari Lee, Niklas Bruun, and Mingde Li, 43–64. Cheltenham: Edward Elgar Publishing.

Franck, Thomas. 1995. *Fairness in International Law and Institutions.* Oxford: Oxford University Press.

Jacobson, Harold K., and Edith Brown Weiss. 1998a. Assessing the Record and Designing Strategies to Engage Countries. In *Engaging Countries: Strengthening Compliance with International Environmental Accords,* ed. Edith Brown Weiss and Harold K. Jacobson. Cambridge, MA: The MIT Press.

———. 1998b. A Framework for Analysis. In *Engaging Countries: Strengthening Compliance with International Environmental Accords,* ed. Edith Brown Weiss and Harold K. Jacobson. Cambridge, MA: The MIT Press.

Koh, Harold Hongju. 1996. Transnational Legal Process (The 1994 Roscoe Pound Lecture). *Nebraska Law Review* 75(1): 181–207.

Neuhold, Hanspeter. 1999. The Foreign Policy 'Cost-Benefit Analysis' Revisited. *German Yearbook of International Law* 42: 84–124.

Ruse-Khan, Henning Grosse. 2011. Protecting Intellectual Property Rights under BITs, FTAs and TRIPS: Conflicting Regimes or Mutual Coherence? In *Evolution in Investment Treaty Law and Arbitration,* ed. Chester Brown and Kate Miles, 485–515. Cambridge: Cambridge University Press.

Slaughter, Anne-Marie. 2000. A Liberal Theory of International Law. *Proceedings of the Annual Meeting (American Society of International Law)* 94: 240–253.

Taubman, Antony, Hannu Wager, and Jayashree Watal, eds. 2012. *A Handbook on the WTO TRIPS Agreement.* Cambridge: Cambridge University Press.

World Trade Organisation. 2016. The Doha Agenda. http://www.wto.org/english/thewto_e/whatis_e/tif_e/doha1_e.htm. Accessed 1 Sept 2016.

Yu, Peter K. 2016. The Transplant and Transformation of Intellectual Property Laws in China. In *Governance of Intellectual Property Rights in China and Europe,* ed. Nari Lee, Niklas Bruun, and Mingde Li, 20–64. Cheltenham: Edward Elgar Publishing.

APPENDIX 1:

QUESTIONNAIRE ON INTELLECTUAL PROPERTY IN CHINA

The aim of this questionnaire is to evaluate the effectiveness of the intellectual property (IP) system in China and identify ways in which the system could be improved. Your cooperation with this survey is very much appreciated. Please answer the questions in as much detail as possible, according to your firm's experiences in China.

本调查问卷的目的是为了评价知识产权制度在中国的有效性,并据此识别用何种方法可改善该制度。非常感谢您对此调查的合作。请根据贵司在中国的经验,尽可能详细地回答问题。

All information given will be treated as strictly confidential and will be made anonymous. No names or company names will be used under any circumstances.

如前所述,所有被提供的信息都将被严格保密并以匿名显示。在任何情况下,个人或公司的名字都不会被使用。

1. Please choose one of the following options to describe the goods or services that your company provides:贵司提供何种产品或服务?
   - ☐ Agriculture; 农业
   - ☐ Aviation; 航空
   - ☐ Banking, Finance, Insurance; 银行业, 金融, 保险
   - ☐ Education and Training; 教育,培训
   - ☐ Energy, Utilities, Environment; 能量,公用事业, 环境
   - ☐ Fashion and Luxury Goods; 流行式样,奢侈品
   - ☐ Food & Beverage; 食物, 饮料
   - ☐ Leisure, Tourism, Hospitality; 闲暇, 旅行业
   - ☐ Manufacturing; 制造业
   - ☐ Media and Advertising; 传播媒介, 广告
   - ☐ Professional & Business Services; 职业的, 商业的服务行业
   - ☐ Technology, Telecommunications; 工艺学, 电信

© The Author(s) 2017
K. Thomas, *Assessing Intellectual Property Compliance in Contemporary China*, Palgrave Series in Asia and Pacific Studies, DOI 10.1007/978-981-10-3072-7

☐ Wholesale, Retail; 批发商, 零售商
☐ Other (please specify); 其他 (请详细描述)

[ ]

2. How many offices does your company have in China and in which cities are they located? 贵司在中国有多少家办事处,它们位于哪些城市?

[ ]

3. If applicable, how many offices does your company have worldwide and in which countries are they located? 如果适用此情形,贵司有多少家国外的办事处,它们都分布在哪些国家?

[ ]

Where are the headquarters of your company? 贵司的总部在哪国家?
☐ China; 中国
☐ Worldwide; 全世界的

4. How long has your company been operating in China? 贵司在中国开设了多少年?
☐ 0–2 years; 0–2 年
☐ 2–5 years; 2–5 年
☐ 5–10 years; 5–10 年
☐ More than 10 years; 10 年以上

5. Is your company involved with intellectual property in China? 贵司是否涉及到在中国的知识产权?
☐ Yes;是
☐ No;否
☐ Don't Know;不知道

6. If yes, what types of IP do you deal with? (Please choose all that are applicable):如果是,您所涉及的是何种知识产权?请选择所有合适的选项)
☐ Patent; 专利权
☐ Utility Model; 实用新型
☐ Industrial Design; 工业设计
☐ Trademark; 商标权
☐ Copyright; 著作权
☐ Other (e.g.) Trade secrets; 其他如商业秘密

7. Have you noticed any changes in IP protection in China over the past five years? 您是否注意到过去五年知识产权所发生的任何变化?
☐ Yes: 是
☐ No: 否
☐ Don't Know: 不知道

8. If you have noticed a change, would you characterize the change as positive or negative? (−2 = negative change, 0 = no change, 2 = positive change)
如果您已注意到有变化,请描述该变化是积极的还是消极的?
(−2=消极的变化,0=没有变化,2=积极的变化)
☐ −2   ☐ −1   ☐ 0   ☐ 1   ☐ 2

9. Would you please give details on any changes observed: 请详细描述您所观察到的变化:

10. What do you think prompted these changes? 你认为是什么促成了这此变化?

11. In your opinion, how effective is the current system of IP protection in China?
(1 = completely ineffective; 6 = entirely effective) 在您看来,中国现行的知识产权保护体制效力如何?(1=完全没有效率,6=完全有效)
☐ 1   ☐ 2   ☐ 3   ☐ 4   ☐ 5   ☐ 6

12. Has your company ever experienced any problems with protecting IP in China? 您有没有在中国遇到过知识产权的相关问题?
☐ Yes; 是
☐ No; 否
☐ Don't Know; 不知道

13. In your opinion, how serious are the problems you have experienced?
(1 = not at all serious; 6 = extremely serious) 您遇到的问题有多严重?(1=根本不严重,6=极度严重)
☐ 1   ☐ 2   ☐ 3   ☐ 4   ☐ 5   ☐ 6

14. In your opinion, what is the main cause of any problems that you have experienced? 在您看来,问题产生的主要原因是什么?
☐ Poor legislation; 立法不良
☐ Poor enforcement; 执法不力
☐ Both; 都有
☐ Neither; 都不是
☐ Not sure; 不清楚

15. To what extent do you think the following factors contribute to the current state of the IP protection system in China? 在何种程度上,您认为以下因素造成了知识产权保护的状态?
(0 = no contribution; 6 = major contribution)(0=没有贡献,6=主要贡献)

	0	1	2	3	4	5	6
Lack of the concept of individual rights in China: 在中国缺乏个人权利概念	0☐	1☐	2☐	3☐	4☐	5☐	6☐
Influence of Confucianism; 儒教的影响	0☐	1☐	2☐	3☐	4☐	5☐	6☐
Influence of socialism; 社会主义的影响	0☐	1☐	2☐	3☐	4☐	5☐	6☐
Lack of public awareness of IP rights; 缺乏知识产权的社会公共意识	0☐	1☐	2☐	3☐	4☐	5☐	6☐
The role of the government in the economy; 在经济过程中政府的作用	0☐	1☐	2☐	3☐	4☐	5☐	6☐
Perception that IP only benefits foreigners; 感觉知识产权保护只对外国人有利	0☐	1☐	2☐	3☐	4☐	5☐	6☐
Local protectionism; 方保护主义	0☐	1☐	2☐	3☐	4☐	5☐	6☐
Over-reliance on public enforcement mechanisms; 过度依赖公共实施机制	0☐	1☐	2☐	3☐	4☐	5☐	6☐
Lack of consistency in enforcement; 实施缺乏一致性	0☐	1☐	2☐	3☐	4☐	5☐	6☐
Lack of a unified agency for dealing with IP; 缺乏处理知识产权的统一机构	0☐	1☐	2☐	3☐	4☐	5☐	6☐
Weak judicial enforcement; 法院执行不力	0☐	1☐	2☐	3☐	4☐	5☐	6☐
Lack of trained and experienced legal personnel; 缺乏训练有素且经验丰富的法律从业人员	0☐	1☐	2☐	3☐	4☐	5☐	6☐
Lack of transparency; 缺少透明度	0☐	1☐	2☐	3☐	4☐	5☐	6☐
Length of the process; 过程太长	0☐	1☐	2☐	3☐	4☐	5☐	6☐
Inadequate penalties; 惩罚不当	0☐	1☐	2☐	3☐	4☐	5☐	6☐
Lack of powers to enforce court judgments; 执行法院判决时权力缺失	0☐	1☐	2☐	3☐	4☐	5☐	6☐

16. Could you identify any other factors, apart from those listed above, which also contribute to the current state of the IP protection system in China? 除问题15所列的一些因素外,您能否找出导致中国知识产权保护状态的其他因素?

17. How do you think IP protection in China could be improved? 您认为在中国,知识产权保护怎样可以得到改善?
    ☐ More money dedicated to IP protection; 投入更多的知识产权保护专项资金
    ☐ Campaigns for greater public awareness; 加强公众意识的宣传活动
    ☐ Better training for legal personnel; 给予法律从业者更好的培训
    ☐ Better training for customs personnel; 给予海关人员更好的培训
    ☐ Better training for administrative personnel: 给予行政管理人员更好的培训
    ☐ Greater international cooperation; 加强国际合作
    ☐ Stronger commitment from central government; 来自中央政府更有力度的承诺
    ☐ Other; 其它
    (Please give details 请详细描述)

18. What other comments do you have about IP protection in China?
您对中国的知识产权保护还有其它意见吗?

This information will be detached from the survey to ensure confidentiality is maintained. No names or company details will be revealed under any circumstances.
此消息将与调查问卷分离以确保机密性。在任何情况下,个人姓名或公司详细资料都不会被透露

A.1. FOLLOW-UP INTERVIEWS后续访谈

19. Would you be willing to take part in a follow-up interview? 您愿意参加后续的访谈吗?
    □ Yes; 是
    □ No; 否
20. If yes, please indicate which type of communication you would prefer for the follow-up interview: 如果是,请表明在后续访谈中您偏向使用何种类型的交流
    (You can choose more than one 可多项选择)
    □ Telephone; 电话
    □ E-mail; 电子邮件
    □ Face-to-face; 面对面
    □ Mail; 信件
    □ Fax; 传真

A.2. CONTACT DETAILS 联系方式

公司名称 Company Name
联系人姓名 Contact Name
职务 Position
地址 Address
电话号码 Telephone Number
传真号码 Fax Number
电子邮箱 E-mail Address

Thank you very much for your support; your response is invaluable to my research.

Appendix 2:
Sample Interview Questions

1. For how many years have you been working in the IP-related field (in China)?
   您在(中国)与知识产权相关的领域工作了多少年了？
2. For how many years have you had experience of the IP protection system in China?
   您在从事与知识产权保护体系有关的工作有多少年了？
3. What aspects of the IP system have you experienced in that time?
   在此期间您接触到的是知识产权体系的哪些方面？
4. Could you please outline your experiences of the current IP (administrative/judicial) system in China and how it operates in practice?
   能否请您描述一下你对当前的知识产权(行政/司法)系统在中国实施的经历和体验，以及它在实践中是如何运作的？
5. How has the (administrative/ judicial) system of IP protection changed during that time?
   在此期间您认为知识产权保护体系在行政或者司法方面有何变化？
6. Would you characterise the changes as largely positive or largely negative?
   你所体验的变化是以正面还是负面为主？
7. What positive/negative changes have you noticed?
   你注意到的正面或负面的变化有哪些？
8. How have changes to the formal substantive laws affected the enforcement of IP on the ground?
   正式法规制度的变化对知识产权的具体实施有怎样的影响？
9. Why do you think the system of IP protection has changed during that time?
   你觉得知识产权保护体系在这段时间里发生变化的原因有哪些？

© The Author(s) 2017
K. Thomas, *Assessing Intellectual Property Compliance in Contemporary China*, Palgrave Series in Asia and Pacific Studies,
DOI 10.1007/978-981-10-3072-7

10. What further changes do you think are necessary to the current system?
    你认为目前的系统还应该进行怎样的修改和完善?
11. What advice would you give someone seeking to protect their IP in China?
    你对想要在中国保护自己的知识产权的人有何建议?

Index[1]

[1] Note: Page numbers with "n" denote notes.

Printed by Books on Demand, Germany

Printed by Books on Demand, Germany